ABSOLUTE BEGINNER'S GUIDE

TO

Computer Basics, 2nd Edition

Michael Miller

800 East 96th Street,
Indianapolis, Indiana 46240

Absolute Beginner's Guide to Computer Basics, 2nd Edition

International Standard Book Number: 0-7897-3175-4

Library of Congress Catalog Card Number: 2004100888

Printed in the United States of America

First Printing: June 2004

07 06 05 04   4 3 2 1

Trademarks

All terms mentioned in this book that are known to be trademarks or service marks have been appropriately capitalized. Que cannot attest to the accuracy of this information. Use of a term in this book should not be regarded as affecting the validity of any trademark or service mark.

Warning and Disclaimer

Every effort has been made to make this book as complete and as accurate as possible, but no warranty or fitness is implied. The information provided is on an "as is" basis. The author and the publisher shall have neither liability nor responsibility to any person or entity with respect to any loss or damages arising from the information contained in this book.

Bulk Sales

Que offers excellent discounts on this book when ordered in quantity for bulk purchases or special sales. For more information, please contact:

U.S. Corporate and Government Sales
1-800-382-3419
corpsales@pearsontechgroup.com

For sales outside of the U.S., please contact:

International Sales
+1-317-581-3793
international@pearsontechgroup.com

Associate Publisher
Greg Wiegand

Managing Editor
Charlotte Clapp

Acquisitions Editor
Michelle Newcomb

Development Editor
Kevin Howard

Technical Editor
Greg Perry

Project Editor
Sheila Schroeder

Indexer
John Sleeva

Proofreader
Lisa Wilson

Team Coordinator
Sharry Lee Gregory

Interior Designer
Anne Jones

Cover Designer
Dan Armstrong

Page Layout
Julie Parks

Contents at a Glance

Table of Contents

About the Author

Michael Miller is a successful and prolific author with a reputation for practical advice and technical accuracy and an unerring empathy for the needs of his readers.

Mr. Miller has written more than 50 best-selling books in the past 15 years. His books for Que include *Absolute Beginner's Guide to Upgrading and Fixing Your PC, Absolute Beginner's Guide to eBay,* and *Bargain Hunter's Secrets to Online Shopping.* He is known for his casual, easy-to-read writing style and his practical, real-world advice—as well as his ability to explain a wide variety of complex topics to an everyday audience.

You can email Mr. Miller directly at abg@molehillgroup.com. His Web site is located at www.molehillgroup.com.

Dedication

To my nephews Alec and Ben Hauser—thanks for yet another fun summer vacation!

Acknowledgments

Thanks to the usual suspects at Que Publishing, including but not limited to Greg Wiegand, Michelle Newcomb, Kevin Howard, Greg Perry, Sheila Schroeder, and Sharry Lee Gregory.

Tell Us What You Think!

As the reader of this book, *you* are our most important critic and commentator. We value your opinion and want to know what we're doing right, what we could do better, what areas you'd like to see us publish in, and any other words of wisdom you're willing to pass our way.

As an associate publisher for Que Publishing, I welcome your comments. You can email or write me directly to let me know what you did or didn't like about this book—as well as what we can do to make our books better.

Please note that I cannot help you with technical problems related to the topic of this book. We do have a User Services group, however, where I will forward specific technical questions related to the book.

When you write, please be sure to include this book's title and author as well as your name, email address, and phone number. I will carefully review your comments and share them with the author and editors who worked on the book.

Email: feedback@quepublishing.com

Mail: Greg Wiegand
Associate Publisher
Que Publishing
800 East 96th Street
Indianapolis, IN 46240 USA

For more information about this book or another Que Publishing title, visit our Web site at www.quepublishing.com. Type the ISBN (excluding hyphens) or the title of a book in the Search field to find the page you're looking for.

Introduction

Since this is the *Absolute Beginners Guide to Computer Basics*, let's start at the absolute beginning. Which is this:

Computers aren't supposed to be scary.

Intimidating, sometimes. Difficult to use, perhaps. Inherently unreliable, most definitely. (Although they're better than they used to be.)

But scary? Definitely not.

Computers aren't scary because there's nothing they can do to hurt you. And there's not much you can do to hurt them, either. It's kind of a wary coexistence between man and machine, but the relationship has the potential to be quite beneficial. To you, anyway.

A lot of people think that they're scared of computers because they think they're unfamiliar with them. But that isn't really true.

You see, even if you've never actually used a computer before, you've been exposed to computers and all they can do for at least the last 20 years or so. Whenever you make a deposit at your bank, you're working with computers. Whenever you make a purchase at a retail store, you're working with computers. Whenever you watch a television show, or read a newspaper article, or look at a picture in a magazine, you're working with computers.

That's because computers are used in all those applications. Somebody, somewhere, is working behind the scenes with a computer to manage your bank account.

In fact, it's hard to imagine, here at the dawn of the twenty-first century, how we ever got by without all those keyboards, mice, and monitors. (Or, for that matter, the Internet.)

However, just because computers have been around for awhile doesn't mean that everyone knows how to use them. It's not unusual to feel a little trepidation the first time you sit down in front of that intimidating monitor and keyboard. Which keys should you press? What do they mean by double-clicking the mouse? And what are all those little pictures onscreen?

As foreign as all this might seem at first, computers really aren't that hard to understand—or to use. You have to learn a few basic concepts, of course (all the pressing and clicking and whatnot), and it helps to understand exactly what part of the system does what. But once you get the hang of things, computers really are fairly easy to use.

Which, of course, is where this book comes in.

Absolute Beginner's Guide to Computer Basics, 2nd Edition, will help you figure out how to use your new computer system. You'll learn how computers work, how to connect all the pieces and parts together, and how to start using them. You'll learn about computer hardware and software, about Windows and operating systems, and about the Internet. And after you're comfortable with the basic concepts (which won't take too long, trust me), you'll learn how to actually do stuff.

You'll learn how to do useful stuff, like writing letters and balancing your checkbook and creating presentations. Fun stuff, like listening to music and watching movies and playing games. Online stuff, like searching for information and sending email and chatting with friends via instant messages. And essential stuff, like copying files and troubleshooting problems and protecting against thieves and hackers.

All you have to do is sit yourself down in front of your computer, try not to be scared (there's nothing to be scared of, really), and work your way through the chapters and activities in this book. And remember that computers aren't hard to use, they don't break easily, and they let you do all sorts of fun and useful stuff once you get the hang of them. Really!

How This Book Is Organized

This book is organized into six main parts, as follows:

- **Part 1, Getting Started**, describes all the pieces and parts of your system, and how to connect them together to get your new PC up and running.
- **Part 2, Using Windows**, introduces the backbone of your entire system, the Microsoft Windows operating system. You'll learn how Windows works, and how to use Windows to perform basic tasks, such as copying and deleting files and folders. (You'll also learn fun stuff, like how to change the picture on your computer desktop.)
- **Part 3, Upgrading and Maintaining Your System**, contains all the boring (but necessary) information you need to know to keep your new PC in tip-top shape. You'll learn how to add new pieces of hardware to your system, how to set up either a wired or wireless home network, how to perform routine maintenance, and how to track down and fix common PC problems.
- **Part 4, Using Computer Software**, tells you everything you need to know about running the most popular computer programs. You'll learn how to use Microsoft Works Suite, Microsoft Word, Microsoft Excel, Microsoft PowerPoint, Microsoft Money, and all sorts of other programs—including educational software and PC games.

- ■ **Part 5, Using the Internet**, is all about going online. You'll discover how to surf the Web, send and receive email, use instant messaging and chat, and download files. You'll also learn how to shop online, buy and sell at online auctions, and create your own personal Web page—and how to protect your system from computer viruses, email spam, and other nuisances.

- ■ **Part 6, Working with Music, Movies, and Photos**, shows you how to download and play digital music files, how to burn your own audio CDs, how to watch DVDs on your computer screen, and how to use your PC with your digital camera and camcorder.

Taken together, the 38 chapters in this book will help you progress from absolute beginner to experienced computer user. Just read what you need, and before long you'll be using your computer like a pro!

Conventions Used in This Book

I hope that this book is easy enough to figure out on its own, without requiring its own instruction manual. As you read through the pages, however, it helps to know precisely how I've presented specific types of information.

Menu Commands

Most computer programs operate via a series of pull-down menus. You use your mouse to pull down a menu and then select an option from that menu. This sort of operation is indicated like this throughout the book:

Select File, Save

or

Click the Start button and select All Programs, Accessories, Notepad.

All you have to do is follow the instructions in order, using your mouse to click each item in turn. When there are submenus tacked onto the main menu (as in the All Programs, Accessories, Notepad example), just keep clicking the selections until you come to the last one—which should open the program or activate the command you wanted!

Shortcut Key Combinations

When you're using your computer keyboard, sometimes you have to press two keys at the same time. These two-key combinations are called *shortcut keys* and are shown as the key names joined with a plus sign (+).

For example, Ctrl+W indicates that you should press the W key while holding down the Ctrl key. It's no more complex than that.

Web Page Addresses

There are a lot of Web page addresses in this book. (That's because you'll probably be spending a lot of time on the Internet.) They're noted as such:

`www.molehillgroup.com`

Technically, a Web page address is supposed to start with `http://` (as in `http://www.molehillgroup.com`). Because Internet Explorer and other Web browsers automatically insert this piece of the address, however, you don't have to type it—and I haven't included it in any of the addresses in this book.

Special Elements

This book also includes a few special elements that provide additional information not included in the basic text. These elements are designed to supplement the text to make your learning faster, easier, and more efficient.

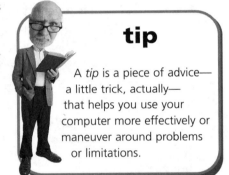

tip

A *tip* is a piece of advice—a little trick, actually—that helps you use your computer more effectively or maneuver around problems or limitations.

note

A *note* is designed to provide information that is generally useful but not specifically necessary for what you're doing at the moment. Some are like extended tips—interesting, but not essential.

caution

A *caution* will tell you to beware of a potentially dangerous act or situation. In some cases, ignoring a caution could cause you significant problems—so pay attention to them!

Let Me Know What You Think

I always love to hear from readers. If you want to contact me, feel free to email me at abg@molehillgroup.com. I can't promise that I'll answer every message, but I will promise that I'll read each one!

If you want to learn more about me and any new books I have cooking, check out my Molehill Group Web site at www.molehillgroup.com. Who knows—you might find some other books there that you'd like to read.

PART I

GETTING STARTED

1

UNDERSTANDING YOUR COMPUTER HARDWARE

Chances are you're reading this book because you just bought a new computer, are thinking about buying a new computer, or maybe even had someone give you his old computer. (Nothing wrong with high-tech hand-me-downs!) At this point you might not be totally sure what it is you've gotten yourself into. Just what is this mess of boxes and cables, and what can you—or *should* you—do with it?

This chapter serves as an introduction to the entire concept of personal computers in general—what they do, how they work, that sort of thing—and computer hardware in particular. It's a good place to start if you're not that familiar with computers, or want a brief refresher course in what all those pieces and parts are, and what they do.

Of course, if you want to skip the background and get right to using your computer, that's okay, too. For step-by-step instructions on how to connect and configure your new PC, go directly to Chapter 2, "Setting Up Your New Computer System."

What Your Computer Can—and *Can't*—Do

What good is a personal computer, anyway?

Everybody has one, you know. (Including you, now!) In fact, it's possible you bought your new computer just so that you wouldn't feel left out. But now that you have your very own personal computer, what do you do with it?

Good for Work

A lot of people use their home PCs for work-related purposes. You can bring your work (reports, spreadsheets, you name it) home from the office and finish it on your home PC, at night or on weekends. Or, if you work at home, you can use your computer to pretty much run your small business—you can use it to do everything from typing memos and reports to generating invoices and setting budgets.

In short, anything you can do with a normal office PC, you can probably do on your home PC.

Good for Play

All work and no play makes Jack a dull boy, so there's no reason not to have a little fun with your new PC. Not only can you use your PC to play some really cool games, you can also use it to track your favorite hobby, create interesting crafts projects, print pictures from your latest family vacation, listen to your favorite music, and watch your favorite videos. In fact, with the right software and hardware, you can even use your PC to edit movies you take with your video camcorder.

Good for Managing Your Finances

You don't have to be a professional accountant to use your PC to manage your finances. Software programs, such as Microsoft Money and Quicken, let you create budgets, write checks, and balance your accounts, right from your computer screen. You can even set up your system to automatically pay bills and do other banking online—no paper checks necessary.

Good for Keeping in Touch

Want to send a letter to a friend? With your new PC (and a word processor program, such as Microsoft Word), it's a cinch. Even better, save a stamp and send that friend an electronic letter—called an *email*—over the Internet. And if that person's online the same time you are, you can chat with him in real time via an instant messaging program. Many families use their PCs for almost all their communications.

Good for Getting Online

Speaking of email, chances are one of the main reasons you got a PC was to get connected to the Internet. The Internet's a great tool; in addition to email and instant messaging, you can join online message boards, participate in public chat rooms, and browse the World Wide Web—which is chock full of interesting and informative content and services. Now you won't feel left out when people start talking about "double-you double-you double-you" this and "dot-com" that—because you'll be online, too.

Getting to Know Your Personal Computer System

Now that you know *why* you have that brand-new personal computer sitting on your desk, you might be interested in just *what* it is that you have. It's important to know what each part of your system is, what it does, and how to hook it all together.

Pieces and Parts—Computer Hardware

We'll start by looking at the physical components of your system—the stuff we call computer *hardware*. As you can see in Figure 1.1, there are a lot of different pieces and parts that make up a typical computer system. You should note, however, that no two computer systems are identical, since you can always add new components to your system—or disconnect other pieces you don't have any use for.

This book is written for users of relatively new personal computers—in particular, PCs running the Windows XP operating system. If you have an older PC, most of the advice here is still good, although not all the step-by-step instructions will apply.

FIGURE 1.1

A typical personal computer system.

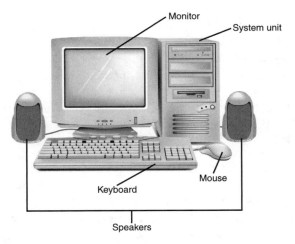

These items are the basic elements you'll find in almost all computer systems. Of course, you can add lots of other items to your personal system, including *printers* (to make printouts of documents and pictures), *scanners* (to change a printed document or picture to electronic format), *PC cameras* (to send live video of yourself to friends and family), *digital cameras* (to transfer your snapshots to electronic format), and *joysticks* (to play the most challenging games). You can even add the appropriate items to connect multiple PCs together in a *network*.

The Right Tools for the Right Tasks— Computer Software

By themselves, all those little beige and black boxes really aren't that useful. You can connect them and set them in place, but they won't do anything until you have some *software* to make things work.

Computer *hardware* are those things you can touch—your system unit, monitor, and the like.

note

Learn more about these pieces and parts in "Computer Hardware Basics," later in this chapter. If you need help connecting all the pieces and parts, turn to Chapter 2. And if you want to add a new piece of hardware to your basic system, check out Chapter 7, "Adding New Hardware and Devices to Your System."

Computer *software*, on the other hand, is something you *can't* touch, because it's nothing more than a bunch of electronic bits and bytes. These bits and bytes, however, combine into computer programs—sometimes called *applications*—that provide specific functionality to your system.

For example, if you want to crunch some numbers, you need a piece of software called a *spreadsheet* program. If you want to write a letter, you need a *word processing* program. If you want to make changes to some pictures you took with your digital camera, you need *graphics editing* software.

In other words, you need separate software for each task you want to do with your computer. Fortunately, most new computer systems come with a lot of this software already installed.

Making Everything Work—with Windows

When you're not using a specific piece of application software, you interface with your computer via a special piece of software called an *operating system*. As the name implies, this program makes your system operate; it's your gateway to the hardware part of your system.

note

If you want or need any additional software, you'll have to buy and install it yourself—as described in Chapter 11, "Installing New Software."

The operating system is also how your application software interfaces with your computer hardware. When you want to print a document from your word processor, that software works with the operating system to send the document to your printer.

Most computers today ship with an operating system called Microsoft Windows. This operating system has been around for over 15 years and is published by Microsoft Corporation.

Windows isn't the only operating system around, however. Computers manufactured by Apple Computing use a different operating system, called the Mac OS. Therefore, computers running Windows and computers by Apple aren't totally compatible with each other. Then there's Linux, which is compatible with most PCs sold today, but used primarily by uber-techie types; it's not an operating system I'd recommend for general users.

But let's get back to Windows, of which there have been several different versions over the years. The current version is called Windows XP, and if you have a new PC, this is probably the version you're using. (Older versions—which look a little different but work pretty much the same—include Windows 95, Windows 98, and Windows Me.) You use Windows to launch specific programs and to perform various system maintenance functions, such as copying files and turning off your computer.

note

You can learn more about Windows in Chapter 3, "Understanding Microsoft Windows XP."

Don't Worry, You Can't Screw It Up—Much

The balance of this chapter goes into a bit more detail about the hardware components of your PC system. Before you proceed, however, there's one other important thing you need to know about computers.

A lot of people are afraid of their computers. They think if they press the wrong key or click the wrong button that they'll break something or will have to call in an expensive repairperson to put things right.

This really isn't true.

The important thing to know is that it's really difficult to break your computer system. Yes, it's possible to break something if you drop it, but in terms of breaking your system through normal use, it just doesn't happen that often.

It *is* possible to make mistakes, of course. You can click the wrong button and accidentally delete a file you didn't want to delete or turn off your system and lose a document you forgot to save. You can even take inadequate security precautions and find your system infected by a computer virus. But in terms of doing serious harm just by clicking your mouse, it's unlikely.

So don't be afraid of the thing. Your computer is a tool, just like a hammer or a blender or a camera. After you learn how to use it, it can be a very useful tool. But it's *your* tool, which means *you* tell *it* what to do—not vice versa. Remember that you're in control and that you're not going to break anything, and you'll have a lot of fun—and maybe even get some real work done!

Computer Hardware Basics

As you just read, computer hardware are those parts of your system you can actually see and touch. This includes your system unit and everything connected to it, including your monitor, keyboard, mouse, and printer.

We'll take a close look at all the various pieces of hardware you can have in a computer system—including those parts you can't always see because they're built in to your system unit. So, if you're curious about microprocessors and memory and modems and monitors, read on—this is the chapter for you!

Your PC's System Unit—The Mother Ship

The most important piece of hardware in your computer system is the *system unit*. This is the big, ugly box that houses your disk drives and many other components. You can find system units that lie horizontally on your desk (like the one in Figure 1.2) or ones that stand straight up (like the one in Figure 1.3). You can even find some computers that build the system unit into the monitor.

FIGURE 1.2

A desktop-type computer system unit.

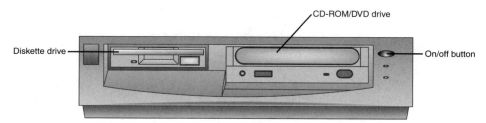

Diskette drive

CD-ROM/DVD drive

On/off button

FIGURE 1.3

A system unit in a mini-tower configuration.

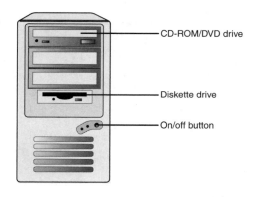

CD-ROM/DVD drive

Diskette drive

On/off button

note

Vertical system units often are called *towers* or *mini-towers*.

The back of the system unit typically is covered with all types of connectors. This is because all the other parts of your computer system connect to your system unit, and they all have to have a place to plug in. And, because each component has its own unique type of connector, you end up with the assortment of jacks (called *ports* in the computer world) that you see in Figure 1.4.

All the good stuff in your system unit is inside the case. With most system units, you can remove the case to peek and poke around inside.

To remove your system unit's case, make sure the unit is unplugged, then look for some big screws or thumbscrews on either the side or back of the case. (Even better—read your PC's instruction manual for instructions specific to your unit.) With the screws loosened or removed, you should then be able to either slide off the entire case, or pop open the top or back.

note

Desktop computer systems are composed of all these separate components. Laptop PCs, on the other hand, have all that stuff crammed into a single case. So, you don't have a separate system unit, monitor, keyboard, and mouse—they're part of one very compact unit. Learn more about laptop computers in the section "Laptop PCs—Lightweight All-in-One Systems," later in this chapter.

FIGURE 1.4

The back of a typical system unit—just look at all those different connectors!

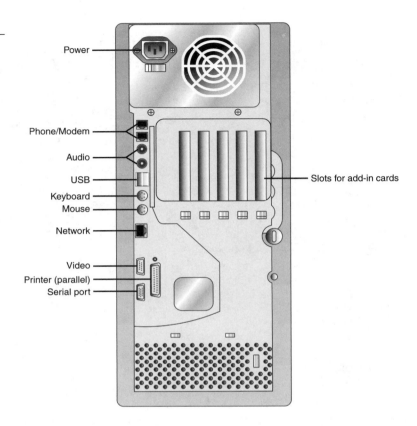

Power

Phone/Modem

Audio

USB

Keyboard

Mouse

Network

Video

Printer (parallel)

Serial port

Slots for add-in cards

When you open the case on your system unit, you see all sorts of computer chips and circuit boards. The really big board located at the base of the computer (to which everything else is plugged into) is called the *motherboard*, because it's the "mother" for your microprocessor and memory chips, as well as for the other internal components that enable your system to function. This motherboard contains several slots, into which you can plug additional *boards* (also called *cards*) that perform specific functions.

As you can see in Figure 1.5, most PC motherboards contain six or more slots for add-on cards. For example, a video card enables your microprocessor to transmit video signals to your monitor. Other available cards enable you to add sound and modem/fax capabilities to your system.

caution

Always turn off and unplug your computer before attempting to remove the system unit's case—and be careful about touching anything inside. If you have any built-up static electricity, you can seriously damage the sensitive chips and electronic components with an innocent touch.

FIGURE 1.5
What your PC looks like on the inside—a big motherboard with lots of add-on boards attached.

Microprocessors: The Main Engine

We're not done looking at the system unit just yet. Buried somewhere on that big motherboard is a specific chip that controls your entire computer system. This chip is called a *microprocessor* or a *central processing unit (CPU)*.

The microprocessor is the brains inside your system. It processes all the instructions necessary for your computer to perform its duties. The more powerful the microprocessor chip, the faster and more efficiently your system runs.

Microprocessors carry out the various instructions that let your computer compute. Every input and output device hooked up to a computer—the keyboard, printer, monitor, and so on—either issues or receives instructions that the microprocessor then processes. Your software programs also issue instructions that must be implemented by the microprocessor. This chip truly is the workhorse of your system; it affects just about everything your computer does.

Different computers have different types of microprocessor chips. Many IBM-compatible computers use chips manufactured by Intel. Some use Intel-compatible chips manufactured by AMD and other firms. But all IBM-compatible computers that run the Windows operating system use Intel-compatible chips.

In addition to having different chip manufacturers (and different chip families from the same manufacturer), you'll also run into microprocessor chips that run at different speeds. CPU speed today is measured in gigahertz (GHz). A CPU with a speed of 1GHz can run at one *billion* clock ticks per second! The bigger the gigahertz number, the faster the chip runs. If you're still shopping for a new PC, look for one with the combination of a powerful microprocessor and a high clock speed for best performance.

note

The Apple Macintosh uses chips made by Motorola that are totally different from the Intel-compatible chips. It's because of the different processor configurations that software written for the Macintosh won't run on IBM-compatible computers—and vice versa.

Computer Memory: Temporary Storage

Speaking of memory, before your CPU can process any instructions you give it, your instructions must be stored somewhere, in preparation for access by the microprocessor. These instructions—along with other data processed by your system—are temporarily held in the computer's *random access memory (RAM)*. All computers have some amount of memory, which is created by a number of memory chips. The more memory that's available in a machine, the more instructions and data that can be stored at one time.

Memory is measured in terms of *bytes*. One byte is equal to approximately one character in a word processing document. A unit equaling approximately one thousand bytes (1,024, to be exact) is called a *kilobyte (KB)*, and a unit of approximately one thousand (1,024) kilobytes is called a *megabyte (MB)*. A thousand megabytes is a *gigabyte (GB)*.

Most computers today come with at least 256MB of memory, and it's not uncommon to find machines with 512MB or more. To enable your computer to run as many programs as quickly as possible, you need as much memory installed in your system as it can accept—or that you can afford. Extra memory can be added to a computer by installing a new memory module, which is as easy as plugging a "stick" directly into a slot on your system's motherboard.

If your computer doesn't possess enough memory, its CPU must constantly retrieve data from permanent storage on its hard disk. This method of data retrieval is slower than retrieving instructions and data from electronic memory. In fact, if your machine doesn't have enough memory, some programs will run very slowly (or you might experience random system crashes), and other programs won't run at all!

Hard Disk Drives: Long-Term Storage

Another important physical component inside your system unit is the *hard disk drive*. The hard disk permanently stores all your important data. Some hard disks today can store up to 300 gigabytes of data—and even bigger hard disks are on the way. (Contrast this to your system's random access memory, which stores only a few hundred megabytes of data, temporarily.)

A hard disk consists of numerous metallic platters. These platters store data *magnetically*. Special read/write *heads* realign magnetic particles on the platters, much like a recording head records data onto magnetic recording tape.

Before data can be stored on any disk, including your system's hard disk, that disk must first be *formatted*. A disk that has not been formatted cannot accept any data. When you format a hard disk, your computer prepares each track and sector of the disk to accept and store data magnetically.

Of course, when you buy a new PC, your hard disk is already formatted for you. (And, in most cases, your operating system and key programs also are preinstalled.)

caution

If you try to reformat your hard disk, you'll erase all the programs and data that have been installed—so don't do it!

Disk Drives: Portable Storage

Along with a hard disk drive, some computers have a *removable disk drive*. This is older technology, however, as these removable disks—often called *floppy disks* or *diskettes*—don't hold a lot of data. (A standard 3 1/2" floppy disk only holds 1.44MB of data.) For that reason, most newer computers no longer include diskette drives—although these drives were standard issue on older model PCs.

If you want to transfer data from one PC to another, there are better technologies available—such as rewritable CDs, discussed next.

CD-ROM Drives: Storage on a Disc

There's a third type of disk that is now standard on personal computer systems. This disc is called a *CD-ROM*. (The initials stand for *compact disc–read-only memory*.)

CD-ROM discs, such as the one in Figure 1.6, look just like the compact discs you play on your audio system. They're also very similar in the way they store data (audio data in the case of regular CDs; computer data in the case of CD-ROMs).

FIGURE 1.6

Store tons of data, digitally, on a shiny CD-ROM disc.

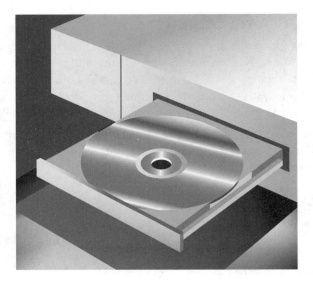

Information is encoded at a disc-manufacturing plant, using an industrial-grade laser. This information takes the form of microscopic pits (representing the 1s and 0s of computer binary language) below the disc's surface. Similar to hard and floppy disks, the information is arranged in a series of tracks and sectors, but the tracks are so close together that the disk surface is highly reflective.

Data is read from the CD-ROM disc via a drive that uses a consumer-grade laser. The laser beam follows the tracks of the disc and reads the pits, translating the data into a form your system can understand.

By the way, the *ROM* part of CD-ROM means that you can only read data from the disk; unlike normal hard disks and disks, you can't write new data to a standard CD-ROM. However, recordable (CD-R) and rewritable (CD-RW) drives are available that *do* let you write data to CD discs—although they're a bit more expensive than standard CD-ROM drives.

DVD Drives: Even More Storage on a Disc

Beyond the CD-ROM is the newer *DVD* medium. DVDs can contain up to 4.7GB of data (compared to 700MB for a typical CD-ROM), and therefore are ideally suited for large applications or games that otherwise would require multiple CDs. Similar to standard CD-ROMs, most DVDs are read-only—although all DVD drives can also read CD-ROM discs. In addition, most DVD drives play full-length DVD movies, which turns your PC into a mini movie machine.

And, just as there are recordable CD-ROM drives, you can also find recordable DVD drives. These DVD-R drives are a little expensive, but the prices are coming down—and they let you record an entire movie on a single disc.

Keyboards: Fingertip Input

Computers receive data by reading it from disk, accepting it electronically over a modem, or receiving input directly from you, the user. You provide your input by way of what's called, in general, an *input device*; the most common input device you use to talk to your computer is the keyboard.

A computer keyboard, similar to the one in Figure 1.7, looks and functions just like a typewriter keyboard, except that computer keyboards have a few more keys. Some of these keys (such as the arrow,

note

DVD really isn't an acronym for anything in particular. Some manufacturers claim that it stands for *digital versatile disc* or *digital video disc*, but it's really just a bunch of initials with no real meaning.

PgUp, PgDn, Home, and End keys) enable you to move around within a program or file. Other keys provide access to special program features. When you press a key on your keyboard, it sends an electronic signal to your system unit that tells your machine what you want it to do.

FIGURE 1.7
A standard PC keyboard.

Most PC keyboards look like the one in Figure 1.7. Some keyboards, however, have an ergonomic design that splits the keyboard into right and left parts and twists and tilts each side for maximum comfort. In addition, some manufacturers make *wireless* keyboards that connect to your system unit via radio signals—thus eliminating one cable from the back of your system.

Mice: Point-and-Click Input Devices

It's a funny name, but a necessary device. A computer *mouse*, like the one shown in Figure 1.8, is a small handheld device. Most mice consist of an oblong case with a roller underneath and two or three buttons on top. When you move the mouse along a desktop, an onscreen pointer (called a *cursor*) moves in response. When you click (press and release) a mouse button, this motion initiates an action in your program.

FIGURE 1.8
Roll the mouse back and forth to move the onscreen cursor.

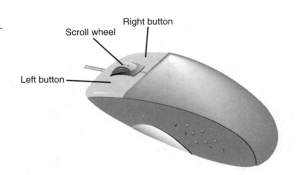

Mice come in all shapes and sizes. Some have wires, and some are wireless. Some are relatively oval in shape, and others are all curvy to better fit in the palm of your hand. Some have the typical roller ball underneath, and others use an optical sensor to determine where and how much you're rolling. Some even have extra buttons that can be programmed for specific functions or a scroll wheel you can use to scroll through long documents or Web pages.

Of course, a mouse is just *one* type of input device you can hook up to your PC. Trackballs, joysticks, game controllers, and pen pads all count as input devices, whether they work in conjunction with a mouse or replace it. You can use one of these alternative devices to replace your original mouse or (in some cases) to supplement it.

If you have a portable PC, you don't have a separate mouse, but rather a built-in pointing device of some sort—a touchpad, rollerball, or TrackPoint (the thing that looks like a little rubber eraser). Fortunately, you don't have to use the built-in pointing device on a portable PC; most portables let you attach an external mouse, which then overrides the internal device.

Modems: Getting Connected

Almost all PC systems today include a *modem*. A modem enables your computer to connect to telephone lines and transmit data to and from the Internet and commercial online services (such as America Online).

Modems come in either internal (card-based) or external (hooking up to an open port on the back of your system) models. *Internal* modems usually fit into a slot on your motherboard and connect

note

The word "modem" stands for "modulate-demodulate," which is how digital data is sent over traditional analog phone lines. The data is "modulated" for transmittal, and "demodulated" upon receipt.

directly to a telephone line. *External* modems are free-standing devices that connect to your system unit by cable and hook directly to a phone line.

If you connect to the Internet via a broadband connection, you probably have an external cable or DSL modem. These devices work just like traditional phone line modems, but are specifically designed to work with the data transmitted over digital cable and DSL lines.

Sound Cards and Speakers: Making Noise

Every PC comes with some sort of speaker system. While some older PCs had a speaker built into the system unit, most systems today come with separate right and left speakers, sometimes accompanied by a subwoofer for better base. (Figure 1.9 shows a typical right-left-subwoofer speaker system.) You can even get so-called 5.1 surround sound speaker systems, with five satellite speakers (front and rear) and the ".1" subwoofer—great for listening to movie soundtracks or playing explosive-laden videogames.

FIGURE 1.9

A typical set of right and left external speakers, complete with subwoofer.

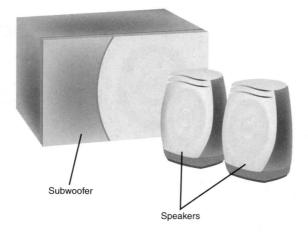

Subwoofer

Speakers

All speaker systems are driven by a sound card that is installed inside your system unit. If you upgrade your speaker system, you also might need to upgrade your sound card accordingly.

Video Cards and Monitors: Getting the Picture

Operating a computer would be difficult if you didn't constantly receive visual feedback showing you what your machine is doing. This vital function is provided by your computer's monitor.

The traditional monitor, similar to the one shown in Figure 1.10, is a lot like a little television set. Your microprocessor electronically transmits words and pictures (*text* and *graphics*, in PC lingo) to your monitor, in some approximation of how these visuals would appear on paper. You view the monitor and respond according to what you see onscreen.

FIGURE 1.10

A traditional tube-type video monitor.

Although the traditional monitor uses a picture tube (called a *cathode ray tube* or *CRT*, similar to that used in a normal television set) to display its picture, another type of monitor does away with the tube. A so-called *flat-screen* monitor, such as the one in Figure 1.11, uses an LCD display instead—which is not only flat, but also very thin. These are the same types of displays used in portable PCs, and are now standard on many new PC systems.

FIGURE 1.11

A space-saving, flat-screen video monitor.

You measure the size of a monitor by measuring from corner to corner, diagonally. The traditional desktop monitor is normally a 14" or 15" monitor; larger 17" and 19" monitors are becoming more common as they become more affordable.

The monitor itself does not generate the images it displays. These images are electronically crafted by a *video card* installed inside your system unit. To work correctly, both video card and monitor must be matched to display images of the same resolution.

Resolution refers to the size of the images that can be displayed onscreen and is measured in pixels. A *pixel* is a single dot on your screen; a full picture is composed of thousands of pixels. The higher the resolution, the sharper the resolution— which lets you display more (smaller) elements onscreen.

tip

The measurement is different for tube-type monitors than it is for flat-screen monitors. This is because a flat-screen monitor displays its images all the way to the edge of the screen, and traditional tube-type monitors don't. For that reason, a 15" flat-screen monitor has the same size picture as a 17" tube-type monitor.

Resolution is expressed in numbers of pixels, in both the horizontal and vertical directions. Older video cards and monitors could only display 640×480 or 800×600 pixel resolution; you want a card/monitor combination that can display at least 1024×768 resolution.

Printers: Making Hard Copies

Your monitor displays images in real time, but they're fleeting. For permanent records of your work, you must add a printer to your system. Printers create hard copy output from your software programs.

You can choose from various types of printers for your system, depending on your exact printing needs. The two main types of printers today are laser and inkjet printers.

Laser printers work much like copying machines, applying toner (powdered ink) to paper by using a small laser. *Inkjet* printers, on the other hand, shoot jets of ink to the paper's surface to create the printed image. Inkjet printers are typically a little lower priced than laser printers, although the price difference is shrinking.

You also can choose from either black-and-white or color printers. Black-and-white printers are faster than color printers and better if you're printing memos, letters, and other single-color documents. Color printers, however, are great if you have kids, and they're essential if you want to print pictures taken with a digital camera.

By the way, there's a type of "combination" printer available that combines a printer with a scanner and a fax machine. If you need all these devices and are short on space, these are pretty good deals.

Laptop PCs—Lightweight All-in-One Systems

Before we wrap up this chapter, we need to discuss a slightly different type of computer. This type of PC combines all the various elements (except for a printer) into a single case and then adds a battery so that you can use it on the go. This type of PC is called a *laptop* or *notebook* computer.

Laptop PCs, like the one in Figure 1.12, feature a flip-up LCD screen. When the screen is folded down, the PC is very portable; when the screen is flipped up, the keyboard is exposed.

FIGURE 1.12

A typical laptop PC—all those components in a single package.

All laptop PCs include some sort of built-in pointing device—but typically not a standalone mouse. A portable might have a touchpad, rollerball, or Trackpoint (which looks like a miniature joystick in the middle of the keyboard). Speakers typically are built into the base of the unit, and various types of disk drives are located on the sides or underneath.

The key thing about laptop PCs—in addition to their small sizes and light weights— is that they can operate on battery power. Depending on the PC (and the battery), you might be able to operate a laptop for four hours or more before switching batteries or plugging the unit into a wall outlet. That makes laptops great for use on airplanes, in coffeshops, or anywhere plugging in a power cord is inconvenient.

The only bad thing about laptop PCs is that they're a little more expensive than a similarly equipped desktop PC. That's because all the normal components used in a desktop PC have to be shrunk down to a more compact size of a laptop model.

THE ABSOLUTE MINIMUM

Here are the key points to remember from this chapter:

- Your computer system is composed of various pieces of hardware, almost all of which plug into that big beige box called the system unit.

- You interface with your computer hardware via a piece of software called an operating system. The operating system on your new computer is probably some version of Microsoft Windows.

- You use specific software programs to perform specific tasks, such as writing letters and editing digital photos.

- The brains and engine of your system is the system unit, which contains the microprocessor, memory, disk drives, and all the connections for your other system components.

- To make your system run faster, get a faster microprocessor or more memory.

- Data is temporarily stored in your system's memory; you store data permanently on some type of disk drive—either a hard disk, floppy disk, or CD-ROM.

2

SETTING UP YOUR NEW COMPUTER SYSTEM

Chapter 1, "Understanding Your Computer Hardware," gave you the essential background information you need to understand how your computer system works. Now it's time to connect all the various pieces and parts of your computer system—and your PC is up and running!

Before You Get Started

It's important to prepare the space where you'll be putting your new PC. Obviously, the space has to be big enough to hold all the components—though you don't have to keep all the components together. You can, for example, spread out your left and right speakers, place your subwoofer on the floor, and separate the printer from the system unit. Just don't put anything so far away that the cables don't reach. (And make sure you have a spare power outlet—or even better, a mutli-outlet power strip—nearby.)

You also should consider the ergonomics of your setup. You want your keyboard at or slightly below normal desktop height, and you want your monitor at or slightly below eye level. Make sure your chair is adjusted for a straight and firm sitting position with your feet flat on the floor, and then place all the pieces of your system in relation to that.

Wherever you put your system, you should make sure that it's in a well-ventilated location free of excess dust and smoke. (The moving parts in your computer don't like dust and dirt or any other such contaminants that can muck up the way they work.) Because your computer generates heat when it operates, you must leave enough room around the system unit for the heat to dissipate. *Never* place your computer in a confined, poorly ventilated space; your PC can overheat and shut down if it isn't sufficiently ventilated.

For extra protection to your computer, connect the power cable on your system unit to a surge suppressor rather than directly into an electrical outlet. A *surge suppressor*—which looks like a power strip, but with an on/off switch—protects your PC from power-line surges that could damage its delicate internal parts. When a power surge temporarily spikes your line voltage (causes the voltage to momentarily increase above normal levels), a surge suppressor shuts down power to your system, acting like a circuit breaker or fuse.

tip

When you unpack your PC, be sure you keep all the manuals, CD-ROMs, and cables. Put the ones you don't use in a safe place, in case you need to reinstall any software or equipment at a later date.

Connecting the Cables

Now it's time to get connected. Position your system unit so that you easily can access all the connections on the back, and carefully run the cables from each of the other components so that they're hanging loose at the rear of the system unit.

Connect in Order

It's important that you connect the cables in a particular order. To make sure that the most critical devices are connected first, follow the instructions in Table 2.1.

Table 2.1 Connecting Your System Components

Order	Connection	Looks Like
1.	Connect your mouse to the mouse connector.	
2.	Connect your keyboard to the keyboard connector.	
3.	Connect your video monitor to the video connector..	
4.	Connect your printer to the parallel connector. This connector is sometimes labeled "printer" or "LPT1." (Note that some printers connect to a USB port instead of the parallel port.)	
5.	Connect a cable from your telephone line to the "line in" connector on your modem or modem board. Connect a cable from the "line out" connector on your modem to your telephone. (You can skip this step if you're using a cable modem or DSL modem to connect to the Internet; wait until you have the rest of your system up and running, then follow the instructions you were given by your Internet service provider.)	
6.	Connect the phono jack from your speaker system to the "audio out" or "sound out" connector.	
7.	Connect any other devices to the appropriate USB, FireWire, parallel, or serial connector.	
8.	Plug the power cable of your video monitor into a power outlet.	

Table 2.1 (continued)

Order	Connection	Looks Like
9.	If your system includes powered speakers, plug them into a power outlet.	
10.	Plug any other powered external component into a power outlet.	
11.	Plug the power cable of your system unit into a power outlet.	

Connect by Color

Most PC manufacturers color-code the cables and connectors to make the connection even easier—just plug the blue cable into the blue connector, and so on. If you're not sure what color cable goes to what device, take a look at the standard cable color coding in Table 2.2.

caution

Before you connect *anything* to your system unit, make sure that it's turned off.

Table 2.2 Connector Color Codes

Connector	Color
VGA (analog) monitor	Blue
Digital monitor	White
Video out	Yellow
Mouse	Green
Keyboard	Purple
Serial	Teal or turquoise
Parallel (printer)	Burgundy
USB	Black
FireWire (IEEE 1394)	Grey
Audio line out (left)	Red
Audio line out (right)	White
Audio line out (headphones)	Lime
Speaker out/subwoofer	Orange

Table 2.2   (continued)

Connector	Color
Right-to-left speaker	Brown
Audio line in	Light blue
Microphone	Pink
Gameport/MIDI	Gold

Turning It On and Setting It Up

Now that you have everything connected, sit back and rest for a minute. Next up is the big step—turning it all on.

It's important that you turn on things in the proper order. Follow these steps:

1. Turn on your video monitor.

2. Turn on your speaker system—but make sure the speaker volume knob is turned down (towards the left).

3. Turn on any other system components that are connected to your system unit—such as your printer, scanner, external modem, and so on.

4. Turn on your system unit.

> **caution**
>
> Make sure that every cable is *firmly* connected—both to the system unit and the specific piece of hardware. Loose cables can cause all sorts of weird problems, so be sure they're plugged in really good.

Note that your system unit is the *last* thing you turn on. That's because when it powers on, it has to sense the other components of your system—which it can do only if the other components are plugged in and turned on.

Powering On for the First Time

The first time you turn on your PC is a unique experience. A brand-new, out-of-the-box system will have to perform some basic configuration operations, which include asking you to input some key information.

This first-time startup operation differs from manufacturer to manufacturer, but typically includes some or all of the following steps:

- **Windows Product Activation**—You may be asked to input the long and nonsensical product code found on the back of your Windows installation CD (or someplace else in the documentation that came with your new PC). Your system then phones into the Microsoft mother ship, registers your system information, and unlocks Windows for you to use. (Many manufacturers "pre-activate" Windows at the factory, so you might not have to go through this process.)

- **Windows Registration**—A slightly different process from product activation, registration requires you to input your name and other personal information, along with the Windows product code. This information then is phoned into the Microsoft mother ship to register your copy of Windows with the company, for warranty purposes.

- **Windows Configuration**—During this process Windows asks a series of questions about your location, the current time and date, and other essential information. You also might be asked to create a username and password.

- **System Configuration**—This is where Windows tries to figure out all the different components that are part of your system, such as your printer, scanner, and so on. Enter the appropriate information when prompted; if asked to insert a component's installation CD, do so.

Windows registration is optional; product activation is mandatory.

Some computer manufacturers supplement these configuration operations with setup procedures of their own. It's impossible to describe all the different options that might be presented by all the different manufacturers, so watch the screen carefully and follow all the onscreen instructions.

After you have everything configured, Windows finally starts, and then *you* can start using your system.

Some installation procedures require your computer to be restarted. In most cases, this happens automatically; then the installation process resumes where it left off.

Powering On Normally

After everything is installed and configured, starting your computer is a much simpler affair. When you turn on your computer, you'll notice a series of text messages flash across your screen. These messages are there to let you know what's going on as your computer *boots up*.

After a few seconds (during which your system unit beeps and whirrs a little bit), the Windows Welcome screen appears. All registered users are listed on this screen. Click your username or picture, enter your password (if necessary), and then press the Enter key or click the green right-arrow button. After you're past the Welcome screen, you're taken directly to the Windows desktop, and your system is ready to run.

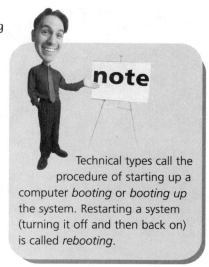

Technical types call the procedure of starting up a computer *booting* or *booting up* the system. Restarting a system (turning it off and then back on) is called *rebooting*.

If you have only a single user on your PC and that user doesn't have a password assigned, Windows moves past the Welcome screen with no action necessary on your part.

THE ABSOLUTE MINIMUM

Here are the key points to remember when connecting and configuring your new computer:

- Most cables plug into only a specific connector—and on most new systems, they're color-coded for easier hookup.

- Make sure your cables are *firmly* connected; loose cables are the cause of many computer problems.

- Connect all the cables to your system unit *before* you turn on the power.

- Remember to turn on your printer and monitor before you turn on the system unit.

PART

USING WINDOWS

3

Understanding Microsoft Windows XP

As you learned back in Chapter 1, "Understanding Your Computer Hardware," it's the software and operating system that make your hardware work. The operating system for most personal computers is Microsoft Windows, and you need to know how to use Windows to use your PC system. This is because Windows pretty much runs your computer for you; if you don't know your way around Windows, you won't be able to do much of anything on your new PC.

What Windows Is—and What It Does

Windows is a piece of software called an *operating system*. An operating system does what its name implies—it *operates* your computer *system*, working in the background every time you turn on your PC.

Equally important, Windows is what you see when you first turn on your computer, after everything turns on and boots up. The "desktop" that fills your screen is part of Windows, as is the taskbar at the bottom of the screen and the big menu that pops up when you click the Start button.

Different Versions of Windows

The version of Windows installed on your new PC is probably Windows XP. Microsoft has released different versions of Windows over the years, and XP is the latest— which is why it comes preinstalled on most new PCs.

If you've used a previous version of Windows—such as Windows 95, Windows 98, or Windows Me—on another PC, Windows XP probably looks and acts a little differently to you. (It's even different from the version of Windows found in most large corporations—Windows 2000.) Don't worry; everything that was in the old Windows is still in the new Windows—it's probably just in a slightly different place.

There are actually two different retail versions of Windows XP. Windows XP Home Edition, which comes with most lower-priced PCs, is the version of XP for home and small-business users. Windows XP Professional Edition, which comes with some higher-priced PCs, is designed for larger businesses and corporate users. They both share the same basic functionality; XP Professional just has a few more features specifically designed for large corporate networks.

Some new "media center" PCs come with a slightly different version of Windows XP called Windows XP Media Center Edition. The Media Center is an optional interface that sits on the top of the normal Windows XP desktop and allows one-button access to key multimedia functions, including My TV, My Music, My Pictures, and My Videos. In fact, PCs equipped with Media Center come with a handheld remote control for quick switching from across the room! If you have Windows XP Media Center, don't panic; underneath the Media Center is the same Windows XP we all know and love, and that is described in this chapter.

Working Your Way Around the Desktop

As you can see in Figure 3.1, the Windows XP desktop includes a number of elements. Get to know the desktop; you're going to be seeing a lot of it from now on.

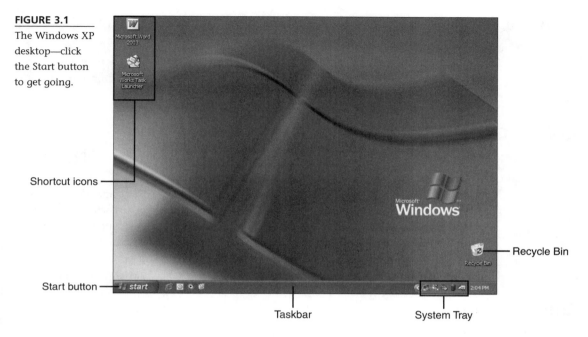

FIGURE 3.1
The Windows XP
desktop—click
the Start button
to get going.

Shortcut icons

Recycle Bin

Start button

Taskbar   System Tray

The major parts of the Windows desktop include

- **Start button**—Opens the Start menu, which is what you can use to open all your programs and documents.
- **Taskbar**—Displays buttons for your open applications and windows, as well as different toolbars for different tasks.
- **System Tray**—The part of the taskbar that holds the clock, volume control, and icons for other utilities that run in the background of your system.
- **Shortcut icons**—These are links to software programs you can place on your desktop; a "clean" desktop includes just one icon, for the Windows Recycle Bin.
- **Recycle Bin**—This is where you dump any files you want to delete.

Important Windows Operations

To use Windows efficiently, you must master a few simple operations, such as pointing and clicking, dragging and dropping, and right-clicking. You perform all these operations with your mouse.

Pointing and Clicking

The most common mouse operation is *pointing and clicking.* Simply move the mouse so that the cursor is pointing to the object you want to select, and then click the left mouse button once. Pointing and clicking is an effective way to select menu items, directories, and files.

Double-Clicking

If you're using Windows XP's default operating mode, you'll need to *double-click* an item to activate an operation. This involves pointing at something onscreen with the cursor and then clicking the left mouse button twice in rapid succession. For example, to open program groups or launch individual programs, simply double-click a specific icon.

Right-Clicking

When you select an item and then click the *right* mouse button, you'll often see a pop-up menu. This menu, when available, contains commands that directly relate to the selected object. Refer to your individual programs to see whether and how they use the right mouse button.

tip

This classic double-click mode is activated by default on most new PCs. Windows XP also includes a new single-click mode, which makes Windows act more like a Web page. In this mode, you hover over an object to select it and single-click to activate it. To learn how to switch to single-click mode, see Chapter 5, "Personalizing Windows."

Dragging and Dropping

Dragging is a variation of clicking. To drag an object, point at it with the cursor and then press and hold down the left mouse button. Move the mouse without releasing the mouse button, and drag the object to a new location. When you're done moving the object, release the mouse button to drop it onto the new location.

You can use dragging and dropping to move files from one folder to another or to delete files by dragging them onto the Recycle Bin icon.

Hovering

When you position the cursor over an item without clicking your mouse, you're *hovering* over that item. Many operations require you to hover your cursor and then perform some other action.

Moving and Resizing Windows

Every software program you launch is displayed in a separate onscreen window. When you open more than one program, you get more than one window—and your desktop can quickly get cluttered.

There are many ways to deal with desktop clutter. One way to do this is to move a window to a new position. You do this by positioning your cursor over the window's title bar (shown in Figure 3.2) and then clicking and holding down the left button on your mouse. As long as this button is depressed, you can use your mouse to drag the window around the screen. When you release the mouse button, the window stays where you put it.

Title bar

FIGURE 3.2

The various parts of a window.

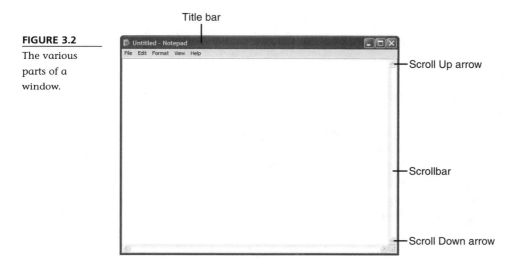

Scroll Up arrow

Scrollbar

Scroll Down arrow

You also can change the size of most windows. You do this by positioning the cursor over the very edge of the window—any edge. If you position the cursor on either side of the window, you can resize the width. If you position the cursor on the top or bottom edge, you can resize the height. Finally, if you position the cursor on a corner, you can resize the width and height at the same time.

After the cursor is positioned over the window's edge, press and hold the left mouse button; then drag the window border to its new size. Release the mouse button to lock in the newly sized window.

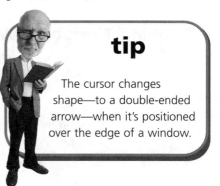

tip

The cursor changes shape—to a double-ended arrow—when it's positioned over the edge of a window.

Maximizing, Minimizing, and Closing Windows

Another way to manage a window in Windows is to make it display full-screen. You do this by maximizing the window. All you have to do is click the Maximize button at the upper-right corner of the window, as shown in Figure 3.3.

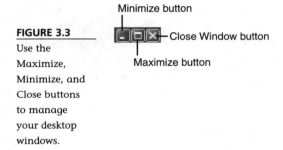

Minimize button

FIGURE 3.3

Use the
Maximize,
Minimize, and
Close buttons
to manage
your desktop
windows.

Close Window button

Maximize button

If the window is already maximized, the Maximize button changes to a Restore Down button. When you click the Restore Down button, the window resumes its previous (pre-maximized) dimensions.

If you'd rather hide the window so that it doesn't clutter your desktop, click the Minimize button. This shoves the window off the desktop, onto the Taskbar. The program in the window is still running, however—it's just not on the desktop. To restore a minimized window, all you have to do is click the window's button on the Windows Taskbar (at the bottom of the screen).

If what you really want to do is close the window (and close any program running within the window), just click the window's Close button.

Scrolling Through a Window

Many windows contain more information than can be displayed at once. When you have a long document or Web page, only the first part of the document or page is displayed in the window. To view the rest of the document or page, you have to scroll down through the window, using the various parts of the scroll bar (shown in Figure 3.4).

caution

If you try to close a window that contains a document you haven't saved, you'll be prompted to save the changes to the document. Because you probably don't want to lose any of your work, click Yes to save the document and then close the program.

FIGURE 3.4

Use the scrollbar to scroll through long pages.

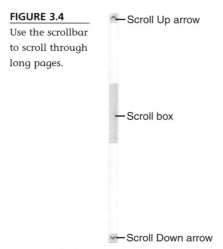

Scroll Up arrow

Scroll box

Scroll Down arrow

There are several ways to scroll through a window. To scroll up or down a line at a time, click the up or down arrow on the window's scrollbar. To move to a specific place in a long document, use your mouse to grab the scroll box (between the up and down arrows) and drag it to a new position. You can also click on the scroll bar between the scroll box and the end arrow, which scrolls you one screen at a time.

If your mouse has a scroll wheel, you can use it to scroll through a long document. Just roll the wheel back or forward to scroll down or up through a window.

Using Menus

Most windows in Windows use a set of pull-down menus to store all the commands and operations you can perform. The menus are aligned across the top of the window, just below the title bar, in what is called a *menu bar*.

You open (or pull down) a menu by clicking the menu's name. The full menu then appears just below the menu bar, as shown in Figure 3.5. You activate a command or select a menu item by clicking it with your mouse.

Menu bar

FIGURE 3.5

Navigating
Windows' menu
system.

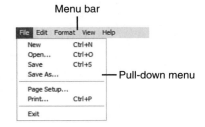

Pull-down menu

Some menu items have a little black arrow to the right of the label. This indicates that additional choices are available, displayed on a submenu. Click the menu item or the arrow to display the submenu.

Other menu items have three little dots (called an *ellipsis*) to the right of the label. This indicates that additional choices are available, displayed in a dialog box. Click the menu item to display the dialog box.

tip

If an item in a menu, toolbar, or dialog box is dimmed (or grayed), that means it isn't available for the current task.

The nice thing is, after you get the hang of this menu thing in one program, the menus should be very similar in all the other programs you use. For example, almost all programs have a File menu that lets you open, save, and close documents, as well as an Edit menu that lets you cut, copy, and paste. While each program has menus and menu items specific to its own needs, these common menus make it easy to get up and running when you install new software programs on your system.

Using Toolbars

Some Windows programs put the most frequently used operations on one or more *toolbars*, typically located just below the menu bar. (Figure 3.6 shows a typical Windows toolbar.) A toolbar looks like a row of buttons, each with a small picture (called an *icon*) and maybe a bit of text. You activate the associated command or operation by clicking the button with your mouse.

If the toolbar is too long to display fully on your screen, you'll see a right arrow at the far-right side of the toolbar. Click this arrow to display the buttons that aren't currently visible.

Toolbar

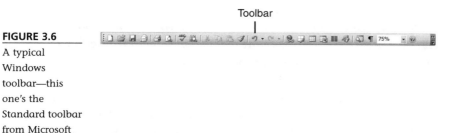

FIGURE 3.6
A typical
Windows
toolbar—this
one's the
Standard toolbar
from Microsoft
Word.

Using Dialog Boxes, Tabs, and Buttons

When Windows or an application requires a
complex set of inputs, you are often presented
with a *dialog box*. A dialog box is similar to a
form in which you can input various parameters
and make various choices—and then register
those inputs and choices when you click the OK
button. (Figure 3.7 shows the Print dialog box,
found in most Windows applications.)

There are several different types of dialog boxes,
each one customized to the task at hand.
However, most dialog boxes share a set of common features, which include the following:

tip

If you're not sure which
button does what, you can
hover the cursor over the
button to display a *tool tip*. A
tool tip is a small text box
that displays the button's
label or other useful
information.

FIGURE 3.7
Use dialog boxes
to control vari-
ous aspects of
your Windows
applications.

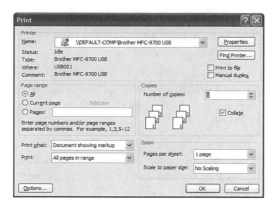

- **Buttons**—Most buttons either register your inputs or open an auxiliary dialog box. The most common buttons are OK (to register your inputs and close the dialog box), Cancel (to close the dialog box without registering your inputs), and Apply (to register your inputs without closing the dialog box). Click a button once to activate it.

- **Tabs**—These allow a single dialog box to display multiple "pages" of information. Think of each tab, arranged across the top of the dialog box, as a "thumbtab" to the individual page in the dialog box below it. Click the top of a tab to change to that particular page of information.

- **Text boxes**—These are empty boxes where you type in a response. Position your cursor over the empty input box, click your left mouse button, and begin typing.

- **Lists**—These are lists of available choices; lists can either scroll or drop down from what looks like an input box. Select an item from the list with your mouse; you can select multiple items in some lists by holding down the Ctrl key while clicking with your mouse.

- **Check boxes**—These are boxes that let you select (or deselect) various stand-alone options.

- **Sliders**—These are sliding bars that let you select increments between two extremes, similar to a sliding volume control on an audio system.

Using the Start Menu

All the software programs and utilities on your computer are accessed via Windows' Start menu. You display the Start menu by using your mouse to click the Start button, located in the lower-left corner of your screen.

As you can see in Figure 3.8, the Windows XP Start menu consists of two columns of icons. Your most frequently used programs are listed in the left column; basic Windows utilities and folders are listed in the right column. To open a specific program or folder, just click the icon.

To view the rest of your programs, click the All Programs arrow. This displays a new menu called the Programs menu. From here you can access various programs, sorted by type or manufacturer. (When more programs are contained within a master folder, you'll see an arrow to the right of the title; click this arrow to display additional choices.)

Frequently used programs

FIGURE 3.8

Access all the
programs on
your system
from the Start
menu.

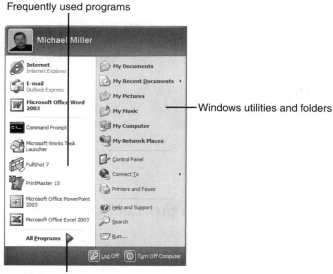

Windows utilities and folders

All Programs arrow

Launching a Program

Now that you know how to work the Start menu, it's easy to start any particular software program. All you have to do is follow these steps:

1. Click the Start button to display the Start menu.

2. If the program is displayed on the Start menu, click the program's icon.

3. If the program isn't visible on the main Start menu, click the All Programs
   button, find the program's icon, and then click it.

Switching Between Programs

After you've launched a few programs, it's easy to switch between one program and
another. To switch to another program (and send all other open programs to the
background), you can do one of the following:

■ Click the application's button in the taskbar, as shown in Figure 3.9.

FIGURE 3.9

Use the taskbar
buttons to
switch between
applications.

- Click any visible part of the application's window—including its title bar.
- Hold down the Alt key and then press the Tab key repeatedly until the application window you want is selected. (This cycles through all open windows.) When you're at the window you want, release the Alt key.

If you have multiple windows open at the same time, you can determine which is currently the active window by its title bar. The title bar for the active program is brighter, and the title bar text is bright white. An inactive title bar is more dull, with off-white text. If you have overlapping windows on your desktop, the window on top is always the active one. The active application's Taskbar button looks like it's pressed in.

Shutting Down Windows—and Your Computer

Windows starts automatically every time you turn on your computer. Although you will see lines of text flashing onscreen during the initial startup, Windows loads automatically and goes on to display the Windows desktop.

When you want to turn off your computer, you do it through Windows. In fact, you don't want to turn off your computer any other way—you *always* want to turn off things through the official Windows procedure.

To shut down Windows and turn off your PC, follow these steps:

1. Click the Start button to display the Start menu.

2. Click the Turn Off Computer button.

3. When the Turn Off Computer dialog box appears, click the Turn Off button.

caution

Do *not* turn off your computer without shutting down Windows. You could lose data and settings that are temporarily stored in your system's memory.

Understanding Files and Folders

All the information on your computer is stored in *files*. A file is nothing more than a collection of data of some sort. Everything on your computer's hard drive is a separate file, with its own name, location, and properties. The contents of a file can be a document from an application (such as a Works worksheet or a Word document), or they can be the executable code for the application itself.

Every file has its own unique name. A defined structure exists for naming files, and its conventions must be followed for Windows to understand exactly what file you want when you try to access one. Each filename must consist of two parts, separated by a period—the *name* (to the left of the period) and the *extension* (to the right of the period). A filename can consist of letters, numbers, spaces, and characters and looks something like this: `this is a filename.ext`.

Windows stores files in *folders*. A folder is like a master file; each folder can contain both files and additional folders. The exact location of a file is called its *path* and contains all the folders leading to the file. For example, a file named `filename.doc` that exists in the `system` folder, that is itself contained in the `windows` folder on your `c:\` drive, has a path that looks like this: `c:\windows\system\filename.doc`.

Learning how to use files and folders is a necessary skill for all computer users. You might need to copy files from one folder to another or from your hard disk to a floppy disk. You certainly need to delete files every now and then. To do this, you use either My Computer or My Documents—two important utilities, discussed next.

> **tip**
>
> By default, Windows XP hides the extensions when it displays filenames. To display extensions, use the Control Panel to open the Folder Options dialog box; then select the View tab. In the Advanced Settings list, *uncheck* the Hide Extensions for Known File Types option, and then click OK.

Managing PC Resources with My Computer

The My Computer utility lets you access each major component of your system and perform basic maintenance functions. For example, you can use My Computer to "open" the contents of your hard disk, and then copy, move, and delete individual files.

To open My Computer, follow these steps:

1. Click the Start button to display the Start menu.
2. Select My Computer.

As you can see in Figure 3.10, the My Computer folder contains icons for each of the major components of your system—your hard disk drive, floppy disk drive, CD-ROM or DVD drive, and so on.

System Tasks panel Hard disk drive

FIGURE 3.10

Use My
Computer to
manage your
hard drive
and other key
components.

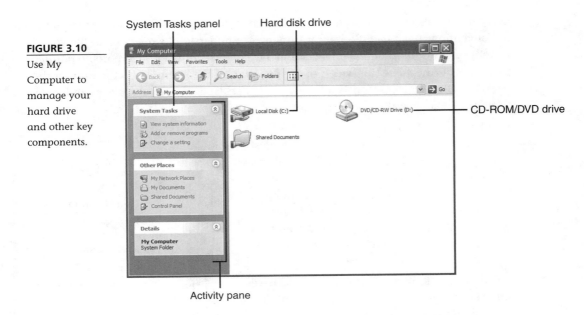

CD-ROM/DVD drive

Activity pane

Each folder in Windows XP contains an *activity pane* (sometimes called a *task pane*) on the left side of the window. This pane lets you view relevant information about and perform key operations on the selected item.

You can also use My Computer to view the contents of a specific drive. When you double-click the icon for that drive, you'll see a list of folders and files located on that drive. To view the contents of any folder, just double-click the icon for that folder.

Managing Files with My Documents

The documents you create with Microsoft Word and other software programs are actually separate computer files. By default, all your documents are stored somewhere in the My Documents folder.

Windows lets you access the contents of your My Documents folder with a few clicks of your mouse. Just follow these steps:

1. Click the Start button to display the Start menu.

2. Click My Documents.

As you can see in Figure 3.11, the My Documents folder not only contains individual files, it also contains a number of other folders (sometimes called *subfolders*), such as My Pictures and My Music. Double-click a subfolder to view its contents, or use the options in the Files and Folders Tasks panel to perform specific operations—including moving, copying, and deleting.

FIGURE 3.11
Access your
important docu-
ment files from
the My
Documents
folder.

Files and Folders task panel   Subfolder

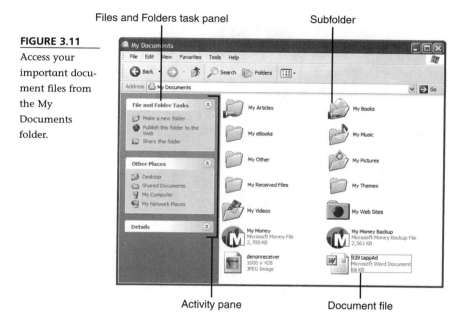

Activity pane   Document file

Managing Windows with the Control Panel

There's one more Windows utility, similar to My Computer and My Documents, that you need to know about. This utility, the Control Panel, is used to manage most (but not all) of Windows' configuration settings. The Control Panel is actually a system folder (like My Computer and My Documents) that contains a number of individual utilities that let you adjust and configure various system properties.

To open the Control Panel, follow these steps:

1. Click the Start button to display the Start menu.
2. Click Control Panel.

When the Control Panel opens, as shown in Figure 3.12, you can select a particular category you want to configure. When the Pick a Task page appears, either click a task or click an icon to open a specific configuration utility. (When you click a task, the appropriate configuration utility is launched.)

FIGURE 3.12

The Windows XP Control Panel—configuration tasks organized by category.

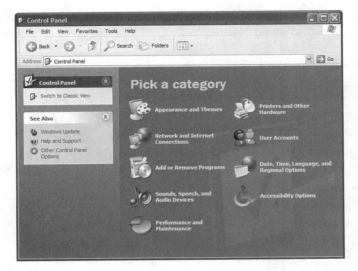

When you open a configuration utility, you'll see a dialog box for that particular item. You can then change the individual settings within that dialog box; click the OK button to register your new settings.

note

To learn more about configuring various Windows settings, see Chapter 5, "Personalizing Windows."

All the Other Things in Windows

Windows is more than just a pretty desktop and some configuration utilities. Windows also includes a large number of accessory programs and system tools you can use to perform other basic system operations.

Accessories

Windows includes a number of single-function accessory programs, all accessible from the Start menu. These programs include a calculator, some games, two basic word processors (Notepad and WordPad), a drawing program (Paint), a player for audio and video files (Windows Media Player), and a digital video editing program (Windows Movie Maker). You access most of these accessories by clicking the Start button and selecting All Programs, Accessories.

Internet Utilities

In addition to the aforementioned Windows accessories, Windows XP also gives you three important Internet utilities. These include a Web browser (Internet Explorer), an email program (Outlook Express), and an instant messaging program (Windows Messenger). You access these three utilities by clicking the Start button and selecting All Programs.

System Tools

Windows XP includes a handful of technical tools you can use to keep your system running smoothly. You can access all these tools by clicking the Start button and selecting All Programs, Accessories, System Tools.

Getting Help in Windows

When you can't figure out how to perform a particular task, it's time to ask for help. In Windows XP, this is done through the Help and Support Center.

note

To learn about the practical uses of these and other system tools, turn to Chapter 9, "Performing Routine Maintenance."

To launch the Help and Support Center, follow these steps:

1. Click the Start button to display the Start menu.
2. Click Help and Support.

The Help and Support Center lets you search for specific answers to your problems, browse the Help contents by topic, connect to another computer for remote assistance, go online for additional help, and access Windows's key system tools. Click the type of help you want, and follow the onscreen instructions from there.

THE ABSOLUTE MINIMUM

This chapter gave you a lot of background about Windows and the other software programs installed on your PC system. Here are the key points to remember:

- You use Windows to manage your computer system and run your software programs.

- Most functions in Windows are activated by clicking or double-clicking an icon or a button.

- All the programs and accessories on your system are accessed via the Start menu, which you display by clicking the Start button.

- Use My Computer to manage the main components of your system.

- Use My Documents to manage your document files and folders.

- Use the Control Panel to manage Windows' configuration settings.

- When you can't figure out how to do something, click the Start button and select Help and Support.

4

TAKING WINDOWS FOR A SPIN

Now that you have everything connected, configured, and powered up—and you know a little about how Windows works—it's time to take your new computer for a test drive. Just to get the feel of things, you know—open a few documents, print a few pages, that sort of thing. That's what this chapter is about.

Playing a Game

Let's assume you followed the instructions in Chapter 2, "Setting Up Your New Computer System," and that you have all the components connected and your system up and running. You should now be looking at an empty Windows desktop, similar to the one shown in Figure 4.1.

FIGURE 4.1

Start with the
Windows
desktop.

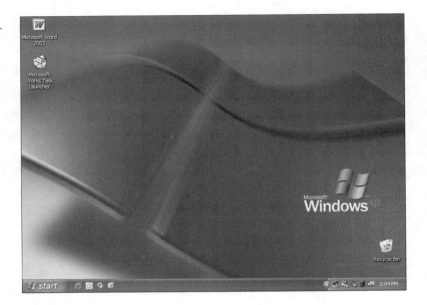

Let's have a little fun—and play a simple computer game.

Windows XP comes with a handful of computer games already installed. The game you're probably most familiar with is Solitaire, so let's launch Solitaire and play a game or two.

All you have to do is follow these steps:

1. Click the Start button in the lower-left corner of the screen.
2. When the Start menu appears, as shown in Figure 4.2, click the All Programs button.
3. When the Programs menu appears, as shown in Figure 4.3, click the item labeled Games.

FIGURE 4.2

Click the Start button to display the Start menu.

FIGURE 4.3

Click the All Programs button to display all the programs installed on your system.

4. This displays a submenu listing all the games available in Windows. Move your cursor down to the one labeled Solitaire, and then click it.

5. Windows now launches the Solitaire program and displays it in a small window on your desktop, as shown in Figure 4.4.

6. Before you start playing, you probably should resize the window. Move your cursor to the lower-right corner of the Solitaire window, and then drag the window border down and to the right. When the window is large enough for you, release the mouse button.

7. That was good, but maybe the game would be easier to play if it were displayed full-screen, as shown in Figure 4.5. Click the Maximize button (upper-right corner of the window, in the middle) to maximize the Solitaire window.

8. Now it's time to play. To move a card, grab it with your mouse and drag it onto another card. To turn over cards from the main deck, click the deck. To start a new game, pull down the Game menu and select Deal.

9. When you're done playing, close the Solitaire window by either clicking the window's Close button or pulling down the Game menu and selecting Exit.

tip

Solitaire is also a good way to practice your mouse skills. You get to practice dragging and dropping (by moving cards from stack to stack) and double-clicking (to move cards to the top rows).

FIGURE 4.5

Playing
Solitaire,
full-screen.

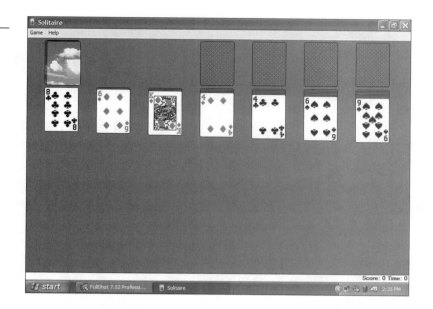

Launching a Program—and Printing and Saving a Document

That was fun. Now let's try something a little more productive—like creating a short note. We'll use Notepad, which is a basic word processor that's part of Microsoft Windows.

Opening Notepad

To open the Notepad program, follow these steps:

1. Click the Start button to display the Start menu.

2. Click the All Programs button to display the Programs menu.

3. Click the item labeled Accessories, then click the item labeled Notepad.

4. The Notepad program now launches in its own window, as shown in Figure 4.6.

note

Throughout the rest of this chapter and the book, this type of operation will be combined into a single action, as in "select All Programs, Accessories, Notepad."

FIGURE 4.6

Writing a note
with Notepad.

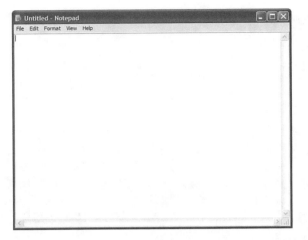

FIGURE 4.6

Writing a note
with Notepad.

Writing Your Note

The blank white space in the middle of the screen is a new Notepad document—kind of like a blank sheet of paper. To write a note, position the cursor within the window and type the following text, using your computer keyboard:

`This is my very first note in Notepad.`

Printing Your Note

Now let's print a copy of your note. Make sure your printer is connected to your computer, and then follow these steps:

1. Pull down the File menu and select Print.

2. When the Print dialog box appears (shown in Figure 4.7), make sure the correct printer is selected in the Select Printer section; then click the Print button.

FIGURE 4.7

Printing a
document.

Your printer should now come to life and, after a few moments, spit out a piece of paper. When you look at the paper, you should see your note printed at the top.

Saving Your File

Any document you create needs to be saved to your hard disk; otherwise, it won't exist after you close the program. To save your current note as a new file, follow these steps:

1. Pull down the File menu and select Save As.

2. When the Save As dialog box appears (shown in Figure 4.8), click the My Documents button on the left side of the dialog box; then type `my new file` in the File Name box.

3. Click the Save button.

FIGURE 4.8

Saving a new file in the My Documents folder.

What you've done here is saved your document as a file named `my new file`. You saved it in the My Documents folder, which is where Windows stores all new documents by default.

Closing the Program

To close Notepad, pull down the File menu and select Exit.

Viewing Your Documents

Now that you've created a document, let's take a look at it. If you remember, you saved the file in the My Documents folder, so let's open that folder and take a peek around.

Follow these steps:

1. Click the Start button to display the Start menu.
2. Select My Documents to open the My Documents folder, shown in Figure 4.9.
3. Hover your cursor over the my new file icon.

FIGURE 4.9

Examining the contents of your My Documents folder.

4. Information about your file is displayed in the Details panel of the activity pane, and basic tasks are displayed in the File and Folder Tasks panel.

   To open this file for further editing, double-click the file icon. This launches Notepad with the my new file file already loaded and ready to edit.

Examining Your Hard Disk

Before we finish our quick spin around the desktop, let's examine the My Computer folder and see what's on your hard disk. Follow these steps:

1. Click the Start button to display the Start menu.
2. Select My Computer to open the My Computer folder, shown in Figure 4.10.

FIGURE 4.10

The contents of
your My
Computer folder.

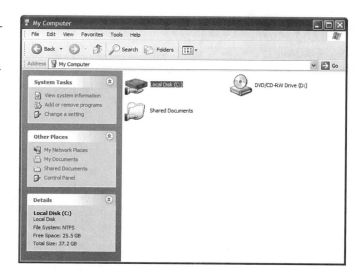

3. Hover your cursor over your local hard disk drive—typically labeled drive C.

4. Information about your hard disk is displayed in the Details panel of the activity pane, and basic operations are displayed in the System Tasks panel.

5. Position your cursor over the hard disk icon, and click your *right* mouse button (in other words, *right-click* the icon).

6. This displays a pop-up menu. Select Properties from this menu.

7. When the Properties dialog box appears, select the General tab. As you can see in Figure 4.11, this tab displays a pie chart that represents how much of your hard disk is currently used and how much free space is available.

8. Click OK to close the dialog box.

FIGURE 4.11

Viewing interest-
ing information
about your hard
disk.

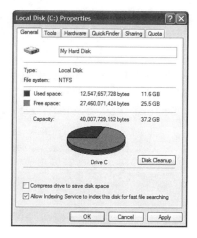

Shutting Down Your System

Now that our test drive is over, let's turn off things and settle in for the day. While you *could* turn off your system by pressing the big button on the front of your system unit, this isn't the *proper* way to shut off your system. The proper procedure uses Windows to shut down everything, nice and orderly.

Just follow these steps:

1. Click the Start button to display the Start menu.

2. Select Turn Off Computer.

3. When the Turn Off Computer box appears, select Turn Off.

Windows will now do what it needs to do to properly close all of its system files. When the screen goes blank and your system unit stops making noise, your system is shut down.

tip

To turn your computer back on, press the power button on the front of your PC's system unit.

THE ABSOLUTE MINIMUM

That was a fun little trip of discovery, wasn't it? Here are the key points to remember:

- Just about everything you could want to launch or open is somewhere on the Start menu.

- After you have a window open on your desktop, you can use your mouse to resize it—or you can maximize it to display full-screen.

- When you want to print a file in a Windows application, pull down the File menu and select Print.

- When you want to save a file in a Windows application, pull down the File menu and select Save As.

- When you want to close a Windows application, pull down the File menu and select Exit—or just click the window's Close button.

- To turn off your computer, use the Turn Off Computer command on the Windows Start menu.

Personalizing Windows

When you first turn on your new computer system, you see the Windows desktop as Microsoft set it up for you. If you like the way it looks, great. If not, you can change it.

Windows presents a lot of different ways to personalize the look and feel of your desktop. In fact, one of the great things about Windows is how quickly you can make the desktop look like *your* desktop, different from anybody else's.

Changing the Look of Your Desktop

One of the first things that most users want to personalize is the look of the Windows desktop itself. Read on to learn what you can customize—and how.

Changing the Desktop Size

You can configure your computer's display so that the desktop is larger or smaller than normal. A larger desktop lets you view more things onscreen at the same time—even though each item is smaller than before. A smaller desktop displays fewer items, but they're larger. (Great if your eyesight is less than perfect.)

Changing the size of the desktop is accomplished by changing Windows's *screen resolution*. You do this by following these steps:

tip

You can also open the Display Properties dialog box from the Windows Control panel; just open the Control Panel folder, select Appearance and Themes, and then select Display.

1. Right-click anywhere on the desktop to display a pop-up menu.

2. Select Properties from the pop-up menu; this displays the Display Properties dialog box.

3. Select the Settings tab (shown in Figure 5.1).

FIGURE 5.1

Use the Display Properties dialog box to configure Windows' display settings.

4. Adjust the Screen Resolution slider. (The sample display changes to reflect your new settings.)

While you're on this tab, you can also change the number of colors displayed. (More is better.) Just choose the desired setting from the Color Quality drop-down list, and then click OK when done.

Selecting a New Desktop Theme

Desktop *themes* are specific combinations of background wallpaper, colors, fonts, cursors, sounds, and screensavers—all arranged around a specific look or topic. When you choose a new theme, the look and feel of your entire desktop changes.

To change desktop themes, follow these steps:

1. Open the Display Properties dialog box and select the Themes tab.

2. Select a new theme from the Theme drop-down list.

3. Click OK when done.

Personalizing the Desktop Background

Although changing themes is the fastest way to change the look of all your desktop elements, you can also change each element separately.

For example, you can easily change your desktop's background pattern or wallpaper. You can choose from the many patterns and wallpapers included with Windows or select a graphic of your own choosing.

Just follow these steps:

1. Open the Display Properties dialog box and select the Desktop tab, shown in Figure 5.2.

2. To choose one of Windows's built-in backgrounds, make a selection from the Background list.

tip

To best use all the features of Windows XP, go for a 1024×768 resolution. If this setting makes things look too small (a problem if you have a smaller monitor), try the 800×600 resolution. As for color, 16-bit is my recommended minimum for Windows XP, but 32-bit is better for displaying fast-moving games or video.

tip

You can find additional themes in the Microsoft Plus! for Windows add-on pack. Learn more at the Microsoft Plus! Web site (www.microsoft.com/windows/plus/).

FIGURE 5.2

Use the Display Properties dialog box to select a new desktop background.

3. To select your own graphics file, click the Browse button and navigate to the file you want to use. Click the Open button to add this file to the Background list.

4. To determine how the image file is displayed on your desktop, select one of the items from the Position pull-down list: Center, Tile, or Stretch.

5. If you'd rather display a solid background color with no graphic, select None from the Background list and select a color from the Color list.

6. Click OK to register your changes.

Changing the Color Scheme

The default Windows XP desktop uses a prede-fined combination of colors and fonts. If you don't like this combination, you can choose from several other predefined schemes.

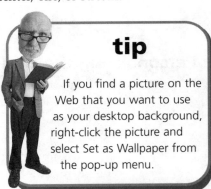

tip

If you find a picture on the Web that you want to use as your desktop background, right-click the picture and select Set as Wallpaper from the pop-up menu.

To change to a new color scheme, follow these steps:

1. Open the Display Properties dialog box and select the Appearance tab.

2. Pull down the Color Scheme list, and select a new theme.

3. Click OK when done.

Organizing Desktop Icons

Desktop icons—those little pictures on your desktop—function as shortcuts for starting applications and opening documents. Placing a shortcut on your desktop is an alternative to launching items from the Start menu.

Creating New Shortcuts on the Desktop

To put a new shortcut on your desktop, follow these steps:

1. From within My Computer or any Windows folder, navigate to the application or document for which you want to create a shortcut.

2. Right-click the file icon, and then select Send To, Desktop (Create Shortcut).

To remove a shortcut icon from the desktop, just drag it into the Recycle Bin.

tip

You can also create a shortcut by right-dragging a file icon directly to the desktop, or by right-clicking on the desktop and selecting New, Shortcut from the pop-up menu.

Changing the Name of a Shortcut

When you create a new shortcut icon, its name is automatically prefixed with the words "Shortcut to...." To change the name of a shortcut, follow these steps:

1. Right-click the shortcut on your desktop.

2. When the pop-up menu appears, select Rename.

3. The shortcut's name is now highlighted on your desktop. Use the Delete or Backspace keys to erase parts of the existing name, and then type a new name. Press Enter when you've finished entering the new name.

Arranging Icons on the Desktop

All those desktop icons let you quickly open your most-used programs, but they can really clutter up the look of your Windows desktop. To better arrange your icons, right-click a blank area of the desktop and choose from one of the following options:

- **Name**—Sorts items alphabetically by filename
- **Size**—Sorts items by file size, from smallest to largest
- **Type**—Sorts items by file type so that files with the same extension are grouped together
- **Modified**—Sorts items by date, from oldest to most recent

In addition, you can choose to Auto Arrange the items, which automatically arranges the icons along the left side of your desktop, or Align to Grid, which makes all your icons snap to an invisible grid.

Cleaning Up Your Desktop Shortcuts

tip

You can't choose Align to Grid and Auto Arrange at the same time. If you want to spread your icons across the desktop (but aligned to the invisible grid), turn off Auto Arrange and Align to Grid on.

Windows XP includes a Desktop Cleanup Wizard that sweeps all your unused desktop icons into an Unused Desktop icons folder, thus cleaning up a cluttered desktop. Windows XP automatically runs the Desktop Cleanup Wizard every 60 days, but you can also run the wizard manually. Just follow these steps:

1. Open the Display Properties dialog box, select the Desktop tab, and then click the Customize Desktop button.

2. When the Desktop Items dialog box appears, select the General tab.

3. Click the Clean Desktop Now button to run the Wizard now.

Changing the Way the Start Menu Works

You use the Start menu every time you launch a program. Windows offers a few ways for you to customize the way the Start menu works for you.

Applying Start Menu Special Effects

Windows XP applies a handful of special effects to the Start menu. You can animate the Start menu when it opens, force submenus to open when you hover over them, and highlight new applications.

To change these special effects, follow these steps:

1. Right-click the Start button and select Properties from the pop-up menu; this displays the Taskbar and Start Menu Properties dialog box.

2. Select the Start Menu tab.

3. Click the Customize button to display the Customize Start Menu dialog box.

4. Select the Advanced tab, as shown in Figure 5.3.

FIGURE 5.3

Use the Customize Start Menu dialog box to change the way the Start menu works.

5. To make submenus open when you point at them, check the Open Submenus When I Pause On Them With My Mouse option.

6. To highlight the newest applications, check the Highlight Newly Installed Programs option.

7. Click OK when done.

Displaying More—or Fewer—Programs on the Start Menu

By default, the Start menu displays the five most-recent applications you've run. You can reconfigure the Start menu to display more (up to nine) or fewer (as few as zero) applications at a time.

To display more or fewer programs, follow these steps:

1. Right-click the Start button and select Properties from the pop-up menu to display the Taskbar and Start Menu Properties dialog box.

2. Select the Start Menu tab.

3. Click the Customize button to display the Customize Start Menu dialog box.

4. Select the General tab.

5. Select a new number from the Number of Programs on Start Menu list.

6. Click OK when done.

Selecting Which Icons to Display on the Start Menu—and How

The default Start menu also displays icons for the Control Panel, My Computer, My Documents, My Pictures, My Music, Network Connections, Help and Support, and the Run command. You can configure Windows XP to not display any of these icons—or to display some of the icons as expandable menus. Just follow these steps:

1. Right-click the Start button and select Properties from the pop-up menu to display the Taskbar and Start Menu Properties dialog box.

2. Select the Start Menu tab.

3. Click the Customize button to display the Customize Start Menu dialog box.

4. Select the Advanced tab.

5. In the Start Menu Items list, click Display As a Link to display an icon as a link to the main item (in a separate window), Display As a Menu to display a pop-up menu when an icon is clicked, or Don't Display This Item to not display an item.

6. Repeat step 5 for each of the items listed.

7. Click OK when done.

Adding a Program to the Start Menu—Permanently

If you're not totally comfortable with the way programs come and go from the Start menu, you can add any program to the Start menu—*permanently*. All you have to do is follow these steps:

1. Click the Start button to display the Start menu.

2. Click the All Programs button to open the Programs menu.

3. Navigate to a specific program.

4. Right-click that program to display the pop-up menu.

5. Select Pin to Start Menu.

The program you selected now appears on the Start menu, just below the browser and email icons.

To remove a program you've added to the Start menu, right-click its icon and select Unpin from Start Menu.

Activating Special Effects

Windows XP includes all sorts of special effects, not all of which are turned on by default. These effects are applied to the way certain elements look or the way they pull down or pop up onscreen.

Enabling ClearType

ClearType is a new display technology in Windows XP that effectively triples the horizontal resolution on LCD displays. (In other words, it makes things look sharper—and smoother.) If you have a flat-panel monitor or a portable PC, you definitely want to turn on ClearType.

To turn on ClearType, follow these steps:

1. Open the Display Properties dialog box and select the Appearance tab.
2. Click the Effects button to display the Effects dialog box.
3. Check the Use the Following Method to Smooth Edges of Screen Fonts option.
4. Select ClearType from the pull-down list.
5. Click OK when done.

Using the Effects Dialog Box

Some Windows special effects are activated from the Effects dialog box, which you access via the Display Properties dialog box. To change these special effects, follow these steps:

1. Open the Display Properties dialog box and select the Appearance tab.
2. Click the Effects button to display the Effects dialog box, shown in Figure 5.4.

FIGURE 5.4

Activating special effects via the Effects dialog box.

3. Make the appropriate choices from the options available.
4. Click OK.

The Effects dialog box offers a variety of special effects. You can choose to add transition effects for menus, display drop shadows under menus, display large icons on the desktop, display the contents of windows when they're dragged, and hide the underlined letters on menu items.

Using the Performance Options Dialog Box

Even more special effects are activated from the Systems Property dialog box. You access these effects by following these steps:

1. Click the Start button to display the Start menu.
2. Select Control Panel to open the Control Panel folder.
3. Select Performance and Hardware, and then select System to open the Systems Properties dialog box.
4. Select the Advanced tab and click the Settings button in the Performance section.
5. When the Performance Options dialog box appears, click the Visual Effects tab, as shown in Figure 5.5.

FIGURE 5.5

Use the Performance Options dialog box to select more subtle display effects.

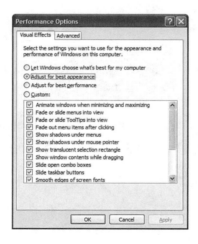

6. Choose which effects you want to activate.
7. Click OK when done.

Most of the effects in the Performance Options dialog box are self-explanatory, although some are extremely subtle. If you aren't sure which effects to choose, select either the Adjust for Best Appearance or Adjust for Best Performance option. The first option turns on all the special effects, and the second option turns them all off. Even better is the Let Windows Choose What's Best for My Computer option, which activates a select group of effects that won't slow down your system's performance.

Changing Your Click

How do you click? Do you like to double-click the icons on your desktop? Would you prefer to single-click your icons the same way you click hyperlinks on a Web page? Should the names of your icons be plain text or underlined like a hyperlink?

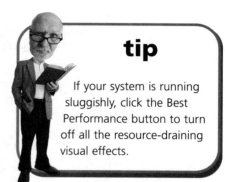

tip

If your system is running sluggishly, click the Best Performance button to turn off all the resource-draining visual effects.

Windows XP comes from the factory set up for traditional double-clicking. (This is where you single-click an item to select it and double-click to open it.) To change Windows's click mode, just follow these steps:

1. Click the Start button to display the Start menu.
2. Select Control Panel to open the Control Panel folder.
3. Select Appearance and Themes, and then Folder Options to display the Folder Options dialog box, shown in Figure 5.6.

FIGURE 5.6

Change Windows XP to single-click operation.

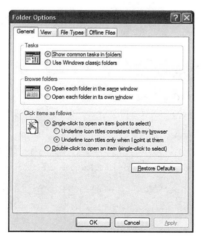

4. Select the General tab.
5. If you want to use traditional double-clicking, check the Double-Click to Open an Item option. If you want to use Web-like single-clicking, check the

Single-Click to Open an Item option. (In this mode, you select an item by hovering your cursor over it and open items with a single click.)

6. Click OK.

Using a Screensaver

Screensavers display moving designs on your computer screen when you haven't typed or moved the mouse for a while. This prevents static images from burning into your screen—and provides some small degree of entertainment if you're bored at your desk.

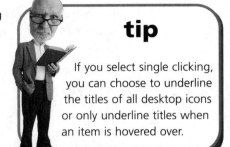

tip

If you select single clicking, you can choose to underline the titles of all desktop icons or only underline titles when an item is hovered over.

To activate one of the screensavers included with Windows XP, follow these steps:

1. Open the Display Properties dialog box and select the Screen Saver tab.

2. Select a screensaver from the Screen Saver drop-down list.

3. Click the Settings button to configure that screensaver's specific settings (if available).

4. Return to the Display Properties dialog box and select the number of minutes you want the screen to be idle before the screensaver activates.

5. Click OK when done.

Resetting the Time and Date

The time and date for your system should be automatically set when you first turn on your computer. If you find that you need to change or reset the time or date settings, all you have to do is follow these steps:

1. Double-click the time display in the Windows Tray (at the bottom right of your screen) to display the Date and Time Properties dialog box.

2. Select the Date & Time tab; then select the correct month and year from the pull-down lists, click the correct day of the month on the calendar, and set the correct time on the clock.

3. Select the Time Zone tab; then select the correct time zone from the pull-down list. (For most states, you should also select Automatically Adjust Clock for Daylight Saving Changes.)

4. Select the Internet Time tab; then check the Automatically Synchronize with an Internet Time Server option. (This automatically synchronizes your PC's internal clock with an ultra-accurate time server on the Internet.)

5. Click OK when done.

Setting Up Additional Users

Chances are you're not the only person using your computer; it's likely that you'll be sharing your PC to some degree with your spouse and kids. Fortunately, you can configure Windows so that different people using your computer sign on with their own custom settings—and access to their own personal files.

You should assign each user in your household his own password-protected *user account*. Anyone trying to access another user's account and files without the password will then be denied access.

There are three different types of user accounts you can establish on your computer—computer administrator, limited, and guest. You'll want to set yourself up as the computer administrator because only this account can make systemwide changes to your PC, install software, and access all the files on the system. Set up other household members with limited accounts; they'll be able to use the computer and access their own files but won't be able to install software or mess up the main settings. Any guests to your household, then, can sign on via the guest account.

tip

There can be more than one administrator account per PC, so you might want to set up your spouse with an administrator account, too.

Only the computer administrator can add a new user to your system. To set up a new account on your machine, be sure that you're logged on via an administrator account and then follow these steps:

1. Click the Start button to open the Start menu.

2. Select Control Panel to open the Control Panel folder.

3. Select User Accounts, and then select Create a New Account.

4. When the User Accounts screen appears, enter a name for the account and click Next.

5. On the next screen, check either the Computer Administrator or Limited option; then click the Create Account button.

Windows XP now creates the new account and randomly assigns a picture that will appear next to the username. You or the user can change this picture at any time by returning to the User Accounts utility, selecting the account, and then selecting the Change My Picture option.

By default, no password is assigned to the new account. If you want to assign a password, return to the User Accounts utility, select the account, and then select the Create a Password option.

caution

If you create a password for your account, you better remember it. You won't be able to access Windows—or any of your applications and documents—if you forget the password!

THE ABSOLUTE MINIMUM

Here are the key points to remember from this chapter:

- ■ To change most display options (color, resolution, and so on), right-click anywhere on the desktop to display the Display Options dialog box.

- ■ To change the way the Start menu looks and acts, right-click the Start button and select Properties from the pop-up menu.

- ■ If you're using a laptop PC or a desktop with an LCD flat-screen display, make sure that you activate the ClearType option.

- ■ If you have multiple users in your household, create a user account for each person, and assign each user his own password. (Just make sure that you remember your password—or you won't be able to log in to Windows!)

6

WORKING WITH FILES AND FOLDERS

As you learned in Chapter 3, "Understanding Microsoft Windows XP," all the documents and programs on your computer are stored in electronic files. These files are then arranged into a series of folders and subfolders—just as you'd arrange paper files in a series of file folders in a filing cabinet.

Since all your important data is stored in files, it's important that you learn how to work with Windows' files and folders. Every user needs to know how to copy, move, and delete files—none of which, fortunately, are that hard to do.

Viewing Folders and Files

In Windows XP you use either My Computer or My Documents (both accessible from the Windows Start menu) to view the folders and files on your system. Both of these tools work similarly and enable you to customize the way they display their contents.

As you can see in Figure 6.1, the My Documents folder contains not only individual files, but also other folders—called *subfolders*—that themselves contain other files. Most of the file-related operations you want to undertake are accessible directly from the File and Folder Tasks section in the Tasks pane, located at the left of the My Documents window.

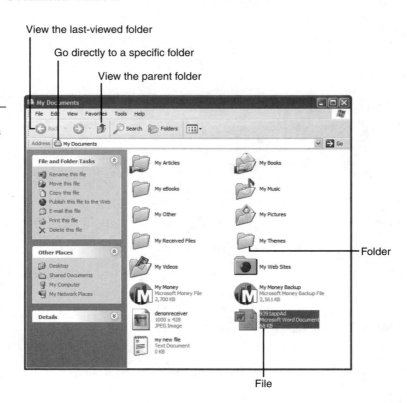

View the last-viewed folder

Go directly to a specific folder

View the parent folder

FIGURE 6.1
Manage your folders and files with the My Documents folder.

Changing the Way Files Are Displayed

You can choose to view the contents of a folder in a variety of ways. Just follow these steps:

1. Click the Views button on the My Documents toolbar; this displays a pop-up menu, shown in Figure 6.2.
2. Select from the Thumbnails, Tiles, Icons, List, or Details views.

FIGURE 6.2

Click the Views button to change the way files are displayed.

The default view is the Tiles view, shown in Figure 6.1; experiment with each view to determine which you like best.

> **tip**
>
> Thumbnails view is best for working with graphics files. Details view is best if you're looking for files by date or size.

Sorting Files and Folders

When viewing files in My Computer or My Documents, you can sort your files and folders in a number of ways. To do this, follow these steps:

1. Pull down the View menu and select Arrange Icons By.
2. Choose to sort by Name, Size, Type, or Modified.

If you want to view your files in alphabetical order, choose to sort by Name. If you want to see all similar files grouped together, choose to sort by Type. If you want to sort your files by the date and time they were last edited, choose the Modified option.

Grouping Files and Folders

You can also configure Windows XP to group the files in your folder, which can make it easier to identify particular files. For example, if you sorted your files by time and date modified, they'll now be grouped by date (Today, Yesterday, Last Week, and so on), as shown in Figure 6.3. If you sorted your files by type, they'll be grouped by file extension, and so on.

To turn on grouping, follow these steps:

1. Pull down the View menu and select Arrange Icons By.
2. Check the Show in Groups option.

Windows now groups your files and folders by the criteria you used to sort those items.

FIGURE 6.3

Files grouped by date.

Saving Your Settings, Universally

By default, when you customize a folder, that view is specific to that folder. To apply a folder view to all the folders on your system, follow these steps:

1. Start by configuring the current folder the way you want.

2. Select Tools, Folder Options to display the Folder Options dialog box.

3. Select the View tab, shown in Figure 6.4.

4. Click the Apply to All Folders button, and then click OK.

FIGURE 6.4

Use the Folder Options dialog box to make all your folders look alike.

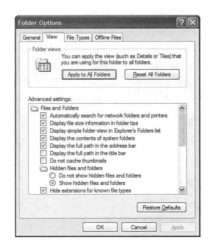

tip

To return your folders to their original states, click the Reset All Folders button.

Navigating Folders

You can navigate through the folders and subfolders in My Computer, My Documents, and other folders in several ways:

■ To view the contents of a disk or folder, double-click the selected item.

■ To move up the hierarchy of folders and subfolders to the next highest item, click the Up button on the toolbar.

■ To move back to the disk or folder previously selected, click the Back button on the toolbar.

■ To choose from the history of disks and folders previously viewed, click the down arrow on the Back button (shown in Figure 6.5) and select a disk or folder.

FIGURE 6.5

View a list of previously viewed folders by clicking the down arrow on the Back button.

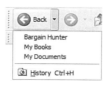

■ If you've moved back through multiple disks or folders, you can move forward to the next folder by clicking the Forward button.

■ Go directly to any disk or folder by entering the path in the Address Bar (in the format *x:\folder\subfolder*) and pressing Enter or clicking the Go button.

You can also go directly to any folder by clicking the Folders button to display the Folders pane, shown in Figure 6.6. You can then select the folder you want from the Folders list.

FIGURE 6.6

Display the Folders pane to go directly to any folder on your computer's hard disk.

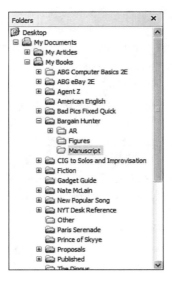

Creating New Folders

The more files you create, the harder it is to organize and find things on your hard disk. When the number of files you have becomes unmanageable, you need to create more folders—and subfolders—to better categorize your files.

To create a new folder, follow these steps:

1. Navigate to the drive or folder where you want to place the new folder.

2. Select Make a New Folder from the File and Folder Tasks panel; a new, empty folder now appears, with the filename `New Folder` highlighted.

3. Type a name for your folder (which overwrites the `New Folder` name), and press Enter.

Renaming Files and Folders

When you create a new file or folder, it helps to give it a name that somehow describes its contents. Sometimes, however, you might need to change a file's name. Fortunately, Windows makes it relatively easy to rename an item.

caution

Folder and filenames can include up to 255 characters—including many special characters. Some special characters, however, are "illegal," meaning that you *can't* use them in folder or filenames. Illegal characters include the following: \ / : * ? " < > |.

To rename a file (or folder), follow these steps:

1. Select the file or folder you want to rename.

2. Select Rename This File from the File Tasks list, or press F2; this highlights the filename.

3. Type a new name for your folder (which overwrites the current name), and press Enter.

Copying Files

Now it's time to address the most common things you do with files—copying and moving them from one location to another. These operations, like most file operations, can be accessed directly from the Tasks pane in any Windows folder.

It's important to remember that copying is different from moving. When you *copy* an item, the original item remains in its original location— plus you have the new copy. When you *move* an item, the original is no longer present in the original location—all you have is the item in the new location.

caution

The one part of the filename you should never change is the extension—the part that comes after the "dot." That's because Windows and other software programs recognize different types of program files and documents by their extension. For example, program files always have an .EXE extension, and Microsoft Word documents always have a .DOC extension. Try to change the extension, and Windows will warn you that you're doing something wrong.

The Easy Way to Copy

To copy a file or a folder with Windows XP, follow these steps:

1. Select the item you want to copy.

2. Select Copy This File from the File Tasks list; this opens the Copy Items dialog box, shown in Figure 6.7.

3. Navigate to and select the new location for the item.

4. Click the Copy button.

tip

If you want to copy the item to a new folder, click the New Folder button before you click the Copy button.

That's it. You've just copied the file from one location to another.

FIGURE 6.7

Use the Copy Items dialog box to copy a file or folder.

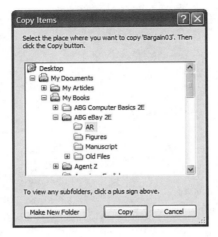

Other Ways to Copy

The method just presented is just one of many ways to copy a file. Windows XP provides several other methods, including:

- Pull down the File menu and select Copy (or Copy to Folder), then paste to the new location.
- Right-click a file and select Copy from the pop-up menu, then paste to the new location.
- Right-click a file and select Send To from the pop-up menu, then select a location from the choices listed.
- Hold down the Ctrl key and then use your mouse to drag the file or folder from one location to another within the My Documents or My Computer folders.
- Drag the file or folder while holding down the *right* mouse button. When you drop the file into a new location, you see a pop-up menu that asks whether you want to move it or copy it. Select the copy option.

Moving Files

Moving a file (or folder) is different from copying it. Moving cuts the item from its previous location and places it in a new location. Copying leaves the original item where it was *and* creates a copy of the item elsewhere.

In other words, when you copy something you end up with two of it. When you move something, you only have the one thing.

The Easy Way to Move

To move a file, follow these steps:

1. Select the item you want to move.
2. Select Move This File from the File Tasks list.
3. When the Move Items dialog box appears (looks just like the Copy Items dialog box), navigate to and select the new location for the item.
4. Click the Move button.

Other Ways to Move a File

Just as Windows provides several other ways to copy a file, you also have a choice of alternative methods for moving a file, including the following:

- Pull down the File menu and select Move (or Move to Folder), then paste it to the new location.
- Right-click a file name and select Cut from the pop-up menu, then paste it to the new location.
- Use your mouse to drag the file from one location to another.
- Drag the file or folder while holding down the *right* mouse button. When you drop the file into a new location, you see a pop-up menu that asks whether you want to move it or copy it. Select the move option.

Deleting Files

Too many files eat up too much hard disk space—which is a bad thing, since you only have so much disk space. (Music and video files, in particular, can chew up big chunks of your hard drive.) Because you don't want to waste disk space, you should periodically delete those files (and folders) you no longer need.

The Easy Way to Delete

Deleting a file is as easy as following these two simple steps:

1. Select the file.
2. Select Delete This File from the File Tasks list.

This simple operation sends the file to the Windows Recycle Bin, which is kind of a trash can for deleted files. (It's also a trash can that periodically needs to be dumped—as discussed later in this activity.)

Restoring Deleted Files

Have you ever accidentally deleted the wrong file? If so, you're in luck. For a short period of time, Windows stores the files you delete in the Recycle Bin. The Recycle Bin is actually a special folder on your hard disk; if you've recently deleted a file, it should still be in the Recycle Bin folder.

To "undelete" a file from the Recycle Bin, follow these steps:

1. Double-click the Recycle Bin icon on your desktop (shown in Figure 6.8) to open the Recycle Bin folder.
2. Select the file you want to restore.
3. Select Restore This Item from the Recycle Bin Tasks list.

This copies the deleted file back to its original location, ready for continued use.

note

You can also delete a file by dragging it from the folder window onto the Recycle Bin icon on the desktop, or by highlighting it and pressing the Del key.

FIGURE 6.8
The Recycle Bin, where all your deleted files end up.

Recycle Bin

Managing the Recycle Bin

Deleted files do not stay in the Recycle Bin indefinitely. By default, the deleted files in the Recycle Bin can occupy 10% of your hard disk space. When you've deleted enough files to exceed this 10%, the oldest files in the Recycle Bin are automatically and permanently deleted from your hard disk.

If you'd rather dump the Recycle Bin manually (and thus free up some hard disk space), follow these steps:

1. Double-click the Recycle Bin icon on your desktop to open the Recycle Bin folder.
2. Select Empty the Recycle Bin from the Recycle Bin Tasks list.
3. When the Confirm File Delete dialog box appears, click Yes to completely erase the files, or click No to continue storing the files in the Recycle Bin.

Working with Compressed Folders

Really big files can be difficult to move or copy. They're especially hard to transfer to other users, whether by floppy disk or email.

Fortunately, Windows XP includes a way to make big files smaller. *Compressed folders* take big files and compress them down in size, which makes them easier to copy or move. After the file has been transferred, you can then uncompress the file back to its original state.

Compressing a File

Compressing one or more files is a relatively easy task from within any Windows folder. Just follow these steps:

1. Select the file(s) you want to compress.

2. Right-click the file(s) to display the pop-up menu.

3. Select Send to, Compressed (zipped) Folder.

Windows now creates a new folder that contains compressed versions of the file(s) you selected. (This folder is distinguished by a little zipper on the folder icon, as shown in Figure 6.9.) You can now copy, move, or email this folder, which is a lot smaller than the original file(s).

The compressed folder is actually a file with a .ZIP extension, so it can be used with other compression/decompression programs, such as WinZip.

FIGURE 6.9
A compressed folder contain-ing one or more files.

Bargain04
13 KB

Extracting Files from a Compressed Folder

The process of decompressing a file is actually an *extraction* process. That's because you *extract* the original file(s) from the compressed folder.

In Windows XP, this process is eased by the use of the Extraction Wizard. Follow these steps:

1. Right-click the compressed folder to display the pop-up menu.

2. Select Extract All.

3. When the Extraction Wizard launches, as shown in Figure 6.10, click the Next button.

FIGURE 6.10

Use the Extraction Wizard to decompress compressed files.

4. Select which folder you want to extract the files to and click Next.

5. The wizard now extracts the files and displays the Extraction Complete page.

6. Click the Finish button to view the files you've just extracted.

THE ABSOLUTE MINIMUM

Here are the key points to remember from this chapter:

■ You can use either the My Documents or My Computer folders to work with your files and folders.

■ Most of the operations you'll want to perform are listed in the Tasks pane, on the left side of the My Documents folder.

■ There are many ways to copy and move files, but the easiest is to select the file, then select either Copy This File or Move This File from the Tasks pane.

■ You can delete a file by selecting Delete This File from the Tasks pane, or by pressing the Del key on your keyboard.

■ If you accidentally delete a file, you may be able to recover it by opening the Recycle Bin window.

■ If you need to share a really big file, consider compressing it into a compressed folder (also called a .ZIP file).

PART III

UPGRADING AND MAINTAINING YOUR SYSTEM

7

ADDING NEW HARDWARE AND DEVICES TO YOUR SYSTEM

If you just purchased a brand-new, right-out-of-the-box personal computer, it probably came equipped with all the components you could ever desire—or so you think. At some point in the future, however, you might want to expand your system—by adding a second printer, a scanner, a PC camera, or something equally new and exciting.

Adding new hardware to your system is relatively easy if you know what you're doing. That's where this chapter comes in.

Most Popular Peripherals

When it comes to adding stuff to your PC, what are the most popular peripherals? Here's a list of hardware you can add to or upgrade on your system:

- **Video card**—To display higher-resolution pictures and graphics, provide smoother playback with visually demanding PC games, or power a second monitor for some high-end programming or development activities.

- **Monitor**—To upgrade to a larger viewing area or a space-saving flat-screen monitor.

- **Sound card**—To improve the audio capabilities of your systems; this is particularly important if you're listening to CDs or MP3 files, watching surround-sound DVD movies, playing PC games, or mixing and recording your own digital audio.

- **Speakers**—To upgrade the quality of your computer's sound system. (Speaker systems with subwoofers are particularly popular.)

- **Keyboard**—To upgrade to a more ergonomic or wireless model.

- **Mouse**—To upgrade to a different type of controller (such as a trackball), a more fully featured unit, or a wireless model.

- **Joystick or other game controller**—To get better action with your favorite games.

- **Modem**—In case your PC doesn't have one, or if you're upgrading to broadband DSL or cable service.

- **CD-ROM drive**—In case your computer doesn't have one.

- **CD-R/RW drive (burner)**—To add recordable/rewritable capabilities to your system.

- **DVD**—To add DVD capability to your system.

- **DVD-R/RW (burner)**—To let you burn your own DVD movies or to back up entire hard disks.

- **Hard drive**—To add more storage capacity to your system. (Can be either external or internal.)

- **Removable drive**—To add more removable storage capacity to your system. (The most popular removable drives today are the so-called "USB drives," which pack a tremendous amount of storage into a keychain-sized device, using flash memory. These devices plug in to your PC's USB port.)

- **Memory card reader**—So you can read data from devices (such as digital cameras) that use various types of flash memory cards.

- **Printer**—To improve the quality of your printouts, to add color to your printouts, or to add photo-quality printing to your system.

- **Scanner**—So that you can scan photographs and documents into a digital format to store on your computer's hard drive.

- **PC camera**—So that you can send real-time video to friends and family or create your own Webcam on the Internet.

- **Network card**—So that you can connect your computer to other computers in a small home network.

- **Wireless network adapter**—So that you can connect your computer to a wireless network.

- **Digital media server**—To connect your PC to your home audio system so that you can listen to digital audio files and Internet radio on your home system.

Understanding Ports

Everything that's hooked up to your PC is connected via some type of *port*. A port is simply an interface between your PC and another device—either internally (inside your PC's system unit) or externally (via a connector on the back of the system unit).

Internal ports are automatically assigned when you plug a new card in to its slot inside the system unit. As for external ports, many types are available—each optimized to send and receive specific types of data. Different types of hardware connect via different types of ports.

The most common types of external ports are shown in Table 7.1.

Table 7.1   External Ports

Connector	Type	Uses	Description
	Serial	Modems, printers, mice	Enables communication one bit at a time, in one direction at a time.
	Parallel	Printers, scanners	Enables communications going in two directions at once.
	USB	Almost anything—portable devices, printers, scanners, modems, external sound cards, mice, keyboards, joysticks, CD/DVD drives, hard drives, digital cameras	A newer, faster, more intelligent type of serial port. USB devices can be added while your computer is still running, which you can't do with older types of ports.
	FireWire	Digital cameras, digital camcorders, hard drives, CD/DVD burners	Also called IEEE 1394, this is a newer interface standard that enables hot-pluggable, high-speed data transmission.
	SCSI	Hard drives, CD/DVD drives, tape backups	The *small computer system interface* (SCSI) port is a high-speed parallel interface.
	Gameport	Joysticks and other game controllers, MIDI devices	This port is typically used to connect gaming controllers; also functions as a MIDI port with the appropriate adapter.
	Keyboard/Mouse	Keyboards, mice, other input devices	Sometimes called a PS/2 port, used to connect both wired and wireless input devices.

Adding New External Hardware

The easiest way to add a new device to your system is to connect it externally—which saves you the trouble of opening your PC's case.

Connecting via USB or FireWire Ports

The most common external connector today is the USB port. USB is a great concept (and truly "universal") in that virtually every type of new peripheral comes in a USB version. Want to add a second hard disk? Don't open the PC case; get the USB version. Want to add a new printer? Forget the parallel port; get the USB version. Want to add a wireless network adapter? Don't bother with Ethernet cards; get the USB version.

note

No matter how you're connecting a new device, make sure to read the installation instructions for the new hardware and follow the manufacturer's instructions and advice.

USB is so popular because it's so easy to use. When you're connecting a USB device, not only do you not have to open your PC's case, but also you don't even have to turn off your system when you add the new device. That's because USB devices are *hot swappable*. That means you can just plug the new device in to the port, and Windows will automatically recognize it in real-time.

The original USB standard, version 1.1, has been around for awhile and, if your PC is more than two years old, is probably the type of USB you have installed. The newer USB 2.0 protocol is much faster than USB 1.1, and is standard on most

tip

If you connect too many USB devices, it's possible to run out of USB connectors on your PC. If that happens to you, buy an add-on USB hub, which lets you plug multiple USB peripherals in to a single USB port.

new computers. USB 2.0 ports are fully backward compatible with older USB 1.1 devices.

And let's not forget FireWire. Like USB devices, FireWire devices are hot-swappable, and very easy to connect. Like USB 2.0, FireWire is a very fast standard, which makes it ideal for connecting devices that move a lot of data, such as hard drives and camcorders. (It's also a little more expensive, which is why USB is still preferred for most devices.)

To connect a new USB or FireWire device, follow these steps:

1. Find a free USB or FireWire port on the back of your system unit and connect the new peripheral.

2. Windows should automatically recognize the new peripheral and either install the proper device driver automatically or prompt you to provide a CD or disk containing the driver file. Follow the onscreen instructions to finish installing the driver.

That's it! The only variation on this procedure is if the peripheral's manufacturer recommends using its own installation program, typically provided on an installation CD. If this is the case, follow the manufacturer's instructions to perform the installation and setup.

A *device driver* is a small software program that enables your PC to communicate with and control a specific device. Windows XP includes built-in device drivers for many popular peripherals. If Windows doesn't include a particular driver, you typically can find the driver on the peripheral's installation disk or on the peripheral manufacturer's Web site.

Connecting via Parallel or Serial Ports

Connecting a new device to a parallel or serial port is slightly more involved in that you have to turn off your system first, connect the new device, and then restart your system. Follow these steps:

1. Close Windows and turn off your computer.

2. Find an open port on the back of your system unit and connect the new peripheral.

3. Restart your system.

4. As Windows starts, it should recognize the new device and either install the proper drivers automatically or ask you to supply the device drivers (via CD-ROM or disk).

5. Windows installs the drivers and finishes the startup procedure. Your new device should now be operational.

Adding New Internal Hardware

Adding an internal device—usually through a plug-in card—is slightly more difficult than adding an external device primarily because you have to use a screwdriver and get "under the hood" of your system unit. Other than the extra screwing and plugging, however, the process is much the same as with external devices.

Follow these steps to add a new card to your system:

1. Turn off your computer, and unplug the power cable.

2. Take the case off your system unit, per the manufacturer's instructions.

3. If the new card has switches or jumpers that need to be configured, do this before inserting the card into your system unit.

4. Find an open card slot inside the system unit and insert the new card according to the manufacturer's instructions.

5. After the card is appropriately seated and screwed in, put the case back on the system unit, plug back in the power, and restart your system.

6. After Windows starts, it should recognize the new device and automatically install the appropriate driver.

Using the Add Hardware Wizard

In most cases, both your system and Windows will recognize the new card without any manual prompting. If, however, Windows doesn't recognize your new device, you can install it manually via the Add Hardware Wizard. To use the Add Hardware Wizard, follow these steps:

> **caution**
>
> You probably want to see whether the new component configures properly and works fine before you close up your system unit. For that reason, you might want to leave the case off until you're convinced everything is working okay and you don't need to do any more fiddling around inside your PC.

1. Click the Start button to display the Start menu.

2. Select Control Panel to open the Control Panel folder.

3. Select Printers and Other Hardware, and then Add Hardware to open the Add Hardware Wizard, shown in Figure 7.1.

FIGURE 7.1

Use the Add Hardware Wizard to add new hardware to your computer system.

4. Click the Next button.

5. If you're asked whether you've already installed any new hardware, select Yes and click Next.

6. Windows now evaluates your system and displays a list of installed devices. To add a new device, select Add a New Hardware Device from the list, and click the Next button.

7. When the next screen appears, select Search For and Install the Hardware Automatically; then click Next.

8. Windows now looks for new plug-and-play hardware. If it can identify the new hardware, the wizard continues with the installation. If it can't find a new device, it tells you so. If this is your situation, click Next to begin a manual installation.

9. Select the type of device you want to install, and then click Next.

10. On the next screen, select the manufacturer and specific device. If you want to install the drivers that came with the device, click the Have Disk button. To use a built-in Windows driver, click the Next button.

11. When the necessary files have been loaded, follow the onscreen instructions to complete the installation.

Note, however, that in most cases new hardware is detected automatically by Windows, thus eliminating the need for this somewhat more complicated procedure.

Connecting Portable Devices to Your PC

These days, a lot of the devices you connect to your PC really aren't computer peripherals. Instead, these are gadgets that you use on their own, but plug in to your PC in order to share files.

What kinds of portable devices are we talking about? Here's a short list:

- Personal digital assistants (PDAs), such as Palm and Pocket PC devices
- Portable music players, such as Apple's popular iPod player
- Digital cameras
- Digital camcorders

Most of these devices connect to a USB port; some digital cameras and camcorders might use a FireWire connection. As you remember, both USB and FireWire ports are hot-swappable, which means that all you have to do is connect the device to the proper port—no major configuration necessary. In most cases, the first time you connect your device to your PC, you'll need to run some sort of installation utility to install the device's software on your PC's hard drive. Each subsequent time you connect the device, your PC should recognize it automatically and launch the appropriate software program.

Once your portable device is connected to your PC, what you do next is up to you. Most of the time, you'll be transferring files either from your PC to the portable device, or vice versa. Use the device's software program to perform these operations, or use Windows' My Computer or My Document folders to copy files back and forth.

For example, most PDAs connect to your PC via a docking cradle. The cradle plugs in to a USB port on your PC, and you "dock" the PDA by inserting it into the cradle. When the PDA is in the cradle, the data on your PDA—contacts, appointments, files, you name it—are automatically synchronized with those on your PC. The synchronization program compares files found on both your PDA and your PC, and identifies the most recent versions, which are then copied from one device to another. It all happens automatically in the background; there are no buttons to push or dialog boxes to deal with.

For more detailed information, see the instructions that came with your portable device.

note

Learn more about connecting a portable music player in Chapter 34, "Using Your PC with a Portable Music Player." Learn more about connecting a digital camera in Chapter 37, "Connecting a Digital Camera or Scanner."

THE ABSOLUTE MINIMUM

Here's what you need to know if you're adding new equipment to your computer system:

- The easiest way to connect a new peripheral is via an external USB or FireWire connection.
- When you're installing an internal card, make sure that you turn off your PC before you open the system unit's case.
- In most cases, Windows automatically recognizes your new hardware and automatically installs all the necessary drivers.
- If Windows doesn't recognize the new piece of hardware, run the Add Hardware Wizard.
- Connecting a portable device, such as a portable music player or PDA, is typically done via an external USB port.

8

SETTING UP A HOME NETWORK

When you need connect two or more computers together, you need to create a computer *network*.

Why would you want to connect two computers together? Maybe you want to transfer files from one computer to another. Maybe you want to share an expensive piece of hardware (such as a printer) instead of buying one for each PC. Maybe you want to connect all your computers to the same Internet connection. Whatever your reasons, Windows XP makes it easy to create simple home networks. Read on to learn how!

How Networks Work

When it comes to physically connecting your network, you have two ways to go—wired or wireless. A wireless network is more convenient (no wires to run), but a wired network is faster. Which you choose depends on how you use the computers you network together.

If you use your network primarily to share an Internet connection or a printer or to transfer the occasional word processing file, wireless should work just fine. However, if you plan on transferring a lot of big files from one PC to another, or using your network for multiplayer gaming, you'll want to stick to a faster wired network.

tip

There are several different ways to feed your Internet connection into your home network and share it among multiple computers. Learn more in Chapter 21, "Connecting to the Internet."

Wired Networks

A *wired network* is the kind that requires you to run a bunch of cables from one PC to the next. In a wired network, you install a *network interface card (NIC)* in each PC and connect the cards via Ethernet cable. (Note that many new PCs come with built-in Ethernet capability, so you don't have to purchase an additional card.) Although this type of network is easy enough to set up and is probably the lowest-cost alternative, you still have to deal with all those cables—which can be a hassle if your computers are in different areas of your house.

Most wired networks transfer data at either 10Mbps or 100Mbps, depending on what equipment you install. A 10Mbps network is called *10Base-T*; a 100Mbps network is called *Fast Internet*; networking equipment that can work at either 10Mbps or 100Mbps rates is labeled *10/100*.

note

How quickly data is transferred across a network is measured in megabits per second, or Mbps. The bigger the Mbps number, the faster the network—and faster is always better than slower.

Wireless Networks

The alternative to a wired network is a *wireless network*. Wireless networks use radio frequency (RF) signals to connect one computer to another. The advantage of wireless, of course, is that you don't have to run any cables. This is a big plus if you have a large house with computers on either end or on different floors.

The most popular wireless networks use the Wi-Fi standard. The original Wi-Fi standard, known as 802.11b, transfers data at 11Mbps—slower than Fast Ethernet, but fast enough for most practical purposes.

If you want a faster wireless connection, look for the latest version of Wi-Fi, called 802.11g, that transmits data at a blazing 54Mbps rate. If you tend to copy a lot of big files from one PC to another, this is definitely the way to go.

note

Wi-Fi is short for *wireless fidelity*.

Connecting and Configuring

Whether you're going wired or wireless, you can probably find everything you need to create your network in a preassembled networking kit. These kits contain all the cards, cables, and hubs you need to create your network, along with easy-to-follow instructions. (And if you don't want to open up your computer, you can even find kits that include external network adapters that connect via USB!)

After you have installed and connected all your equipment, you then have to configure all the PCs on your network. Assuming that you're running Windows XP, the configuration process is handled by Windows' Network Setup Wizard. You launch the wizard by opening the Control Panel and selecting Network and Internet Connections, and then Network Connections. When the Network Connections utility opens, select Set Up a Home or Small Office Network from the Network Tasks panel.

You run the Network Setup Wizard on each PC connected to the network. During the process, you provide details about your network connections, including any and all devices or connections you want to share—such as a printer or your broadband Internet connection. The wizard does all the hard work, and when it's done, your network is up and running and ready to use.

tip

If your network hardware comes with its own configuration software, you should run that instead of (or addition to) the Network Setup Wizard. And always make sure to follow the specific instructions that come with your network hardware!

Setting Up a Wired Network

Connecting multiple computers in a wired network is actually fairly simple. Just make sure that you do the proper planning beforehand and buy the appropriate hardware and cables; everything else is a matter of connecting and configuration.

How It Works

The first thing you need to do is install a network interface card (NIC) in each computer in your wired network. Each NIC then connects, via Ethernet cable, to the network *hub*, which is a simple device that functions like the hub of a wheel and serves as the central point in your network. Then, after you make the physical connections, each computer has to be configured to function as part of the network and to share designated files, folders, and peripherals.

When complete, the whole thing should resemble the network in Figure 8.1.

FIGURE 8.1

Setting up a wired Ethernet network.

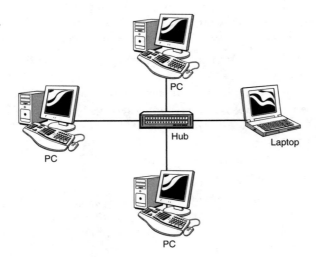

What You Need

Here's the specific hardware you'll need to set up your wired network:

- Network interface cards (one for each PC, and possibly a second card for your gateway PC)
- Ethernet network hub (one for the entire network)
- Router or residential gateway device (optional, for sharing an Internet connection; see Chapter 21 for more information)
- Enough Ethernet cables to run from each PC to the hub

Making the Connections

Naturally, you should follow the instructions that come with your networking hardware to properly set up your network. In general, however, here are the steps to take:

1. Power down your main computer and remove the system unit case.

2. Install a network interface card into an open expansion slot.

3. Close up the case, reboot the computer, and run the NIC installation software.

4. Connect your network hub to a power source.

5. Run an Ethernet cable from your main computer to the network hub.

6. Run the network configuration utility (or the Windows XP Network Setup Wizard) to set up your network.

7. Move on to the second computer in your network and repeat steps 1–3.

8. Run the network configuration utility on the second computer to connect it to your new network.

9. Repeat steps 7 and 8 for each computer on your network.

> **note**
>
> If your host PC has built-in Ethernet networking, you can skip steps 1–3.

After you've connected all the computers on your network, you can proceed to connect your broadband modem, as well as configure any devices (such as printers) you want to share over the network. For example, if you want to share a single printer over the network, it connects to one of the network PCs (*not* directly to the hub), and then is shared through that PC.

Setting Up a Wireless Network

If you don't want to run all those cables, you need a wireless network. The setup is similar, but with some important differences.

How It Works

In a wireless network, the hub function is performed by a *wireless router*, sometimes called a *base station* or an *access point*. This device can make both wireless and wired connections; most base stations include four or more Ethernet connectors in addition to wireless capabilities.

As shown in Figure 8.2, you connect your main PC directly to the base station using an Ethernet cable. All the other PCs in your network can connect either wirelessly or via Ethernet.

FIGURE 8.2

Setting up a wireless network.

The wireless PCs on your network must be connected to or contain *wireless adapters*. These devices function as mini-transmitters/receivers to communicate with the base station. Wireless adapters can be small external devices that connect to the PC via USB, expansion cards that install inside your system unit, or PC cards that insert into a portable PC's card slot.

note

Many newer portable PCs come with wireless functionality built in. Intel's new Centrino chip set was designed around this mobile technology.

What You Need

Here's the specific hardware you'll need to set up your wireless network:

- Network interface card (one for the host PC)
- Wireless network adapters (one for each client PC)
- Wireless network router/base station (one for the entire network)
- One Ethernet cable (to connect your host PC to the wireless base station)

In addition, if you're connecting a broadband Internet modem to your network, you'll need to run a second Ethernet cable from the modem to the wireless base station. (See Chapter 21 for more details.)

Making the Connections

Just as when you're setting up a wired network, you should follow the instructions that come with your wireless base station to properly set up your wireless network. In general, however, here are the steps to take:

1. Power down your main computer and remove the system unit case.

2. Install a network interface card into an open expansion slot.

3. Close up the case, reboot the computer, and run the NIC installation software.

4. Connect your wireless base station to a power source.

5. Run an Ethernet cable from your main computer to the wireless base station.

6. Run the network configuration utility (or Windows XP's Network Setup Wizard) on your main computer to set up your network.

7. Move on to the second computer in your network and install a wireless networking adapter—either internally, via an expansion card, or externally via USB. (Or, if your second PC is a laptop, insert a wireless networking PC card.)

8. Run the installation software to properly configure the wireless adapter.

9. Run the network configuration utility on the second computer to connect it to your new network.

10. Repeat steps 7 and 8 for each additional computer on your network.

note

If your host PC has built-in Ethernet networking, you can skip steps 1–3.

caution

Most wireless networks include some sort of wireless security to prevent outsiders from tapping into your network computers and illicitly accessing your PCs and computer files. In many cases, this security consists of a rather long and involved encrypted password or security key that must be applied to each authorized computer. Make sure that you know where this setting is stored on your main PC so that you can write it down and enter it when prompted when configuring the other computers on your network.

After you've connected all the computers on your network, you can proceed to connect your broadband modem, as well as configure any devices (such as printers) you want to share over the network. For example, if you want to share a single printer over the network, it connects to one of the network PCs (*not* directly to the router), and then is shared through that PC.

Sharing Files and Folders Across Your Network

Once you have your network up and running, it's time to take advantage of it—by copying or moving files from one computer to another. To share files between the PCs on your network, you have to enable Windows XP's file sharing on the PC that contains those files. You do this by following these steps:

1. Use My Computer to navigate to the folder that contains the file you want to share.

2. Right-click the folder icon and select Sharing and Security from the pop-up menu; this displays the Properties dialog box.

3. Select the Sharing tab, shown in Figure 8.3.

4. Check the Share This Folder on the Network option.

5. Click OK when done—then repeat this procedure for every folder you want to share on every computer connected to your network.

caution

Be cautious about turning on file sharing. When you let a folder be shared, anyone accessing your network can access the contents of the folder.

FIGURE 8.3

Enable file sharing so that other computers can access the files in a particular folder.

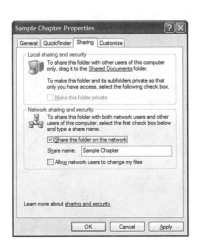

THE ABSOLUTE MINIMUM

Here are the key things to remember about networking and the Internet:

- To share information or hardware between two or more computers, you have to connect them in a network.

- There are two basic types of networks—wired and wireless (using radio frequencies).

- The quickest, easiest, and cheapest way to put together a home network is to use a commercial home networking kit.

- Once you have all the networking hardware installed and connected, use Windows XP's Network Setup Wizard to configure all the PCs on your network.

- To share folders between computers on your network, enable Windows XP's file sharing feature.

9

PERFORMING ROUTINE MAINTENANCE

"An ounce of prevention is worth a pound of cure."

That old adage might seem trite and clichéd, but it's also true—especially when it comes to your computer system. Spending a few minutes a week on preventive maintenance can save you from costly computer problems in the future.

To make this chore a little easier, Windows XP includes several utilities to help you keep your system running smoothly. You should use these tools as part of your regular maintenance routine—or if you experience specific problems with your computer system.

Free Up Disk Space by Deleting Unnecessary Files

Even with today's humongous hard disks, you can still end up with too many useless files taking up too much hard disk space. Fortunately, Windows XP includes a utility that identifies and deletes unused files. The Disk Cleanup tool is what you want to use when you need to free up extra hard disk space for more frequently used files.

To use Disk Cleanup, follow these steps:

1. Click the Start button to display the Start menu.

2. Select All Programs, Accessories, System Tools, Disk Cleanup.

3. Disk Cleanup starts and automatically analyzes the contents of your hard disk drive.

4. When Disk Cleanup is finished analyzing, it presents its results in the Disk Cleanup dialog box, shown in Figure 9.1.

FIGURE 9.1

Use Disk Cleanup to delete unused files from your hard disk.

5. Select the Disk Cleanup tab.

6. You now have the option of permanently deleting various types of files: downloaded program files, temporary Internet files, deleted files in the Recycle Bin, setup log files, temporary files, WebClient/Publisher temporary files, and catalog files for the Content Indexer. Select which files you want to delete.

7. Click OK to begin deleting.

note

You can safely choose to delete all these files *except* the setup log and Content Indexer files, which are often needed by the Windows operating system.

Make Your Hard Disk Run Better by Defragmenting

If you think that your computer is taking longer than usual to open files or notice that your hard drive light stays on longer than usual, you might need to *defragment* your hard drive.

File fragmentation is sort of like taking the pieces of a jigsaw puzzle and storing them in different boxes along with pieces from other puzzles. The more dispersed the pieces are, the longer it takes to put the puzzle together. Spreading the bits and pieces of a file around your hard disk occurs whenever you install, delete, or run an application or when you edit, move, copy, or delete a file.

If you notice that your system takes longer and longer to open and close files or run applications, it's because these file fragments are spread all over the place. You fix the problem when you put all the pieces of the puzzle back in the right boxes—which you do by defragmenting your hard disk.

You use Windows XP's Disk Defragmenter utility to defragment your hard drive. Follow these steps:

1. Click the Start button to display the Start menu.

2. Select All Programs, Accessories, System Tools, Disk Defragmenter to open the Disk Defragmenter utility, shown in Figure 9.2.

3. Select the drive you want to defragment, typically drive C:.

4. Click the Defragment button.

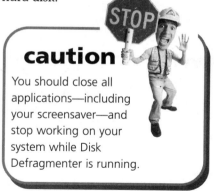

caution

You should close all applications—including your screensaver—and stop working on your system while Disk Defragmenter is running.

FIGURE 9.2

Use Windows XP's Disk Defragmenter to make your hard drive run faster.

Defragmenting your drive can take awhile, especially if you have a large hard drive or your drive is really fragmented. So, you might want to start the utility and let it run while you are at lunch.

Perform a Hard Disk Checkup with ScanDisk

Any time you run an application, move or delete a file, or accidentally turn the power off while the system is running, you run the risk of introducing errors to your hard disk. These errors can make it harder to open files, slow down your hard disk, or cause your system to freeze when you open or save a file or an application.

Fortunately, you can find and fix most of these errors directly from within Windows XP. All you have to do is run the built-in ScanDisk utility.

To find and fix errors on your hard drive, follow these steps:

1. Click the Start button to display the Start menu.

2. Select My Computer to open the My Computer folder.

3. Right-click the icon for the drive you want to scan, and then select the Properties option from the pop-up menu; this displays the Properties dialog box.

4. Select the Tools tab.

5. Click the Check Now button to display the Check Disk dialog box, shown in Figure 9.3.

6. Check both the options (Automatically Fix File System Errors and Scan for and Attempt Recovery of Bad Sectors).

7. Click Start.

Windows now scans your hard disk and attempts to fix any errors it encounters.

tip

Windows XP includes a Scheduled Tasks utility that lets you automatically run essential system maintenance tasks while you're away from your computer. To use this utility, click the Start button; then select All Programs, Accessories, System Tools, Scheduled Tasks. When the Scheduled Tasks window opens, click the icon for a specific task to display its scheduling dialog box. Click the Schedule tab, and then select how often you want to run the task. Click OK to schedule the task.

FIGURE 9.3

Use ScanDisk to check your hard disk for errors.

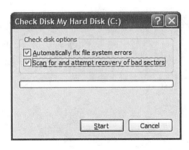

Keep Your Hardware in Tip-Top Condition

There's also a fair amount of preventive maintenance you can physically perform on your computer hardware. It's simple stuff, but can really extend the life of your PC.

System Unit

Your PC system unit has a lot of sensitive electronics inside—everything from memory chips to disk drives to power supplies. Check out these maintenance tips to keep your system unit from flaking out on you:

- Position your system unit in a clean, dust-free environment. Keep it away from direct sunlight and strong magnetic fields. In addition, make sure that your system unit and your monitor have plenty of air flow around them to keep them from overheating.

- Hook up your system unit to a surge suppressor to avoid deadly power spikes.

- Avoid turning on and off your system unit too often; it's better to leave it on all the time than incur frequent "power on" stress to all those delicate components. However...

- Turn off your system unit if you're going to be away for an extended period—anything longer than a day or two.

- Check all your cable connections periodically. Make sure that all the connectors are firmly connected and all the screws properly screwed—and make sure that your cables aren't stretched too tight or bent in ways that could damage the wires inside.

Keyboard

Even something as simple as your keyboard requires a little preventive maintenance from time to time. Check out these tips:

- Keep your keyboard away from young children and pets—they can get dirt and hair and Silly Putty all over the place, and they have a tendency to put way too much pressure on the keys.

- Keep your keyboard away from dust, dirt, smoke, direct sunlight, and other harmful environmental stuff. You might even consider putting a dust cover on your keyboard when it's not in use.

- Use a small vacuum cleaner to periodically sweep the dirt from your keyboard. (Alternately, you can use compressed air to *blow* the dirt away.) Use a cotton swab or soft cloth to clean between the keys. If necessary, remove the keycaps to clean the switches underneath.

■ If you spill something on your keyboard, disconnect it immediately and wipe up the spill. Use a soft cloth to get between the keys; if necessary, use a screwdriver to pop off the keycaps and wipe up any seepage underneath. Let the keyboard dry thoroughly before trying to use it again.

Mouse

If you're a heavy Windows user, you probably put thousands of miles a year on your mouse. Just like a car tire, anything turning over that often needs a little tender loving care. Check out these mouse maintenance tips:

■ Periodically open up the bottom of your mouse and remove the roller ball. Wash the ball with water (or perhaps a mild detergent). Use a soft cloth to dry the ball before reinserting it.

■ While your mouse ball is removed, use compressed air or a cotton swab to clean dust and dirt from the inside of your mouse. (In extreme cases, you might need to use tweezers to pull lint and hair out of your mouse— or use a small knife to scrape packed crud from the rollers.)

■ Always use a mouse pad—they really do help keep things rolling smoothly; plus, they give you good traction. (And while you're at it, don't forget to clean your mouse pad with a little spray cleaner—it can get dirty, too.)

note

If you have an optical mouse, you can skip these steps; there aren't any mouse balls to clean. (However, you still might need to keep pieces of lint from clogging the optical sensor.)

Monitor

If you think of your monitor as a little television set, you're on the right track. Just treat your monitor as you do your TV, and you'll be okay. That said, look at these preventive maintenance tips:

■ As with all other important system components, keep your monitor away from direct sunlight, dust, and smoke. Make sure that it has plenty of ventilation, especially around the back; don't cover the rear cooling vents with paper or any other object, and don't set anything bigger than a small plush toy on top of the cabinet.

■ Don't place any strong magnets in close proximity to your monitor. (This includes external speakers.)

- *With your monitor turned off,* periodically clean the monitor screen. Spray standard glass cleaner on a soft cloth (antistatic type, if possible), and then wipe the screen clean.

- Don't forget to adjust the brightness and contrast controls on your monitor every now and then. Any controls can get out of whack—plus, your monitor's performance will change as it ages, and simple adjustments can often keep it looking as good as new.

Printer

Your printer is a complex device with a lot of moving parts. Follow these tips to keep your printouts in good shape:

- Use a soft cloth, mini-vacuum cleaner, and/or compressed air to clean the inside and outside of your printer on a periodic basis. In particular, make sure that you clean the paper path of all paper shavings and dust.

- If you have an ink-jet printer, periodically clean the ink jets. Run your printer's cartridge cleaning utility, or use a small pin to make sure that they don't get clogged.

- If you have a laser printer, replace the toner cartridge as needed. When you replace the cartridge, remember to clean the printer cleaning bar and other related parts, per the manufacturer's instructions.

- *Don't* use alcohol or other solvents to clean any rubber or plastic parts—you'll do more harm than good!

THE ABSOLUTE MINIMUM

Here are the key points to remember from this chapter:

- Dedicating a few minutes a week to PC maintenance can prevent serious problems from occurring in the future.

- To delete unused files from your hard disk, use the Disk Cleanup utility.

- To defragment a fragmented hard disk, use the Disk Defragmenter utility.

- To find and fix hard disk errors, use the ScanDisk utility.

- Make sure that you keep all your computer hardware away from direct sunlight, dust, and smoke, and make sure that your system unit has plenty of ventilation.

- Invest in a small handheld vacuum cleaner or a can of compressed air to better clean dust out of the small spaces in your system.

10

DEALING WITH COMMON PROBLEMS

Computers aren't perfect. It's possible—although unlikely—that at some point in time, something will go wrong with your PC. It might refuse to start, it might freeze up, it might crash and go dead. Yikes!

When something goes wrong with your computer, there's no need to panic. (Even though that's what you'll probably feel like doing.) Most PC problems have easy-to-find causes and simple solutions. The key thing is to keep your wits about you, and attack the situation calmly and logically—following the advice you'll find in this chapter.

How to Troubleshoot Computer Problems

No matter what kind of computer-related problem you're experiencing, there are seven basic steps you should take to track down the cause of the problem. Work through these steps calmly and deliberately, and you're likely to find what's causing the current problem—and then be in a good position to fix it yourself:

1. **Don't panic!**—Just because there's something wrong with your PC is no reason to fly off the handle. Chances are there's nothing seriously wrong. Besides, getting all panicky won't solve anything. Keep your wits about you and proceed logically, and you can probably find what's causing your problem and get it fixed.

2. **Check for operator errors**—In other words, something *you* did wrong. Maybe you clicked the wrong button, or pressed the wrong key, or plugged something into the wrong jack or port. Retrace your steps and try to duplicate your problem. Chances are the problem won't recur if you don't make the same mistake twice.

3. **Check that everything is plugged into the proper place and that the system unit itself is getting power**—Take special care to ensure that all your cables are *securely* connected—loose connections can cause all sorts of strange results.

4. **Make sure you have the latest versions of all the software installed on your system**—While you're at it, make sure you have the latest versions of device drivers installed for all the peripherals on your system.

5. **Try to isolate the problem by *when* and *how* it occurs**—Walk through each step of the process to see if you can identify a particular program or driver that might be causing the problem.

note

Does a particular computer problem have you stumped? Then learn more about troubleshooting computer problems in my companion book, *Absolute Beginner's Guide to Upgrading and Fixing Your PC* (Que, 2003), available wherever computer books are sold.

6. **When all else fails, call in professional help**—If you think it's a Windows-related problem, contact Microsoft's technical support department. If you think it's a problem with a particular program, contact the tech support department of the program's manufacturer. If you think it's a hardware-related problem, contact the manufacturer of your PC or the dealer you bought it from. (And don't rule out where you purchased the computer—many computer dealers have helpful tech support departments.) The pros are there for a reason—when you need technical support, go and get it.

Using Windows Troubleshooters

Windows XP includes several interactive utilities that can help you diagnose and fix common system problems. These utilities are called Troubleshooters, and they walk you step-by-step through a series of questions. All you have to do is answer the questions in the Troubleshooter, and you'll be led to the probable solution to your problem.

To run a Troubleshooter, follow these steps:

1. Click the Start button to display the Start menu.
2. Select Help and Support to open the Help and Support Center.
3. Click the Fixing a Problem link.
4. When the next screen appears, click the link for the type of problem you're having, and then click the link to start a specific Troubleshooter.

All you have to do now is follow the interactive directions to troubleshoot your particular hardware problem.

Troubleshooting in Safe Mode

If you're having trouble getting Windows to start, it's probably because some setting is set wrong or some driver is malfunctioning. The problem is, how do you get into Windows to fix what's wrong, when you can't even start Windows?

The solution is to hijack your computer before Windows gets hold of it and force it to start *without* whatever is causing the problem. You do this by watching the screen as your computer boots up and pressing the F8 key just before Windows starts to load. This displays the Windows startup menu, where you select Safe mode.

Safe mode is a special mode of operation that loads Windows in a very simple configuration. Once in Safe mode, you can look for device conflicts, restore incorrect or corrupted device drivers, or restore your system to a prior working configuration (using the System Restore utility, discussed later in this chapter).

Depending on the severity of your system problem, Windows might start in Safe mode automatically.

What to Do When Windows Freezes

Probably the most common computer trouble is the freeze-up. That's what happens when your PC just stops dead in its tracks. The screen looks normal, but nothing works—you can't type onscreen, you can't click any buttons, nothing's happening.

If your system happens to freeze up, the good news is that there's probably nothing wrong with your computer hardware. The bad news is that there's probably something funky happening with your operating system.

This doesn't mean your system is broken. It's just a glitch. And you can recover from glitches. Just remember not to panic and to approach the situation calmly and rationally.

What Causes Windows to Freeze?

What causes Windows to freeze? There can be many different causes of a Windows freeze, including the following:

- You might be running an older software program or game that isn't compatible with Windows XP. If so, upgrade the program.

- A memory conflict might exist between applications, or between an application and Windows itself. Try running fewer programs at once, or running problematic programs one at a time to avoid potential memory conflicts.

- You might not have enough memory installed on your system. Upgrade the amount of memory in your PC.

- You might not have enough free hard disk space on your computer. Delete any unnecessary files from your hard drive.

- Your hard disk might be developing errors or bad sectors. Check your hard disk for errors. (See the ScanDisk section in Chapter 9, "Performing Routine Maintenance.")

Dealing with Frozen Windows

When Windows freezes, you need to get it unfrozen and up and running again. The way to do this is to shut down your computer, either by pressing Ctrl+Alt+Del (maybe a few times) or, if that doesn't work, by using the On/Off button on your system unit. Then you can start your computer up again. Chances are everything will be working just fine.

If your system crashes or freezes frequently, however, you should call in a pro. These kinds of problems can be tough to track down by yourself when you're dealing with Windows.

Dealing with a Frozen Program

Sometimes Windows works fine but it's an individual software program that freezes. Fortunately, Windows XP is an exceptionally safe environment. When an individual application crashes or freezes, it seldom messes up your entire system. You can use a utility called the Windows Task Manager to close the problem application without affecting other Windows programs.

When a Windows application freezes or crashes, press Ctrl+Alt+Del; this opens the Windows Task Manager, shown in Figure 10.1. Select the Applications tab and then select the frozen application from the list. Now click the End Task button. After a few seconds, a Wait/Shutdown window appears; confirm that you want to shut down the selected application; then, click the End Task button.

FIGURE 10.1

Use the Windows Task Manager to end non-responding programs.

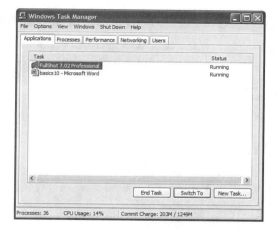

This closes the offending application and lets you continue your work in Windows.

If you have multiple applications that crash on a regular basis, the situation probably can be attributed to insufficient memory. See your computer dealer about adding more RAM to your system.

Dealing with a Major Crash

Perhaps the worst thing that can happen to your computer system is that it crashes—completely shuts down, without any warning. If this happens to you, start by not panicking. Stay calm, take a few deep breaths, and then get ready to get going again.

You should always wait about 60 seconds after a computer crashes before you try to turn on your system again. This gives all the components time to settle down and—

in some cases—reset themselves. Just sit back and count to 60 (slowly), then press your system unit's "on" button.

Nine times out of 10, your system will boot up normally, as if nothing unusual has happened. If this is what happens for you, great! If, on the other hand, your system doesn't come back up normally, you'll need to start troubleshooting the underlying problem, as discussed later in this chapter.

Even if your system comes back up as usual, the sudden crash might have done some damage. A system crash can sometimes damage any software program that was running at the time, as well as any documents that were open when the crash occurred. You might have to reinstall a damaged program or recover a damaged document from a backup file.

Undoing the Damage with System Restore

Perhaps the best course of action when your system crashes is to use Microsoft's System Restore utility. This Windows XP utility can automatically restore your system to the state it was in before the crash occurred—and save you the trouble of reinstalling any damaged software programs. It's a great safety net for when things go wrong.

Setting System Restore Points

System Restore works by monitoring your system and noting any changes that are made when you install new applications. Each time it notes a change, it automatically creates what it calls a *restore point*. A restore point is basically a "snapshot" of key system files just before the new application is installed.

Just to be safe, System Restore also creates a new restore point after every 10 hours of system use. You can also choose to manually create a new restore point at any moment in time. It's a good idea to do this whenever you make any major change to your system, such as installing a new piece of hardware.

To set a manual restore point, follow these steps:

1. Click the Start button to display the Start menu.
2. Select All Programs, Accessories, System Tools, System Restore to open the System Restore window.
3. Select Create a Restore Point and click Next.
4. You'll now be prompted to enter a description for this new restore point; do this.
5. Click the Create button.

That's all you have to do. Windows notes the appropriate system settings and stores them in its System Restore database.

Restoring Your System

If something in your system goes bad, you can run System Restore to set things right. Pick a restore point before the problem occurred (such as right before a new installation), and System Restore will then undo any changes made to monitored files since the restore point was created. This restores your system to its pre-installation—that is, *working*—condition.

To restore your system from a restore point, follow these steps:

1. Click the Start button to display the Start menu.

2. Select All Programs, Accessories, System Tools, System Restore to open the System Restore window.

3. Select Restore My Computer to an Earlier Time option, then click Next.

4. When the Select a Restore Point screen appears, you'll see a calendar showing the current month, as shown in Figure 10.2; any date highlighted in bold contains a restore point. Select a restore point, and then click the Next button.

5. When the confirmation screen appears, click Next.

FIGURE 10.2

Use the System Restore utility to restore damaged programs or system files.

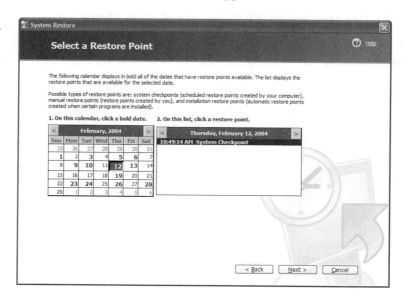

Windows now starts to restore your system. You should make sure that all open programs are closed because Windows will need to be restarted during this process.

When the process is complete, your system should be back in tip-top shape. Note, however, that it might take a half-hour or more to complete a system restore—so you'll have time to order a pizza and eat dinner before the operation is done!

caution

System Restore will help you recover any damaged programs and system files, but it won't help you recover any damaged documents or data files.

The Absolute Minimum

Here are the key points to remember from this chapter:

- If something strange happens to your computer system, the first thing to do is *not panic!*

- Most so-called computer problems are actually caused by operator error, so back up and do whatever it is you did one more time—carefully, this time.

- You can shut down frozen programs from the Windows Task Manager, which you display by pressing Ctrl+Alt+Del.

- Press Ctrl+Alt+Del a second time to reboot your computer.

- Some problems can be fixed from Windows Safe mode; to enter Safe mode, restart your computer and press F8 before the Windows start screen appears.

- If your system misbehaves after installing new software or hardware, use the System Restore utility to return your system to its pre-installation state.

Using Computer Software

11

Installing New Software

Your new computer system probably came with a bunch of programs preinstalled on its hard disk. As useful as these programs are, at some point you're going to want to add something new. Maybe you want to upgrade from Microsoft Works to the more full-featured Microsoft Office. Maybe you want to add some educational software for the kids or a productivity program for yourself. Maybe you just want to play some new computer games.

Whatever type of software you're considering, installing it on your computer system is easy. In most cases software installation is so automatic you don't have to do much more than stick a disc in the CD-ROM drive and click a few onscreen buttons. Even when it isn't that automatic, Windows will walk you through the installation process step-by-step—and you'll be using your new software in no time!

Automatic Installation

Almost all software programs have their own built-in installation programs. Installing the software is as easy as running this built-in program.

If the program you're installing comes on a CD-ROM, just insert the program's main or installation CD in your computer's CD-ROM drive. The program's installation program should then start automatically, and all you have to do is follow the onscreen instructions.

If the installation program *doesn't* start automatically, you have to launch it manually. To do this, follow these steps:

1. Click the Start button to display the Start menu.

2. Select Run.

3. When the Run dialog box appears, as shown in Figure 11.1, enter `x:\setup` in the Open box. (Replace *x* with the letter of your CD-ROM drive; if your CD-ROM is drive D, you'd enter `d:\setup`.)

4. Click OK.

> **tip**
>
> If this process doesn't work, try entering `install` instead of `setup`. (Some older programs have this different name for their installation programs.)

FIGURE 11.1

Enter the location and name of the installation program in the Run dialog box.

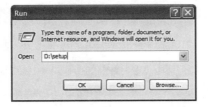

Manual Installation

If the program you're installing doesn't have an automated setup program, you can install the program by using Windows's Add or Remove Programs utility.

Follow these steps:

1. Click the Start button to display the Start menu.

2. Select Control Panel to open the Control Panel folder.

3. Select Add or Remove Programs to display the Add or Remove Programs dialog box.

4. Click the Add New Programs button.

5. When the next screen appears, as shown in Figure 11.2, click the CD or Floppy button.

6. Insert the program's installation disc or disk, and then follow the onscreen instructions to complete the installation.

FIGURE 11.2

Use the Add or Remove Programs utility to manually install a new program.

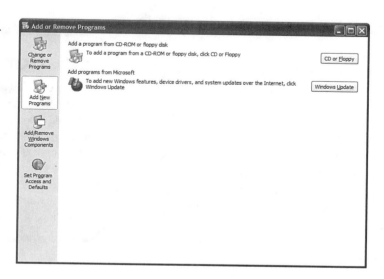

Installing Software from the Internet

Nowadays, many software publishers make their products available via download from the Internet. Some users like this because they can get their new programs immediately. However, downloading software like this can take quite a long time, especially if you have a normal dial-up Internet connection, because the program files are so big.

When you download a program from a major software publisher, the process is generally easy to follow. You probably have to read a page of do's and don'ts, agree to the publisher's licensing agreements, and then click a button to start the download. After you specify where (which folder on your hard disk) you want to save the downloaded file, the download begins.

tip

Most software publishers let you order CD versions of their software—although you might have to pay extra to get a physical copy.

When the download is complete, you should be notified via an onscreen dialog box. From this point, installing the program is almost identical to installing from CD or floppy disk—except that you have to enter the complete path to the installation file in the Run dialog box. (And even this is easy—just click the Browse button to find the folder where you saved the file.)

Removing Old Programs

Chances are you got a *lot* of different software programs with your new PC. Chances are also that some of these are programs you'll never use—and are just taking up space on your hard disk.

For example, your new computer might have come with both Microsoft Money and Quicken installed—and you'll only use one of these two programs. Or your system might include multiple applications for accessing the Internet, from different ISPs. Again, you'll use only one of these, which means you can delete the ones you *don't* use.

caution

Unless you're downloading a program from a trusted download site, the downloaded file could contain a computer virus. See Chapter 30, "Protecting Your PC from Viruses, Spam, and Other Nuisances," for more information.

If you're sure you won't be using a particular program, you can use Windows's Add or Remove Programs utility to remove the software from your hard disk. This frees up hard disk space for other programs you might install in the future.

To remove a software program from your PC, follow these steps:

1. Click the Start button to display the Start menu.
2. Select Control Panel to open the Control Panel folder.
3. Select Add or Remove Programs to display the Add or Remove Programs dialog box.
4. Click the Change or Remove Programs button.
5. The next screen, shown in Figure 11.3, displays a list of all the currently installed programs on your PC. Select the program's name from the Currently Installed Programs list, and then click either the Change/Remove or Remove button.

note

Some programs might require you to insert the original installation disks or CD to perform the uninstall.

6. If prompted, confirm that you want to continue to uninstall the application. Answer any other prompts that appear onscreen; then the uninstall process will start.

After the uninstall routine is complete, click the Close button to close the Add or Remove Programs utility.

FIGURE 11.3

Choose a program to remove from your system.

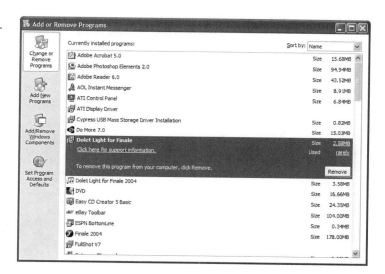

THE ABSOLUTE MINIMUM

Here are the key points to remember from this chapter:

- Most programs come with their own built-in installation programs; the installation should start automatically when you insert the program's installation CD.

- If the program doesn't come with its own self-starting installation program, you can install the program by using Windows's Add or Remove Programs utility.

- The Add or Remove Programs utility can also be used to remove unused programs from your system.

- You also can download some programs from the Internet—just be careful about catching a computer virus!

12

USING SUITES AND BUNDLES

If you just purchased a new PC, chances are it came with a "suite," or bundle of useful programs pre-installed. For many users, this suite of programs will be all you need to perform basic computer tasks such as letter writing and number crunching.

This chapter takes a look at the most popular suites installed on new PCs today—Microsoft Works, Microsoft Works Suite, Microsoft Office, and Corel WordPerfect Office.

Evaluating the Most Popular Software Bundles

When you first turned on your new PC, you might have been surprised to see your desktop already populated with a bunch of shortcut icons for different programs. These are the programs that were pre-installed by your PC's manufacturer. Which particular programs were pre-installed on your PC depends on what sort of arrangements the PC manufacturer made with the software publishers.

If you purchased a low-priced PC, chances are it came with either Microsoft Works or Microsoft Works Suite pre-installed. If you purchased a higher-priced PC, chances are it came with Microsoft Office pre-installed. And if your PC manufacturer didn't cut a deal with Microsoft, your PC probably came with Corel WordPerfect Suite pre-installed. We'll look at each of these bundles separately.

Microsoft Works

Microsoft Works is suite of five basic applications, all tied together by an interface called the Task Launcher (discussed later in this chapter). The key components of Works are

- **Works Word Processor**—A simple word processing program you can use to write letters, memos, and notes.
- **Works Spreadsheet**—A simple spreadsheet program that lets you enter rows and columns of numbers and other data, and then performs basic calculations and analysis on those numbers.
- **Works Database**—A simple database program that functions more-or-less like a giant electronic filing cabinet. (Learn more in Chapter 15, "Working with Databases.")
- **Works Calendar**—A schedule management program.
- **Address Book**—An all-purpose contact manager you can use to store names, addresses, phone numbers, and email addresses.

Microsoft Works Suite

Microsoft Works Suite takes the basic Microsoft Works program and supplements it with a variety of other software programs, all tied together by the Task Launcher. The programs that Microsoft packages in Works Suite differ from year to year, but in the Works Suite 2004 version, they include

- **Microsoft Word**—A full-featured word processor that replaces the Works Word Processor in the basic version of Microsoft Works. (Learn more in Chapter 13, "Working with Words.")

- **Microsoft Money**—A personal finance program that lets you write checks and manage your banking and investment accounts. (Learn more in Chapter 17, "Managing Your Finances.")
- **Microsoft Picture It! Photo**—A graphics program that lets you edit and manage your digital photos.
- **Microsoft Streets & Trips**—Used to generate maps and driving directions.
- **Microsoft Encarta Encyclopedia**—A first-class electronic encyclopedia.
- **Works Spreadsheet**—A basic number-crunching application.
- **Works Database**—A basic flat-file storage program.
- **Works Calendar**—A simple appointment scheduler.
- **Address Book**—Used to store contact information.

Microsoft Office

Microsoft Office is a suite of professional-level applications, just like those used in corporations around the world. These programs are more fully featured than the ones in Works and Works Suite, even though they aren't tied together by a common "launcher" interface.

There have been numerous versions of Office over the years. The current version is called Office 2003; the previous version was called Office XP. Within each version, Microsoft sells several different "editions." Each edition contains a different bundle of programs; which Office programs you get depends on the edition of Office you have.

The edition of Microsoft Office bundled on most new PCs is called the Standard Edition, and it includes the following programs:

- **Microsoft Word**—A full-featured word processing program, discussed previously.
- **Microsoft Excel**—A full-featured spreadsheet program. (Learn more in Chapter 14, "Working with Numbers.")
- **Microsoft PowerPoint**—A program that creates professional-level presentations. (Learn more in Chapter 16, "Working with Presentations.")
- **Microsoft Outlook**—A full-featured scheduling/contact/email program.

note

Don't confuse Microsoft Outlook with Outlook Express. Outlook Express is an email-only program, whereas Microsoft Outlook adds contact management and scheduling functionality. (Learn more about Outlook Express in Chapter 25, "Sending and Receiving Email.")

The Small Business Edition adds Microsoft Publisher, which is a graphics program you can use to create brochures and other projects. The Professional Edition adds both Publisher and Microsoft Access, a sophisticated database program.

The programs in Microsoft Office are the most popular programs used by computer users worldwide. It's hard to find someone who *isn't* using Microsoft Word as their word processor; if you're a serious number cruncher, there's just no substitute for Excel; and even kids in grade school use PowerPoint to prepare slide shows and electronic presentations. This ubiquity translates to almost-universal compatibility, which means that if you're using Office, you won't have any problems sharing files with other computer users.

> **tip**
>
> If you're currently using Microsoft Works or Works Suite and want to upgrade to Microsoft Office, I recommend purchasing the Microsoft Office Student and Teacher Edition. This version is identical to the Standard Edition (Word, Excel, PowerPoint, and Outlook) and costs just $149. And you don't have to be a teacher or student to purchase it.

Corel WordPerfect Suite

Although most of the world is standardized on Microsoft products, there are still some who prefer a non-Microsoft alternative. For them, Corel publishes the WordPerfect Suite, which includes the following programs:

- **WordPerfect**—A Word-like word processing program.
- **Quattro Pro**—An Excel-like spreadsheet program.
- **Paradox**—An Access-like database program.

Some manufacturers that opt for the WordPerfect suite also bundle a copy of Intuit's Quicken personal finance program with their new PCs. (Learn more about Quicken in Chapter 17.)

Working with Works

Because so many low-priced PCs come with either Works or Works Suite installed, we'll take a quick look at how these programs work. To make things easy, we'll focus on Microsoft Works Suite 2004; other versions offer similar features and work in a similar fashion.

You start Microsoft Works Suite by following these steps:

1. Click the Windows Start button to display the Start menu.
2. Select All Programs to open the Programs menu.
3. Select Microsoft Works Task Launcher.

Finding Your Way Around the Task Launcher

When you launch Works Suite, the Works Task Launcher appears onscreen. Along the top of the Task Launcher are buttons that link to five different pages; each page represents a different way to enter a program or document.

Here are the four pages you can link to from the Task Launcher:

■ **Home.** The Home page, shown in Figure 12.1, is what you see when you first launch Works Suite. The Home page includes tabs to view your Calendar and Contacts, as well as a Quick Launch bar that lets you launch any Works Suite application directly.

FIGURE 12.1

The Home page of the Works Suite Task Launcher.

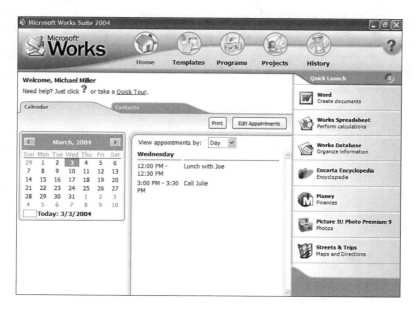

■ **Templates**. Use the Templates page to identify a particular type of document you want to create—select the template, and the Task Launcher will launch the appropriate program, with the appropriate template already loaded.

■ **Programs.** Use the Programs page to launch a specific Works Suite program—then select the task you want that program to perform.

■ **Projects.** Use the Tasks page to create large-scale projects or open pre-existing projects—select the project, and the Task Launcher will launch the appropriate program along with a step-by-step wizard to get you started.

■ **History.** Use the History page to reload any document you've recently edited with any Works Suite application.

When Task Launcher is launched, select a page, select a program or task, and then you're ready to work!

Launching a Program

You use the Programs page to launch individual Works Suite applications. Just follow these steps:

1. From the Works Task Launcher, select the Programs page (shown in Figure 12.2).

2. From the Choose a Program list, select a program.

3. From the tasks displayed for that program, click a task.

FIGURE 12.2

Use the Programs page to launch a specific Works Suite program.

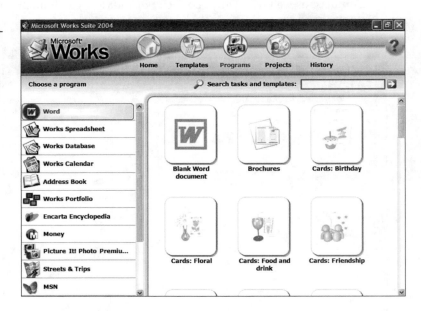

The Task Launcher now launches the program you selected with the appropriate task-based template or wizard loaded.

Creating a New Document

To create a specific type of document—and have Works load the right program for that task, automatically—you use the Templates page, as shown in Figure 12.3. Just follow these steps:

1. From the Works Task Launcher, select the Templates page.

2. From the Choose a Category list, select a particular type of template.

3. From the templates displayed for that category, click a specific template.

note

In older versions of Works, the Templates page is called the Tasks page.

FIGURE 12.3

Click the
Templates page
to get started
with a specific
task—and let
Works Suite fig-
ure out which
program to
launch.

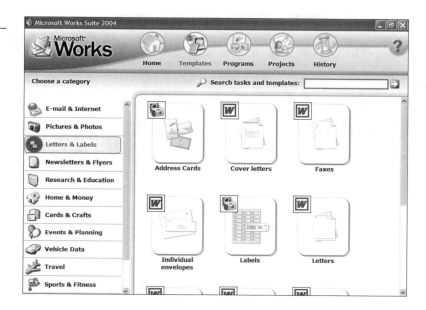

The Task Launcher now launches the appropriate program for your selected template with that template already loaded.

Opening an Existing Document

If you've been working with Works for awhile, you can use the History page to reopen documents you previously created.

The History page, shown in Figure 12.4, lists all your recently used files, newest files first. For each file, the Task Launcher includes the filename, the date it was originally created, the type of template it's based on (when known), and the program associated with that file. You can re-sort the list of files by any column by clicking on the column header. For example, if you wanted to sort files by name, you'd click on the Name header; click a second time to sort in the reverse order.

To open a file listed in the History pane, just click its name. Task Launcher will launch the program associated with that file, and then load the selected file into the program.

tip

If the file you want isn't listed on the History tab, Task Launcher lets you search for that file. When you click the Find Files and Folders link, Task Launcher displays a Windows file/folder window with the search function enabled. You can use this window to search your entire system for specific files.

FIGURE 12.4

Click the History page to view a list of recent files—click a column header to sort items by that column.

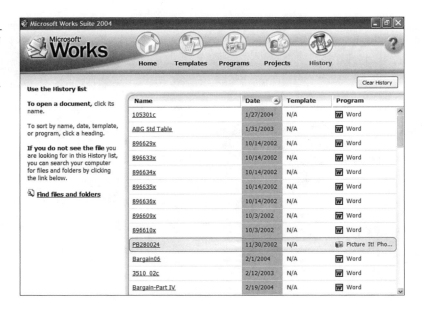

THE ABSOLUTE MINIMUM

Here are the key points to remember from this chapter:

- ■ Most new PCs come with a suite or bundle of applications pre-installed.
- ■ The most popular software suites are Microsoft Works, Microsoft Works Suite, Microsoft Office, and Corel WordPerfect Suite.
- ■ Microsoft Works and Works Suite use a Task Launcher as an interface to all of their programs.
- ■ Task Launcher lets you launch individual programs, create new documents by choosing a particular template or project, or open old documents you've worked on.

13

WORKING WITH WORDS

When you want to write a letter, fire off a quick memo, create a report, or create a newsletter, you use a type of software program called a *word processor*. For most computer users, Microsoft Word is the word processing program of choice. Word is a full-featured word processor, and it's included with both Microsoft Works Suite and Microsoft Office. You can use Word for all your writing needs—from basic letters to fancy newsletters, and everything in between.

Word isn't the only word processor out there, of course. For very basic word processing, the Works Word Processor included in Microsoft Works is often adequate. And if you're not a Microsoft fan, Corel's WordPerfect offers the same kind of professional features you find in Microsoft Word, and works in a similar fashion. But it you want maximum document compatibility with your friends, family, and co-workers, Word is the way to go.

Exploring the Word Interface

Before we get started, let's take a quick tour of the Word workspace—so you know what's what and what's where.

You start Word either from the Windows Start menu (select Start, All Programs, Microsoft Word) or, if you're using Microsoft Works Suite, from the Works Task Launcher. When Word launches, a blank document appears in the Word workspace.

What's Where in Word

The Word workspace, shown in Figure 13.1, is divided into eight main parts:

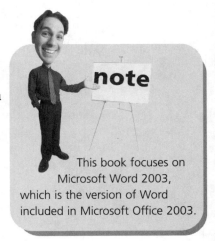

note

This book focuses on Microsoft Word 2003, which is the version of Word included in Microsoft Office 2003.

Title Bar   Menu Bar   Ruler

FIGURE 13.1

The Word work-space—to perform most tasks, just pull down a menu or click a toolbar button.

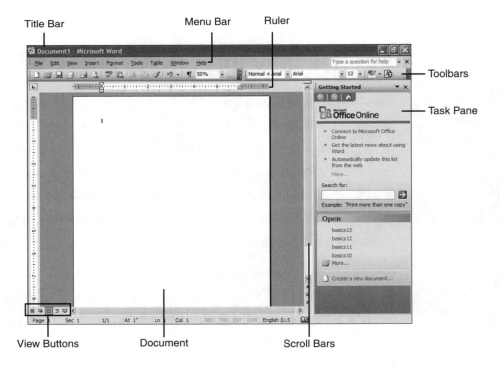

Toolbars

Task Pane

View Buttons   Document   Scroll Bars

- **Title bar.** This is where you find the filename of the current document, as well as buttons to minimize, maximize, and close the window for the current Word document.

■ **Menu bar.** This collection of pull-down menus contains virtually all of Word's commands. Use your mouse to click a menu item, and then the menu pulls down to display a full range of commands and options.

■ **Toolbars.** By default, two toolbars—Standard and Formatting—are docked at the top of the workspace, just underneath the menu bar. Word includes a number of different toolbars that you can display anywhere in the Word workspace. Click a button on any toolbar to initiate the associated command or operation. (To display additional toolbars, pull down the View menu and select Toolbars; when the list of toolbars appears, check those toolbars you want to display, and uncheck those you want to hide.)

> **tip**
>
> If two toolbars docked side-by-side are longer than the available space, buttons at the end of one or both of the toolbars will not be displayed. Instead, you'll see a More Buttons arrow; click this double-arrow to display a submenu of the leftover buttons.

■ **Ruler.** This allows you to measure the width of a document—and set tabs and margins.

■ **Document.** This main space displays your current Word document.

■ **View buttons.** The View buttons let you switch between different document views.

■ **Scroll bars.** The scroll bar at the bottom of the page lets you scroll left and right through the current page; the scroll bar along the side of the workspace lets you scroll through a document from top to bottom.

■ **Status bar.** This provides information about your current document—including what page you're on.

■ **Task pane.** This pane is displayed automatically when you're performing particular tasks, or hidden during most normal operations. It's similar to the Task pane found in Windows XP's My Documents and My Computer folders, and contains commands related to what you're currently doing in Word. You can display the Task Pane manually by selecting View, Task Pane, or by pressing Ctrl+F1.

> **tip**
>
> If you're not sure just what button on which toolbar does what, you're not alone—those little graphics are sometimes hard to decipher. To display the name of any specific button, just hover your cursor over the button until the descriptive *ScreenTip* appears.

Viewing a Word Document—in Different Ways

Word can display your document in one of five different *views*. You select a view by using the View buttons at the bottom left of the Word window, or by making a selection from the View menu.

Each view is a particular way of looking at your document:

- **Normal.** This is primarily a text-based view, because certain types of graphic objects—backgrounds, headers and footers, and some pictures—aren't displayed. This is *not* a good view for laying out the elements on your page.

- **Web Layout**. This is the view you use when you're creating a document to be displayed on the Web. In this view all the elements in your document (including graphics and backgrounds) are displayed as they would be if viewed by a Web browser.

- **Print Layout**. This is the view you use to lay out the pages of your document—with *all* elements visible, including graphics and backgrounds.

- **Reading Layout.** This is a new view with Word 2003 that makes it easier to read documents that you don't need to edit. This view hides all toolbars and resizes the text for better viewing.

- **Outline.** This is a great view for looking at the structure of your document, presenting your text (but *not* graphics!) in classic outline fashion. In this view you can collapse an outlined document to see only the main headings or expand a document to show all (or selected) headings and body text.

Zooming to View

If Word displays a document too large or too small for your tastes, it's easy to change the size of the document display. The Standard toolbar includes a pull-down Zoom list, from which you can select a pre-set zoom level (from 10 percent to 500 percent). You can also choose to have your document automatically fill up the entire width of your screen by selecting the Page Width option.

Another way to change the onscreen size of your document is to pull down the View menu and select Zoom to display the Zoom dialog box. This dialog box lets you choose from both pre-selected and custom zoom levels—and previews your selected zoom level.

Working with Documents

Anything you create with Word is called a *document*. A document is nothing more than a computer file that can be copied, moved, and deleted—or edited, from within Word.

Creating a New Document

Any new Word document you create is based on what Word calls a *template*. A template combines selected styles and document settings—and, in some cases, prewritten text or calculated fields—to create the building blocks for a specific type of document. You can use templates to give yourself a head start on specific types of documents.

To create a new Word document based on a specific template, follow these steps:

1. Pull down Word's File menu and select New; this displays the New Document pane, shown in Figure 13.2.

2. To select a recently used template, go to the Recently Used Templates section of the New Document pane and click a template name.

3. To select another template, go to the Templates section of the New Document pane and click On My Computer.

4. This opens the Templates dialog box, shown in Figure 13.3; select one of the prepared templates listed there.

5. Click OK.

> **note**
>
> If your version of Word is installed as part of Works Suite, you can view additional Works-related templates by selecting File, New Works Template.

FIGURE 13.2

Use the New Document pane to open new and existing Word documents.

FIGURE 13.3

Select a tab to select templates of a specific type.

If you don't know which template to use for your new document, just click the Blank Document link in the New section of the New Document pane. This opens a new document using Word's Normal template. This is a very basic template, with just a few text styles defined.

Opening an Existing Document

To open a previously created document, follow these steps:

1. Select File, Open to display the Open dialog box.

2. Navigate to and select the file you want to open.

3. Click Open.

Saving the Document

Every document you make—that you want to keep—must be saved to a file.

The first time you save a file, you have to specify a filename and location. Do this by following these steps:

1. Pull down the File menu and select Save As to display the Save As dialog box.

2. Navigate to the folder where you want to save the file.

3. Enter a name for the new file.

4. Click the Save button.

When you make additional changes to a document, you must save those changes. Fortunately, after you've saved a file once, you don't need to go through the whole Save As routine again. To "fast save" an existing file, all you have to do is click the Save button on Word's Standard toolbar—or pull down the File menu and select Save.

Working with Text

Now that you know how to create and save Word documents, let's examine how you put specific words on paper—or, rather, on screen.

Entering Text

You enter text in a Word document at the *insertion point*, which appears onscreen as a blinking cursor. When you start typing on your keyboard, the new text is added at the insertion point.

You move the insertion point with your mouse by clicking on a new position in your text. You move the insertion point with your keyboard by using your keyboard's arrow keys.

Editing Text

After you've entered your text, it's time to edit. With Word you can delete, cut, copy, and paste text—or graphics—to and from anywhere in your document, or between documents.

Before you can edit text, though, you have to *select* the text to edit. The easiest way to select text is with your mouse; just hold down your mouse button and drag the cursor over the text you want to select. You also can select text using your keyboard; use the Shift key—in combination with other keys—to highlight blocks of text. For example, Shift+Left Arrow selects one character to the left; Shift+End selects all text to the end of the current line.

Any text you select appears as white text against a black highlight. After you've selected a block of text, you can then edit it in a number of ways, as detailed in Table 13.1.

Table 13.1   Word Editing Operations

Operation	Keystroke	Menu Location
Delete	Del	Edit, Clear
Copy	Ctrl+Ins or Ctrl+C	Edit, Copy
Cut	Shift+Del or Ctrl+X	Edit, Cut
Paste	Shift+Ins or Ctrl+V	Edit, Paste

Formatting Text

After your text is entered and edited, you can use Word's numerous formatting options to add some pizzazz to your document. It's easiest to edit text when you're working in Print Layout view because this displays your document as it will look when printed. To switch to this view, pull down the View menu and select Print Layout.

Formatting text is easy—and most achievable from Word's Formatting toolbar. This toolbar, located at the top of the screen, includes buttons for bold, italic, and underline, as well as font, font size, and font color. To format a block of text, highlight the text and then click the desired format button.

More text formatting options are available in the Font dialog box. To display this dialog box, pull down the Format menu and select Font. From here, you can perform both basic formatting (font, font style, font color, and so on) and advanced formatting (strikethrough, superscript, subscript, shadow, outline, emboss, engrave, character spacing, and text animation). Just select the formatting you want and click OK.

Checking Spelling and Grammar

If you're not a great speller, you'll appreciate Word's automatic spell checking. You can see it right on screen; just deliberately misspell a word, and you'll see a squiggly red line under the misspelling. That's Word telling you you've made a spelling error.

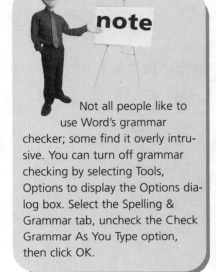

When you see that squiggly red line, position your cursor on top of the misspelled word, then right-click your mouse. Word now displays a pop-up menu with its suggestions for spelling corrections. You can choose a replacement word from the list, or return to your document and manually change the misspelling.

Sometimes Word meets a word it doesn't recognize, even though the word is spelled correctly. In these instances, you can add the new word to Word's spelling dictionary by right-clicking the word and selecting Add from the pop-up menu.

Word also includes a built-in grammar checker. When Word identifies bad grammar in your document, it underlines the offending passage with a green squiggly line. Right-click anywhere in the passage to view Word's grammatical suggestions.

note

Not all people like to use Word's grammar checker; some find it overly intrusive. You can turn off grammar checking by selecting Tools, Options to display the Options dialog box. Select the Spelling & Grammar tab, uncheck the Check Grammar As You Type option, then click OK.

Printing a Document

When you've finished editing your document, you can instruct Word to send a copy to your printer.

Previewing Before You Print

It's a good idea, however, to preview the printed document onscreen before you print it—so you can make any last-minute changes without wasting a lot of paper.

To view your document with Word's Print Preview, click the Print Preview button on Word's Standard toolbar (or pull down the File menu and select Print Preview).

The to-be-printed document appears onscreen with each page of the document presented as a small thumbnail. To zoom in or out of the preview document, click the Magnifier button and then click the magnifier cursor anywhere on your document. When you're done previewing your document, click the Close button.

Basic Printing

The fastest way to print a document is with Word's fast print option. You activate a fast print by clicking the Print button on Word's Standard toolbar.

When you do a fast print of your document, you send your document directly to your default printer. This bypasses the Print dialog box (discussed next) and all other configuration options.

Changing Print Options

Sometimes fast printing isn't the best way to print. For example, you might want to print multiple copies, or print to a different (non-default) printer. For these and similar situations, you need to use Word's Print dialog box.

You open the Print dialog box, shown in Figure 13.4, by pulling down the File menu and selecting Print.

After you have the Print dialog box displayed, you can choose any one of a number of options specific to this particular print job. After you've made your choices, click the OK button to start printing.

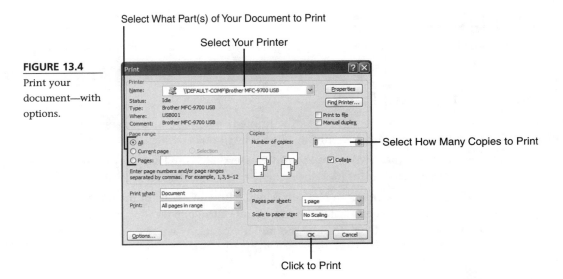

FIGURE 13.4
Print your document—with options.

Formatting Your Document

When you're creating a complex document, you need to format more than just a few words here and there.

Formatting Paragraphs

When you need to format complete paragraphs, you use Word's Paragraph dialog box. You open the Paragraph dialog box by positioning your cursor within a paragraph and then pulling down the Format menu and selecting Paragraph. From here, you can precisely adjust how the entire paragraph appears, including indentation, line spacing, and alignment.

Using Word Styles

If you have a preferred paragraph formatting you use over and over and over, you don't have to format each paragraph individually. Instead, you can assign all your formatting to a paragraph *style* and then assign that style to specific paragraphs throughout your document. Most templates come with a selection of pre-designed styles; you can modify these built-in styles or create your own custom styles. Styles include formatting for fonts, paragraphs, tabs, borders, numbering, and more.

To apply a style to a paragraph, position the insertion point anywhere in the paragraph and then pull down the Style list (in the Formatting toolbar) and select a style. (You don't have to select the entire paragraph; just having the insertion point in the paragraph does the job.)

To modify a style, follow these steps:

1. Pull down the Format menu and select Styles and Formatting; this displays the Styles and Formatting pane, shown in Figure 13.5.

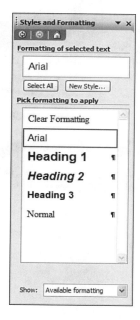

FIGURE 13.5

Use the Styles and Formatting pane to modify and assign Word styles.

2. Hover your cursor over which style you want to edit; this displays a down button.

3. Click the Down button and select Modify; this displays the Modify Style dialog box.

4. Change basic properties from this dialog box, or click the Format button to select other properties to modify.

5. Click OK when done.

Assigning Headings

When you're creating a long document, you probably want to separate sections of your document with headings. Headings appear as larger, bolder text, like mini-headlines.

Word includes several built-in heading styles—Heading 1, Heading 2, Heading 3, and Heading 4. Assign these styles to your document's headings, as appropriate. (And if you don't like the way they look, edit the styles to your liking—as described previously.)

Working with an Outline

If you have a really long document, you might find it easier to work with the various sections in the form of an outline. For this purpose, Word lets you view your document in Outline view, as shown in Figure 13.6. Just pull down the View menu and select Outline.

tip

To force a manual page break in your document—as you might if you want a new section to start on a new page—position the cursor at the front of the line and then press Ctrl+Enter. You can also select Insert, Break to display the Break dialog box, select Page Break, then click OK.

FIGURE 13.6

Use Outline view to reorganize the sections of your document.

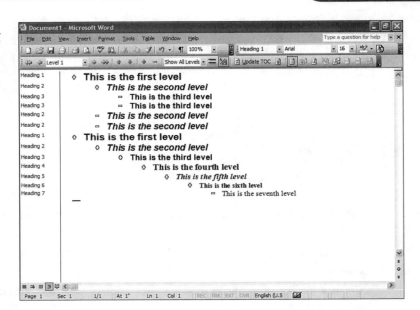

When you're in Outline view, Word displays your headings as different outline levels. Text formatted with the Heading 1 style appears as Level 1 headings in your outline, text formatted as Heading 2 appears as Level 2 headings, and so on.

To make your outline easier to work with, you can select how many levels of headings are displayed. (Just pull down the Show Level list and select the appropriate level number.) You also can choose to expand or contract various sections of the outline by clicking the plus and minus icons to the side of each Level text in your outline.

Outline view makes rearranging sections of your document extremely easy. When you're in Outline view, you can move an entire section from one place to another by selecting the Level heading and then clicking the up and down arrow buttons. (You also can drag sections from one position to another within the outline.)

Working with Pictures

Although memos and letters might look fine if they contain nothing but text, other types of documents—newsletters, reports, and so on—can be jazzed up with pictures and other graphic elements.

Inserting a Picture from the Clip Art Gallery

The easiest way to add a graphic to your document is to use Word's built-in Clip Art Gallery. The Clip Art Gallery is a collection of ready-to-use illustrations and photos, organized by topic, that can be pasted directly into your Word documents.

To insert a piece of clip art, follow these steps:

1. Position your cursor where you want the picture to appear.
2. Select Insert, Picture, Clip Art; this displays the Clip Art pane.
3. Enter one or more keywords into the Search For box, then click Search.
4. Pictures matching your criteria are now displayed in the pane; double-click a graphic to insert it into your document.

tip

If you'd rather browse through available clip art, select Insert, Picture, Clip Collection to display the Insert Clip Art dialog box; select a specific category to display all matching pictures.

Inserting Other Types of Picture Files

You're not limited to using graphics from the Clip Art Gallery. Word lets you insert any type of graphics file into your document—including GIF, JPG, BMP, TIF, and other popular graphic formats.

To insert a graphics file into your document, follow these steps:

1. Position your cursor where you want the picture to appear.
2. Select Insert, Picture, From File; this displays the Insert Picture dialog box.

3. Navigate to and select the picture you want to insert.

4. Click the Insert button to insert that picture into your document.

Formatting the Picture

After you've inserted a picture in your document, you might need to format it for best appearance.

To format the picture itself, double-click the picture. This displays the Format Picture dialog box, which lets you format colors, line, size, layout, brightness, contrast, and other settings.

To move your picture to another position in your document, use your mouse to drag it to its new position. You also can resize the graphic by clicking the picture and then dragging a selection handle to resize that side or corner of the graphic.

To change the way text flows around the graphic, double-click the graphic to display the Format Picture dialog box and then select the Layout tab. You can choose to display the picture inline with the text, wrap around the text as a square, flow in front of the text, or display behind the text.

The Absolute Minimum

Here are the key points to remember from this chapter:

- Microsoft Word is a powerful word processing program included with both Microsoft Works Suite and Microsoft Office.

- Most editing commands are found on Word's Edit menu; most formatting commands are found on the Format menu.

- There are several different ways you can view a Word document, selectable from the small buttons at the lower left corner of the workspace. The most useful views are the Normal and Print Layout views; you can also use the Outline view to display your document as a hierarchical outline.

- If you reuse similar formatting throughout your document, consider using a Word style to apply similar formatting to multiple paragraphs.

- Insert clip art or graphics files by selecting Insert, Picture, and then selecting the appropriate type of picture.

14

WORKING WITH NUMBERS

When you're on your computer and want to crunch some numbers, you use a program called a *spreadsheet*. There are several different spreadsheet programs available for your personal computer. Full-featured spreadsheet programs include Microsoft Excel, Lotus 1-2-3, and Corel's Quattro Pro; for more casual users, there's also the Works Spreadsheet included in Microsoft Works and Works Suite.

The most popular spreadsheet among serious number crunchers is Microsoft Excel, which is included as part of the Microsoft Office suite. That's the spreadsheet we'll look at in this chapter, although the other spreadsheet programs operate in a similar fashion.

Understanding Spreadsheets

A spreadsheet is nothing more than a giant list. Your list can contain just about any type of data you can think of—text, numbers, and even dates. You can take any of the numbers on your list and use them to calculate new numbers. You can sort the items on your list, pretty them up, and print the important points in a report. You can even graph your numbers in a pie, line, or bar chart!

All spreadsheet programs work in pretty much the same fashion. In a spreadsheet, everything is stored in little boxes called *cells*. Your spreadsheet is divided into lots of these cells, each located in a specific location on a giant grid made of *rows* and *columns*. Each single cell represents the intersection of a particular row and column.

As you can see in Figure 14.1, each column has an alphabetic label (A, B, C, and so on). Each row, on the other hand, has a numeric label (1, 2, 3, and so on). The location of each cell is the combination of its column and row locations. For example, the cell in the upper-left corner of the spreadsheet is in column A and row 1; therefore, its location is signified as A1. The cell to the right of it is B1, and the cell below A1 is A2. The location of the selected, or *active*, cell is displayed in the Name box.

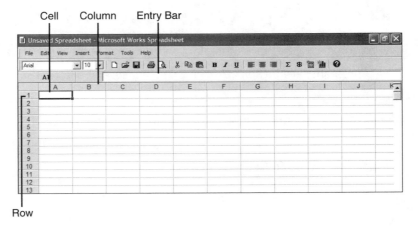

FIGURE 14.1

An Excel spreadsheet— divided into lots of rows and columns.

Next to the Name box is the Formula bar, which echoes the contents of the active cell. You can type data directly into either the Formula bar or active cell.

Entering Data

Entering text or numbers into a spreadsheet is easy. Just remember that data is entered into each cell individually—then you can fill up a spreadsheet with hundreds or thousands of cells filled with their own individual data.

To enter data into a specific cell, follow these steps:

1. Select the cell you want to enter data into.
2. Type your text or numbers into the cell; what you type will be echoed in the Formula bar at the top of the screen.
3. When you're done typing data into the cell, press Enter.

Inserting and Deleting Rows and Columns

Sometimes you need to go back to an existing spreadsheet and insert some new information.

Insert a Row or Column

To insert a new row or column in the middle of your spreadsheet, follow these steps:

1. Click the row or column header *after* where you want to make the insertion.
2. Pull down the Insert menu and select either Insert Row or Insert Column.

Excel now inserts a new row or column either above or to the left of the row or column you selected.

Delete a Row or Column

To delete an existing row or column, follow these steps:

1. Click the header for the row or column you want to delete.
2. Pull down the Edit menu and select Delete.

The row or column you selected is deleted, and all other rows or columns move up or over to fill the space.

Adjusting Column Width

If the data you enter into a cell is too long, you'll only see the first part of that data—there'll be a bit to the right that looks cut off. It's not cut off, of course; it just can't be seen, since it's longer than the current column is wide.

You can fix this problem by adjusting the column width. Wider columns allow more data to be shown; narrow columns let you display more columns per page.

To change the column width, move your cursor to the column header, and position it on the dividing line on the right side of the column you want to adjust. When the cursor changes shape, click the left button on your mouse and drag the column divider to the right (to make a wider column) or to the left (to make a smaller column). Release the mouse button when the column is the desired width.

Using Formulas and Functions

Excel lets you enter just about any type of algebraic formula into any cell. You can use these formulas to add, subtract, multiply, divide, and perform any nested combination of those operations.

tip

To make a column the exact width for the longest amount of data entered, position your cursor over the dividing line to the right of the column header and double-click your mouse. This makes the column width automatically "fit" your current data.

Creating a Formula

Excel knows that you're entering a formula when you type an equal sign (=) into any cell. You start your formula with the equal sign and enter your operations *after* the equal sign.

For example, if you want to add 1 plus 2, enter this formula in a cell: =1+2. When you press Enter, the formula disappears from the cell—and the result, or *value*, is displayed.

Basic Operators

Table 14.1 shows the algebraic operators you can use in Excel formulas.

Table 14.1 Excel Operators

Operation	Operator
Add	+
Subtract	-
Multiply	*
Divide	/

So if you want to multiply 10 by 5, enter =10*5. If you want to divide 10 by 5, enter =10/5.

Including Other Cells in a Formula

If all you're doing is adding and subtracting numbers, you might as well use a calculator. Where a spreadsheet becomes truly useful is when you use it to perform operations based on the contents of specific cells.

To perform calculations using values from cells in your spreadsheet, you enter the cell location into the formula. For example, if you want to add cells A1 and A2, enter this formula: =A1+A2. And if the numbers in either cell A1 or A2 change, the total will automatically change, as well.

An even easier way to perform operations involving spreadsheet cells is to select them with your mouse while you're entering the formula. To do this, follow these steps:

1. Select the cell that will contain the formula.
2. Type =.
3. Click the first cell you want to include in your formula; that cell location is automatically entered in your formula.
4. Type an algebraic operator, such as +, -, *, or /.
5. Click the second cell you want to include in your formula.
6. Repeat steps 4 and 5 to include other cells in your formula.
7. Press Enter when your formula is complete.

Quick Addition with AutoSum

The most common operation in any spreadsheet is the addition of a group of numbers. Excel makes summing up a row or column of numbers easy via the AutoSum function.

All you have to do is follow these steps:

1. Select the cell at the end of a row or column of numbers, where you want the total to appear.
2. Click the AutoSum button, shown in Figure 14.2, on the Standard toolbar.

Excel automatically sums all the preceding numbers and places the total in the selected cell.

FIGURE 14.2
Use AutoSum to automatically add a row or column of numbers.

Other AutoSum Operations

Excel's AutoSum also includes a few other automatic calculations. When you click the down arrow on the side of the AutoSum button, you can perform the following operations:

- **Average**, which calculates the average of the selected cells
- **Count**, which counts the number of selected cells
- **Max**, which returns the largest value in the selected cells
- **Min**, which returns the smallest value in the selected cells

Using Functions

In addition to the basic algebraic operators previously discussed, Excel also includes a variety of *functions* that replace the complex steps present in many formulas. For example, if you wanted to total all the cells in column A, you could enter the formula =A1+A2+A3+A4. Or, you could use the *SUM* function, which lets you sum a column or row of numbers without having to type every cell into the formula. (And when you use AutoSum, it's simply applying the *SUM* function.)

In short, a function is a type of pre-built formula.

You enter a function in the following format: =function(argument), where function is the name of the function and argument is the range of cells or other data you want to calculate. Using the last example, to sum cells A1 through A4, you'd use the following function-based formula: =sum(A1,A2,A3,A4).

> **tip**
>
> When you're referencing consecutive cells in a formula, you can just enter the first and last number or the series separated by a colon. For example, cells A1 through A4 can be entered as A1:A4.

Excel includes hundreds of functions. You can access and insert any of Excel's functions by following these steps:

1. Select the cell where you want to insert the function.
2. Select Insert, Function to display the Insert Function dialog box (shown in Figure 14.3).
3. Select a function category from the Select a Category list, then select a specific function. (Alternatively, you can use the Search for a Function box to search for a specific type of function.)
4. Click the OK button.
5. If the function has related arguments, a Function Arguments dialog box is now displayed; enter the arguments and click OK.
6. The function you selected is now inserted into the current cell. You can now manually enter the cells or numbers into the function's argument.

FIGURE 14.3

Choose from hundreds of functions in the Insert Function dialog box.

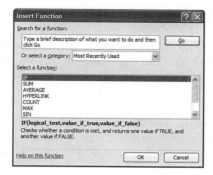

Sorting a Range of Cells

If you have a list of either text or numbers, you might want to reorder the list for a different purpose. Excel lets you sort your data by any column, in either ascending or descending order.

To sort a range of cells, follow these steps:

1. Select all the cells you want to sort.
2. Select Data, Sort to display the Sort dialog box, shown in Figure 14.4.
3. Select whether your list does or doesn't have a header row.
4. Pull down the first Sort By list, and select which column you want to sort by.
5. Choose to sort in either Ascending or Descending order.
6. Repeat steps 4 and 5 to sub-sort on additional columns, using the Then By lists.
7. Click the OK button to sort the data.

FIGURE 14.4

Sort your list by any column, in any order.

Formatting Your Spreadsheet

You don't have to settle for boring-looking spreadsheets. You can format how the data appears in your spreadsheet—including the format of any numbers you enter.

Applying Number Formats

When you enter a number into a cell, Excel applies what it calls a "general" format to the number—it just displays the number, right-aligned, with no commas or dollar signs. You can, however, select a specific number format to apply to any cells in your spreadsheet that contain numbers. Follow these steps:

1. Select the cell (or cells) you want to format.
2. Select Format, Cells to display the Format Cells dialog box, shown in Figure 14.5.
3. Select the Number tab.
4. Check one of the options in the Category list.
5. If the format has additional options (such as decimal points or various date or time formats), configure these as desired.
6. Click OK.

FIGURE 14.5

Use the Format Cells dialog box to change number formats and apply other cell formatting.

Formatting Cell Contents

You can apply a variety of formatting options to the contents of your cells. You can make your text bold or italic, change the font type or size, or even add shading or borders to selected cells.

To format a cell (or range of cells), follow these steps:

1. Select the cell (or range).
2. Select Format, Cells to display the Format Cells dialog box.

3. To change the justification of the cell contents, select the Alignment tab and make the appropriate selections.

4. To change the font size, color, or formatting of the cell contents, select the Font tab and make the appropriate selections.

5. To put a border around the selected cells, select the Border tab and make the appropriate selections.

6. To apply shading to the selected cells, select the Pattern tab and make the appropriate selections.

7. Click OK when done.

tip

You can also apply some basic formatting—alignment, bold, italic, and so on—directly from the Formatting toolbar, at the top of the workspace.

Creating a Chart

Numbers are fine, but sometimes the story behind the numbers can be better told through a picture. The way you take a picture of numbers is with a *chart*, such as the one shown in Figure 14.6.

FIGURE 14.6

Some numbers are better represented via a chart.

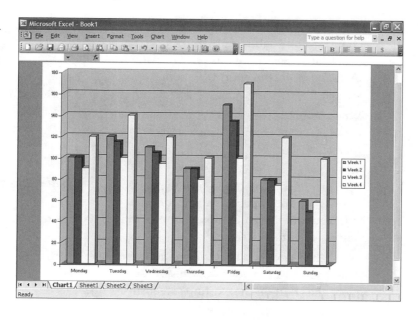

You create a chart based on numbers you've previously entered into your Excel spreadsheet, like this:

1. Select the range of cells you want to include in your chart. (If the range has a header row or column, include that row or column when selecting the cells.)

2. Click the Chart Wizard button to display Step 1 of the Chart Wizard, shown in Figure 14.7.

FIGURE 14.7

Create one of a dozen types of charts to visually represent your data.

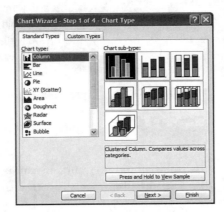

3. Select the Standard Types tab, select a chart type and sub-type, then click Next. (Alternately, select the Custom Types tab to design your own chart type from scratch.)

4. When Step 2 of the Chart Wizard appears, verify the data range selected, then click Next.

5. When Step 3 of the Chart Wizard appears, select each tab in turn to select various formatting options. You can add titles, gridlines, legends, labels, and so forth to your chart. Click Next when you're ready to proceed.

tip

To see how your numbers will appear in a selected chart type, click the Press and Hold to View Sample button.

6. When Step 4 of the Chart Wizard appears, select whether you want to create a new sheet within your worksheet for your chart, or whether you want to place the chart on the existing spreadsheet page.

7. Click Finish to create the chart.

THE ABSOLUTE MINIMUM

Here are the key points to remember from this chapter:

- Popular spreadsheet programs include Microsoft Excel, Lotus 1-2-3, Corel's Quattro Pro, and the Works Spreadsheet included in Microsoft Works and Works Suite.

- A spreadsheet is composed of rows and columns; the intersection of a specific row and column is called a cell.

- Each cell can contain text, numbers, or formulas.

- You start an Excel formula with an = sign, and follow it up with specific numbers (or cell locations) and operators—such as +, -, *, and /.

- To graphically display your spreadsheet data, select the appropriate cells and then click the Chart Wizard button.

15

WORKING WITH A DATABASE

If a spreadsheet is a giant list, a database is a giant file cabinet. Each "file cabinet" is actually a separate database file, and contains individual index cards (called *records*) filled with specific information (arranged in *fields*).

If you want to create a huge industrial-strength database, you'll need to invest in a professional-level database program, such as Microsoft Access or Corel's Paradox. For more casual use, there's always Works Database, included with Microsoft Works and Works Suite. Works Database is the right program to use if you want to create a database that contains all your favorite recipes or the contents of your CD or DVD collection.

Creating a New Database

You launch Works Database the same way you launch most other Works Suite applications, from either the Windows Start menu (select Start, All Programs, Microsoft Works, Microsoft Works Database) or the Works Task Launcher.

Creating a Preformatted Database

Works Database includes a handful of preformatted database applications. These include home inventory worksheets, home lists, and a recipe book. All these databases include ready-made forms and reports specific to that application.

To base your new database on one of these applications follow these steps:

1. Open the Works Task Launcher.
2. Select the Programs page.
3. Select Works Database.
4. Select the application you want.

Creating a Blank Database

You also can use Works Database to create your own customized applications. This means, of course, that you have to design your own fields, forms, and reports.

When you launch Works Database with a blank database, you're presented with the Create Database dialog box, shown in Figure 15.1. Now you're faced with some immediate choices. (Don't worry—if you don't like the choices you make, you can always go back and change them later.)

FIGURE 15.1

Use the Create Database dialog box to design your database.

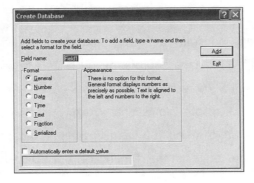

First, you need to decide how many fields to include in your database. In general, you should create one field for each type of information you want to store. If you're creating a database for your movie collection, for example, you might create fields for Movie, Lead Actor, Lead Actress, Director, Running Time, and Year.

Each field you add is assigned a specific *format*. You can select from the following formats: General, Number, Date, Time, Text, Fraction, and Serialized (for automatic consecutive numbers). Select the format that best fits the type of data you'll enter into that field. Click Add to add another field.

After you've finished adding fields to your database, click the Exit button. Works now creates a database, based on your specifications.

Changing Views

You can view your new database in two distinct ways. The default view, called the *List view*, makes your database look a little like a spreadsheet. As you can see in Figure 15.2, the rows are your records, and the columns are your fields.

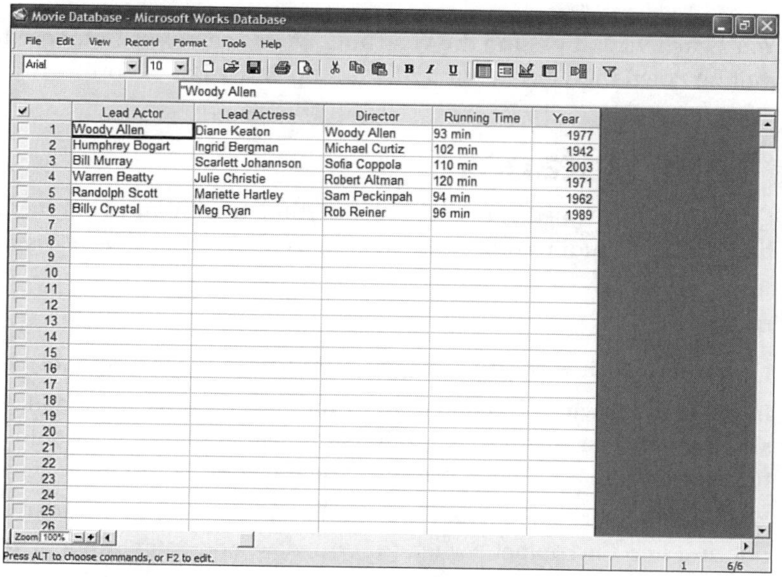

FIGURE 15.2

Viewing a database in List view.

The *Form view*, shown in Figure 15.3 lets you look at one record at a time. You can flip from one record to another by using the arrow keys at the bottom of the screen.

FIGURE 15.3

Viewing an indi-
vidual record in
your database,
AKA Form view.

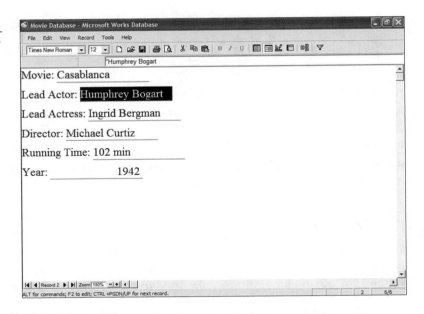

You switch views by using the view buttons on the Works Database toolbar or by
pulling down the View menu and selecting either List or Form.

Editing Your Database

Once you've designed your database, it's time to fill it up. That means entering data
into the individual records—and adding as many records as necessary.

Adding Data

No matter which view you're using, adding data to your database is easy.

If you're in List view, you add data to your database as you'd add data to a spreadsheet. Move your cursor to any particular field, and type your data. Use the Tab key
to move to the next field in a record; use the Enter key to move to the next record.

You might prefer to add data one record at a time, as you'd enter data on an individual card in a file cabinet. Switch to Form view, and enter all the data for the fields in
the current record. Use the Tab key to move from field to field; when you reach the
end of one record, pressing Tab moves you to the first field of the next record.

Adding New Records

If you're in List view, adding a new record is as simple as starting to type in the first
empty record row. If you're in Form view, just click the Insert Record button; a new
blank record appears in the workspace.

Adding New Fields

After you get going in a database, you might discover that you want to include more information for each record. Going back to our movie database example, you might decide that you want to add a field for Category/Genre.

Fortunately, adding new fields to existing databases is easy. All you have to do is follow these steps:

1. Switch to List view.
2. Position your cursor anywhere in the field before where you want to insert the new field.
3. Select Record, Insert Field, After to display the Insert Field dialog box.
4. Enter a name and format for the new field.
5. Click Add.

Works now adds the new field(s) to every record in your database. This field will be blank, of course, so you'll have to go back through your existing records and fill it in, as appropriate.

Sorting and Filtering

You can add records to your database in any order. You don't have to insert new records alphabetically because you can have the program itself re-sort all the records for you; you can filter your information to display only selected records.

Sorting Data

You use List view to display all the records in your database. By default, these records are listed in the order in which they're entered. However, you can sort these records by any field—in either ascending or descending order. Follow these steps:

1. From List view, select Records, Sort Records to display the Sort Records dialog box.
2. Pull down the Sort By list and select the first field by which you want to sort.
3. Select whether you want to sort in Ascending or Descending order.
4. If you want, repeat steps 2 and 3 to sort on a second or third field.
5. Click OK.

Works now re-sorts your database as directed.

Filtering Data

Another option you have in Works Database is to display only those records that match a specific criteria. This is sometimes necessary if your database contains a lot of records and you want to view only a subset of them. This process is called *filtering* the database, and it's easy to do.

For example, in your movie database you might want to display only Humphrey Bogart movies. You would create a filter that looks for all records containing Humphrey Bogart as an actor and displays only those records.

To create a filter, follow these steps:

1. From within List view, select Tools, Filters to display the Filter Name dialog box.
2. Enter a name for the filter, and then click OK.
3. When the Filter dialog box appears, pull down the first Field Name box and select the first field you want to filter.
4. Pull down the first Comparison list and select a criteria (is equal to, does not contain, and so on) for the filter.
5. In the first Compare To box, enter the value for the selected criteria.
6. Repeat steps 4-5 to apply additional parameters for this filter.
7. Click the Apply Filter button.

Using the movie database example, if you wanted to display only Humphrey Bogart movies, you'd select Lead Actor as the Field Name, pull down the Comparison list and select Contains, and then enter `Humphrey Bogart` in the Compare To box. Works Database looks for those records where the Lead Actor field contains Humphrey Bogart and displays only those records.

Creating a Report

Once you have all your data entered, sorted, and filtered, you can print a report of key database information. You can then store this hard copy someplace safe, in case you need it at a future date.

Printing a List

If you want to view all the fields in all the records in your database, all you have to do is print the list of records as they appear in List view. You do this by switching to List view and then clicking the Print button on the toolbar.

If you prefer, you can print only selected records by filtering your database, as explained earlier. Apply the filter, and then print the resulting list of records.

tip

Don't forget to sort your records before you print!

If you just want to print a single record, you don't have to apply some draconian filter. Instead, switch to Forms view, navigate to the record you want to print, and then click the Print button. Works will print only the current form.

Using ReportCreator to Create a Report

Even more useful than printing a list is Works' capability to analyze and summarize the contents of a database in a customized *report*. Works Database includes a special ReportCreator tool that makes creating custom reports a snap.

To create a report, follow these steps:

1. Select Tools, ReportCreator to display the Report Name dialog box.

2. Enter a name for your report and click OK; this displays the ReportCreator dialog box.

3. Select the Title tab, enter or edit the report title, then select an orientation and a font.

4. Select the Fields tab, select those fields you want to include in your report, in the order that you want them to appear, and then click Add. If you want to display the field names at the top of your page, check the Show Field Names at Top of Each Page option; if you want to summarize the data in your fields, check the Show Summary Information Only option.

5. Select the Sorting tab, then select which fields you want to sort by, in either Ascending or Descending order.

6. Select the Grouping tab, then select any fields you want to group or subtotal and how you want them grouped.

7. Select the Filter tab, then select any previously created filter from the Select a Filter list—or click the Create New Filter button to create and apply a new filter.

note

Only sorted fields are available for grouping.

8. Select the Summary tab, then select any fields you want to summarize, how you want to summarize them (sum, average, count, and so on), and where you want to display the summaries (under each column, at the end of the report, and so on).

9. Click the Done button.

10. You're now asked whether you want to preview or modify the report; click Preview.

11. Your report is now displayed onscreen in Preview mode, as shown in Figure 15.4. If you like what you see, click Print. If you don't, click Cancel and edit your report using the report commands on the Tools menu.

FIGURE 15.4

Summarize and analyze your database with custom-created reports.

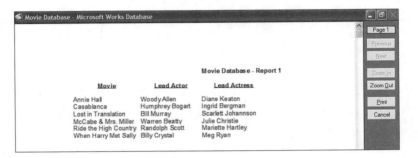

THE ABSOLUTE MINIMUM

Here are the key points to remember from this chapter:

■ A database is like a big electronic filing cabinet.

■ If all you need is a simple database, use Works Database (included with Microsoft Works and Works Suite); if you need a more sophisticated database, use either Microsoft Access or Corel's Paradox.

■ Individual items within a database are called records.

■ Each record can contain a number of fields; all records within a database have the same fields.

■ Works Database lets you view your data in two different views—List view, which looks a little like a spreadsheet (with rows and columns), and Form view, which displays your data one record at a time.

■ Within Works Database, use ReportCreator to create printed reports of your database data.

16

WORKING WITH PRESENTATIONS

When you need to present information to a group of people, the hip way to do it is with a PowerPoint presentation. Whether you use an overhead projector, traditional slides, or a computer projector, PowerPoint can help you create great-looking graphic and bullet-point presentations.

If you work in an office, you probably see at least one PowerPoint presentation a week. Teachers use PowerPoint to present lesson materials in class. Kids even use PowerPoint to prepare what used to be oral reports.

So get with the program—and learn how to create your own great-looking presentations with PowerPoint!

Understanding Microsoft PowerPoint

Microsoft PowerPoint is a presentation program included with most versions of Microsoft Office. We'll look at the latest version of the program, PowerPoint 2003.

The PowerPoint Workspace

As you can see in Figure 16.1, PowerPoint looks like most other Microsoft applications. You have the Standard and Formatting toolbars at the top of the screen, your main document (actually your current slide) in the middle of the screen, and a Task pane at the far right.

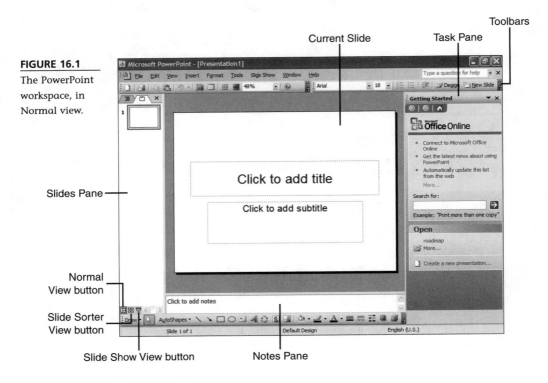

FIGURE 16.1
The PowerPoint workspace, in Normal view.

Opposite the Task pane, on the left side of the workspace, is the Outline/Slides pane, which displays all the slides in your presentation in either text (Outline) or graphic (Slides) views. Below the current slide is a Notes pane, which lets you enter presentation notes. And at the very bottom, in the left-hand corner, are the View buttons, which you use to switch between different views of your presentation.

Changing Views

This default view of the PowerPoint workspace is called, not surprising, Normal view. PowerPoint offers three different ways to view your presentation, all selectable from either the View buttons or the View menu. These views include

- ■ **Normal**, which is the default view complete with Outline/Slides and Notes panes.
- ■ **Slide Sorter**, which displays thumbnails of all the slides in your presentation.
- ■ **Slide Show**, which launches a live full-screen "slide show" of your entire presentation.

Creating a New Presentation

When you launch PowerPoint, a blank presentation is loaded and ready for your input. If you'd rather create a presentation based on a pre-designed template (more on these next), select File, New to display the New Presentation pane. Click From Design Template to display a list of available templates; click a template to get started.

Applying a Template

You don't have to reinvent the wheel when it comes to designing the look of your presentation. PowerPoint includes dozens of *design templates* that you can apply to any presentation, blank or otherwise. A template specifies the color scheme, fonts, layout, and background for each slide you create in your presentation.

To apply a template to an open presentation, follow these steps:

1. Select Format, Slide Design to display the Slide Design pane, shown in Figure 16.2.

2. Scroll through the available templates until you find one you like, then click it.

It's that simple. All the colors and fonts and everything else from the template are automatically applied to all the slides in your presentation—and every new slide you add will also carry the selected design.

FIGURE 16.2

Use the Slide Design pane to apply a design template to your presentation.

Inserting New Slides

When you create a new presentation, PowerPoint starts with a single slide—the *title slide*. Naturally, you'll need to insert additional slides to create a complete presentation. PowerPoint lets you insert different types of slides, with different types of layouts for different types of information.

To insert a new slide, follow these steps:

1. Click the New Slide button on the Formatting Toolbar. (Alternately, select Insert, New Slide—or press Ctrl+M.)

2. The new slide is inserted and the Slide Layout pane, shown in Figure 16.3, is displayed.

3. Scroll through the list of available layouts and click the one you want. This layout is now applied to the slide you just inserted.

Continue adding as many slides as you need to complete your presentation.

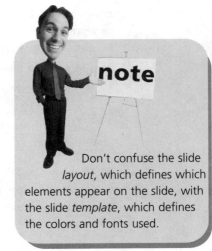

note

Don't confuse the slide *layout*, which defines which elements appear on the slide, with the slide *template*, which defines the colors and fonts used.

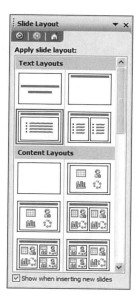

Working from an Outline

Rather than creating a presentation one slide at a time, some people find it easier to outline their entire presentation in advance. To this end, PowerPoint offers the Outline pane, located at the left of the workspace. Select the Outline tab and PowerPoint displays each slide of your presentation, in outline fashion.

To enter text for an outline level, all you have to do is type. To add another slide in your outline, press the Enter key. To add bullet text to a slide, press the Tab key. To add a sub-bullet, press Tab again. When you're done entering bullets, press Shift+Tab to move up the hierarchy and create a new slide.

Adding Text

As you've just seen, one way to add text to your slides is via the Outline pane. You can also enter text directly into each slide. When PowerPoint creates a new slide, the areas for text entry are designated with boilerplate text—"Click to add title" (for the slide's title) or "Click to add text" (for regular text or bullet points). Adding text is as easy as clicking the boilerplate text and then entering your own words and numbers. Press Enter to move to a new line or bullet. To enter a sub-bullet, press the Tab key first; to back up a level, press Shift-Tab.

Formatting Your Slides

You've already seen how to use design templates to format your entire presentation in one go. You can also format slides individually.

Formatting Text

Formatting text on a slide is just like formatting text in a word processing document. Select the text you want to format, and then click the appropriate button on the Formatting menu. (Alternately, you can pull down the Format menu and choose to select the Font, Paragraph, Bullets and Numbering, Alignment, and other attributes.)

Changing Backgrounds

Don't like the slide background from the current template? Then change it! You can create single-color backgrounds, backgrounds that gradate between two different colors, and even backgrounds that incorporate a graphic or photograph.

To apply a new background to the current slide, follow these steps:

1. Select Format, Background to display the Background dialog box, shown in Figure 16.4.

FIGURE 16.4

Use the Background dialog box to change a slide's background.

2. To apply a single-color background from the current color scheme, pull down the Background Fill list and click a color.

3. To apply a different single-color background, pull down the Background Fill list and select More Colors. When the Colors dialog box appears, select a color then click OK.

---

tip

One of the unique formatting operations possible with PowerPoint is the Shadow effect, which you add by clicking the "S" button on the Formatting toolbar. This adds a drop shadow behind the selected text, which can really make the text "pop" off a colored or textured background.

4. To apply a gradated color, pull down the Background Fill list and select Fill Effects. When the Fill Effects dialog box appears, as shown in Figure 16.5, select the gradient tab and then select either a one-color, two-color, or present fill. Select the colors you want, along with the shading style, then click OK.

FIGURE 16.5

Select a variety of background fill effects— including color gradations.

5. To apply a textured background, pull down the Background Fill list and select Fill Effects. When the Fill Effects dialog box appears, select the Texture tab, select a texture, then click OK.

6. To apply a patterned background, pull down the Background Fill list and select Fill Effects. When the Fill Effects dialog box appears, select the Pattern tab and choose a pattern, a foreground color, and a background color, then click OK.

7. To use a picture for the slide's background, pull down the Background Fill list and select Fill Effects. When the Fill Effects dialog box appears, select the Picture tab then click the Select Picture button. When the Select Picture dialog box appears, find and choose a picture file then click Insert.

8. After you've made your background choices, return to the Background dialog box. To apply this background to the current slide only, check the Omit Background Graphics from Master option and click the Apply button.

tip

To apply your new background to all the slides in your presentation, click the Apply to All button in the Background dialog box.

Adding Graphics

An all-text presentation is a little boring. To spice up your slides, you need to add some graphics!

Inserting Pictures

You can insert any type of drawing or photograph into a PowerPoint slide. It's easiest to start with a slide layout that anticipates the addition of a picture, however. Follow these steps:

1. From a blank slide, select Format, Slide Layout to display the Slide Layout pane.

2. Select one of the Content or Text and Content layouts that includes space for a picture.

3. When the new layout is applied to the slide, identify the object labeled "Click icon to add content."

4. To add a clip art drawing, click the Insert Clip Art icon; when the Select Picture dialog box appears, select a drawing and click OK.

5. To add a JPG, GIF, TIF, or other type of picture file, click the Insert Picture icon; when the Insert Picture dialog box appears, find and select a file, then click Insert.

tip

You can add a free-floating graphic to any slide by selecting Insert, Picture, and then selecting the type of graphic you want to add.

Once the graphic is added, you can now format it in a number of ways:

- To rotate the graphic, grab the green handle above the graphic and turn it to the left or right.

- To recolor the graphic or add a border, double-click the graphic to display the Format Picture dialog box, select the Colors and Lines tab, then make the appropriate selections.

- To crop the graphic, double-click the graphic to display the Format Picture dialog box, select the Picture tab, then enter the appropriate dimensions into the Crop From fields.

- To add a drop shadow behind the graphic, make sure the Drawing toolbar is displayed (select View, Toolbars, Drawing), then select the graphic, click the Shadow Style button on the Drawing toolbar, and select a shadow style.

Creating Charts

Another way to spice up your presentation is to display numerical data in chart format. The easiest way to create a chart is to start with a slide layout that includes a chart. Follow these steps:

1. From a blank slide, select Format, Slide Layout to display the Slide Layout pane.

2. Select one of the Content or Text and Content layouts that includes space for a chart.

3. When the new layout is applied to the slide, identify the object labeled "Click icon to add content."

4. Click the Insert Chart icon.

5. Your slide is now displayed with a default bar chart, like the one in Figure 16.6, along with a floating window that contains a data table.

6. Enter new labels and numbers into the data table window.

7. Select a different chart type by clicking the down arrow next to the Chart Type icon on the new Chart toolbar.

8. To format the chart, double-click different areas of the chart and make the appropriate selections.

FIGURE 16.6

Adding a chart to your presentation.

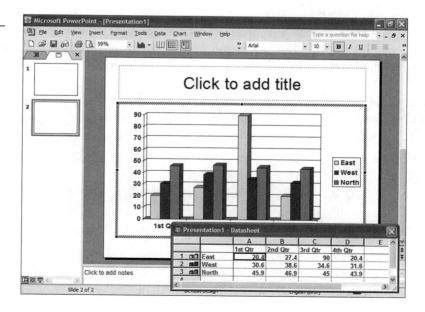

Applying Slide Transitions

If you're presenting your slide show electronically, via a computer attached to a large monitor or projector, then there's one more thing you need to do—add transitions between each slide. PowerPoint lets you use a wide variety of slide transitions, all of which are more interesting than just cutting from one slide to the next.

To apply slide transitions, follow these steps:

1. Click the Slide Sorter View button to switch to Slide Sorter view.
2. Select Slide Show, Slide Transition to display the Slide Transition pane.
3. Select the slides to which you want to add transitions.
4. Select the transition you want to use.
5. Modify the Speed and Sound of the transition, if desired.

tip

You don't have to use the same transitions on every slide. Your presentation will have more visual interest if you use a variety of transitions throughout.

Repeat these steps to add transitions to additional slides.

Start the Show!

To run your slideshow, complete with transitions, click the Slide Show button at the bottom of the PowerPoint workspace, or on the Slide Transition pane. To move from one slide to the next, all you have to do is click your mouse.

THE ABSOLUTE MINIMUM

Here are the key points to remember from this chapter:

■ You use Microsoft PowerPoint to create slides, overhead transparencies, and electronic slideshow presentations.

■ The look and feel of your entire presentation is defined by the design template you choose.

■ Each slide you insert can have a different layout, depending on its function.

■ A slide can include text, bullets, pictures, and charts.

■ When you're presenting an electronic slideshow, add transitions between each slide.

17

MANAGING YOUR FINANCES

Most new computers come with at least one personal finance program installed. That program might be Microsoft Money, or it might be Intuit's Quicken. You can use either of these programs to manage your household budgets, track your bank accounts and investments, write checks, and even pay your bills online.

Both Money and Quicken work similarly, but for the purposes of this book we'll focus on Microsoft Money 2004, because it's fully integrated into the Microsoft Works Suite program. (If you prefer to use Quicken, you'll perform the same operations as described here; make sure you follow that program's specific instructions.)

Getting Started with the Setup Assistant

Before you can use Microsoft Money, you have to configure it with information about your specific banking and financial accounts. The first time you start the program you're presented with the Setup Assistant, which walks you step-by-step through setting up your Money accounts. Make sure you've gathered all your personal financial records beforehand, as you'll need all the account numbers and such to set up the program.

Here's what you'll need to know to complete the Setup Assistant:

note

The Setup Assistant runs any time you create a new Money file—by selecting File, New.

- **Step 1: Sign In.** You can choose to secure your Money account with a password, as well as sign up for a Microsoft Passport to access various online features.

- **Step 2: Personal Information.** This is where you enter your name and your spouse's name, as well as which currency you intend to use.

- **Step 3: Financial Services**. Use this screen to sign up for a Microsoft Bill Pay account, to pay your bills electronically.

- **Step 4: Priorities.** This is a short questionnaire concerning your investment, banking, and planning priorities; your answers to these questions help Money determine how best to set up your accounts.

- **Step 5: Accounts.** Select which of the following accounts you want to monitor: checking, savings, credit card, retirement, brokerage/investment, and money market/cash management. For each account you have, you'll need to enter the bank or broker name, the account number, and your current or starting balance.

- **Step 6: Online Setup.** These questions help configure Money's online features.

- **Step 7: Bills & Paycheck.** Money can be configured to enter your paycheck on a recurring basis; you'll need to know your employer, your take-home pay, and how often you're paid. You should also enter all the different types of bills that you pay regularly—and, for each bill, the payee, estimated amount, and frequency.

After you're finished with the Setup Assistant you can start using Money normally—or you can go back and edit your account information, as necessary.

Navigating Money

Before you start working with your accounts, it's a good idea to get familiar with the way Money works—starting from the My Money Home page.

Home Sweet Home

The My Money Home page, shown in Figure 17.1, is your "home base" for all your Money-related transactions. This page includes links to different activities; you click a link to access that activity.

These links are organized into several sections; which sections you see depends on which view of your My Money Home page you select. You select different views from the Choose a View list.

tip

If you need to add a new account, delete an unused account, or just edit any specific account information, go to the My Money Home page and click the Account List button. To configure other program options, select Tools, Options to access the Options dialog box.

FIGURE 17.1

Start with the My Money Home page, and then click to access different activities and transactions.

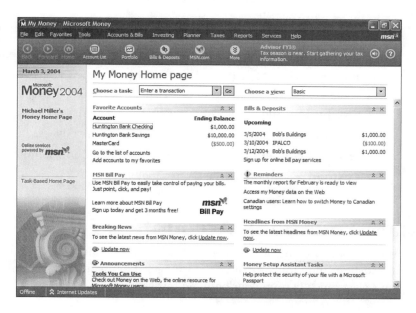

For example, the Basic view displays the tasks shown in Figure 17.1. The Investing view displays only those sections related to your investments; the Normal view displays all available sections.

Money's Financial Centers

Across the top of the My Money Home page are buttons that link to Money's other financial centers. These pages organize tasks and information by specific types of activity.

The buttons across the top of the My Money Home page take you directly to these financial centers:

- **Home.** Takes you back to the My Money Home page, from anywhere in the program.
- **Account List.** View account balances, add new accounts, manage existing accounts, and link directly to each account's register.
- **Portfolio.** View and edit your investment portfolio, record new investment transactions, and go online to get current stock quotes.
- **Bills & Deposits.** Set up new payees, pay bills, and register deposits to your banking accounts.
- **MSN.com.** Connect to the Internet-based financial resources on the MSN.com Web site.
- **Reports.** Create a variety of reports and charts.
- **Cash Flow.** Display a cash flow forecast, based on your current budget.
- **Budget.** Access Money's Budget Planner, which lets you create a budget, create a debt reduction plan, and plan your 401(k).
- **Categories.** Add, delete, and modify the categories used in your accounts.
- **Payees.** Set up and view information about your payees.
- **Money Browser.** Go online to find even more financial information.
- **Customize.** Customize the Money toolbar.

Managing Your Bank Account

Many people use Microsoft Money to track their banking transactions. You can enter transactions manually—or, if you're connected to the Internet, download transactions electronically from your banking institution.

Entering Transactions

Money makes it easy to manually enter transactions into your checking and savings accounts registers. Just follow these steps:

1. From the My Money Home page, click the Account List button; this displays the Pick an Account to Use page.

2. Click the name for your bank account; this displays the account register for that account, as shown in Figure 17.2.

FIGURE 17.2

Enter banking transactions into your account register.

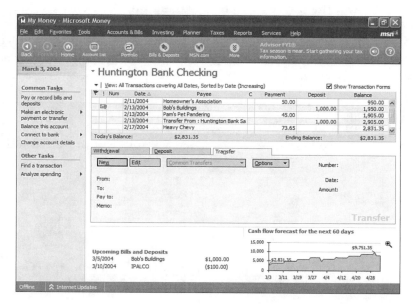

3. To register a withdrawal, click the Withdrawal tab, select the payee from the Pay To list, select a transaction category from the Category list, select a numbering option from the Number list, enter the Date of the transaction, and then enter the Amount of the withdrawal.

4. To register a deposit, select the Deposit tab, select the payer from the From list, select a transaction category from the Category list, select a numbering option from the Number list, enter the Date of the transaction, and then enter the Amount of the deposit.

5. To register a transfer between accounts, select the Transfer tab, select the appropriate accounts from the From and To lists, select a numbering option from the Number list, enter the Date of the transaction, and then enter the Amount of the transfer.

Paying Recurring Bills

Another nice feature of Microsoft Money is being able to schedule recurring payments—so that you don't have to enter the same transaction, month after month after month.

Money lets you set up a list of your recurring transactions. After you've entered a recurring payee, all you have to do is click a few buttons to pay that bill each month, every month.

It's a three-step process that works like this:

1. **Add the payee to your recurring bills list.** Click the Bills & Deposits button to display the Manage Scheduled Bills and Deposits page, shown in Figure 17.3. Click the New button and select Bill to display the Create a Recurring Bill page. Enter the name and other payment information for this bill—including the next payment date and frequency. Click OK when done.

FIGURE 17.3

Scheduling a recurring payment.

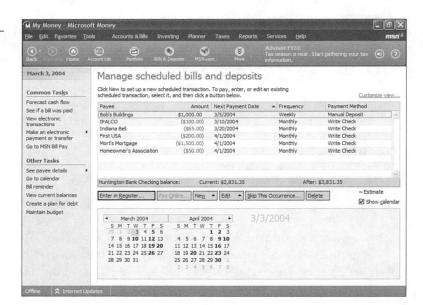

2. **Pay the bill.** Click the Bills & Deposits button to display the Manage Scheduled Bills and Deposits page. Double-click the bill you want to pay; this displays the Record Payment dialog box. Enter the correct payment amount for the bill into the Amount field. Pull down the Number list and select Print This Transaction. Click the Record Payment button. This transaction is now entered in your account register, and the check is sent to Money's "to-do" list for printing at a later time.

3. **Print the check.** Select File, Print Checks to display the Print Checks dialog box. Select which checks you want to print (all or selected), what type of check forms you're using, the number of the first check form in your printer,

and how many checks are on the first page. Make sure you have blank checks loaded into your printer, then click Print to print the selected check(s).

Balancing Your Checkbook

When you receive your monthly statement from your bank, you can have Money automatically reconcile your accounts to your statement—which is a lot easier than trying to do it by hand! It's all done via a wizard, like this:

> **note**
>
> The first time you choose to print a check to a specific payee, Money displays the Print Address dialog box. Enter the appropriate information here (including the payee's address and account number), and then click OK.

1. Open the account register for the account you want to balance.

2. Click Balance This Account from the Common Tasks sidebar; this launches Money's Balance Wizard.

3. When prompted, enter the following information from your monthly statement: statement date, starting balance, ending balance, service charges (if any), and interest earned (if any). Click Next to proceed.

4. Money now displays a Balance page for the selected account. Compare the transactions in the Money register with the transactions on your monthly statement. Click the C column to clear each matching transaction. If a transaction doesn't match, click the transaction and edit it accordingly. If you're missing any transactions (the primary cause of accounts not balancing), click the New button to enter them as new.

5. When you're done balancing, click the Next button in the Common Tasks pane.

6. Money now displays a dialog box telling you that your account is balanced. (Congratulations!) Click the Finish button to close the wizard.

Banking Online

An even easier way to handle your banking needs is to let Money do it automatically, by downloading all your transactions from your bank or credit card company, using the Internet. This way you don't have to enter much of anything—Money interfaces with your financial institutions to track all your transactions.

Setting Up Online Banking

To set up an account for online management, follow these steps:

1. From within Money, select Accounts & Bills, Online Services Manager to open the Online Services Manager page.

2. Find the account you want to connect to, then click Setup Online Services.

3. Money now displays the Online Setup screen. Confirm that your bank is listed here, then click the Next button and follow the onscreen instructions.

If your financial institution is not listed, it does not offer Money-compatible online banking services.

caution

Not all banks or credit card companies offer online banking, and not all online banking services are compatible with Microsoft Money. Some banks let you perform online transactions only from their own Web pages; these banks are not compatible with Money's online banking feature.

Paying Bills Online

If you're tired of dealing with paper checks—even those that Money itself prints—then you need to start paying your bills electronically. Money enables you to sign up with an electronic bill paying service to handle all your bills online, via the Internet.

Money's bill paying service of choice is MSN Bill Pay. (It's also owned by Microsoft.) You can set up a new MSN Bill Pay account from within Money, by following these steps:

note

Most bill payment services charge either a monthly or per-payment fee.

1. From the My Money Home page, select Accounts & Bills, Online Services Manager; this displays the Online Services Manager screen.

2. Click Set Up Electronic Bill Pay Service, to display the Set Up Online Payment Provider page.

3. Pull down the Select an Online Payment Provider list and select a provider, then click the Next button.

4. Money now downloads information specific to the bill pay provider you selected; follow the balance of the onscreen instructions to setup your new account.

Once you're signed up with your bill pay service, paying a bill electronically is as easy as following these steps:

1. Click the Account List button to display the Pick an Account to Use page.

2. Select the account you want to use to pay your bills; this displays the account register.

3. From the Common Tasks pane, select Make an Electronic Payment or Transfer, Make an Electronic Payment; this displays the Record Payment dialog box.

4. Enter the payment information.

5. Make sure you're connected to the Internet, then click Submit Payment.

tip

The first time you enter an electronic payment for a payee, Money prompts you for certain details, such as the payee's name, address, and account number. Be sure you enter the correct information (typically available on your most recent bill from that payee), and then click OK.

THE ABSOLUTE MINIMUM

Here are the key points to remember from this chapter:

■ You can use any financial management program—including Microsoft Money and Quicken—to manage your banking and investment transactions.

■ When you first start Microsoft Money, you need to enter key personal and financial information—including the names and numbers of your banking and investment accounts.

■ Money lets you write checks manually or schedule recurring payments.

■ You can also use Money to download transactions from your bank or credit card company, and to pay your bills electronically.

18

CREATING COOL PROJECTS AND GREETING CARDS

There are many things you can create with your new computer. Sure, you can use Word to write letters and Excel to crunch numbers, but you can also use other software to create other, more fun, types of projects.

For example, did you know you can use your computer to make your own Christmas cards? Or to create invitations and banners for your children's birthday parties? Or even to send electronic greeting cards to friends and family, via the Internet?

That's right, your new personal computer can be your main workstation for all sorts of cool home projects. Read on to learn more—and to get creative!

Designing Simple Home Projects

Microsoft Word is a very versatile word processing program and even includes some very simple home projects. For example, you can use Word to create basic greeting cards. But if you want to really get fancy, you'll want a software program specifically designed for graphic projects—what we call home publishing software.

Popular Home Publishing Programs

Most home publishing programs come with templates for a variety of different home-related projects, including banners, brochures, business cards, calendars, crafts, envelopes, forms, greeting cards, invitations, labels, letterheads, newsletters, postcards, and posters. Most of these programs also include a large number of clip art pictures, which you can use to add visual diversity to your projects. Home publishing programs are typically low-cost (under $50) and easy to use. Here's a quick overview of some of the most popular programs:

- **Greeting Card Factory.** This program does nothing but greeting cards—but it's great at what it does. Nova Development sells several variations of the basic Greeting Card Factory program, including Greeting Card Factory Deluxe, Humorous Greeting Card Factory, and Christian Greeting Card Factory. (Go to www.novadevelopment.com for more information.)

- **Hallmark Card Studio.** Hallmark produces several versions of this low-priced program, each geared around a specific theme: Holiday, Comedy, Christian, Scrapbook, and so on. (Go to www.hallmarksoftware.com for more information.)

- **Microsoft Picture It! Photo.** This program is included as part of Microsoft Works Suite. While it's mainly used for editing digital photos, it also includes quite a few built-in photo-related projects, such as photo albums, picture postcards, and photo greeting cards. (Go to www.microsoft.com/products/imaging/products/ for more information.)

- **Microsoft Publisher.** This is a full-featured publishing program, good for everything from simple projects to sophisticated publications. Publisher is included with some versions of Microsoft Office. (Go to www.microsoft.com/publisher/ for more information.)

- **Print Shop.** Print Shop is one of the most popular home publishing programs. It's affordable, it's easy to use, and it lets you create all manner of fun projects. (Go to www.broderbund.com for more information.)

- **PrintMaster.** Another popular home publishing suite (lower-priced than Print Shop), complete with all manner of home-related projects. (Go to www.broderbund.com for more information.)

Creating a Project

All of these home publishing programs work in a similar fashion. You identify the type of project you want to create, open a template for that project, and then edit it as you like—which typically includes choosing your own color scheme and artwork.

For example, PrintMaster's home page (shown in Figure 18.1) lets you create a new project from scratch or personalize what it calls a "ready-made" project. Whichever route you take, you can choose from all manner of projects, from banners and booklets to post cards and posters. Once you have a project onscreen, you can add your own text and clip art. It's as easy as clicking and dragging!

FIGURE 18.1

Use PrintMaster to create greeting cards, banners, photo albums, and other fun projects.

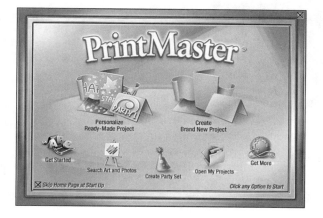

Figure 18.2 shows a birthday party invitation designed in PrintMaster. This took less than five minutes to create, and looks great when printed on a color printer.

Sending Electronic Greeting Cards

You don't have to buy a software program to make your own greeting cards—if you want to send them over the Internet, that is. There are many Web sites that offer free electronic cards that you can personalize and send to friends and family, as easily as you send email messages.

Popular Greeting Card Sites

Most online greeting card sites offer their services for free; they make their money by selling advertising. Other sites charge a small fee or offer basic cards for free and more deluxe cards for a price. In any case, check the terms and requirements before you start clicking.

FIGURE 18.2

A birthday party invitation designed with PrintMaster.

Here are some of the most popular online greeting cards sites on the Web:

- Beat Greets (www.beatgreets.com)
- Birthday Cards.com (www.birthdaycards.com)
- Blue Mountain (www.bluemountain.com)
- DaySpring (www.dayspring.com)
- eFun.com (www.efun.com)
- Hallmark E-Cards (www.hallmark.com)
- Yahoo! Greetings (greetings.yahoo.com)

Sending a Card at Yahoo! Greetings

The two biggest online greeting card sites are Blue Mountain and Yahoo! Greetings. Let's take a quick look at how to send an online card, using Yahoo! Greetings as an example.

1. Launch Internet Explorer and connect to the Yahoo! Greetings Web site (greetings.yahoo. com), shown in Figure 18.3.

note

Learn how to connect to the Internet and use Internet Explorer in Chapters 21 and 22.

FIGURE 18.3
The many different types of online greeting cards available at Yahoo! Greetings.

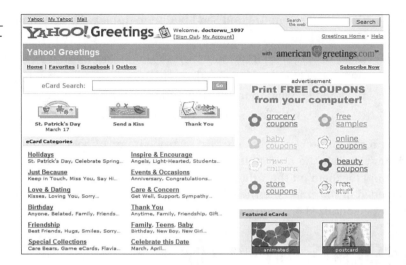

2. Click the type of card you want to send; this displays a selection of available cards.

3. Click the specific card you want to send; this displays the card at full size, as shown in Figure 18.4.

FIGURE 18.4
Sending an online greeting card.

4. Click the Personalize and Send button to display the Personalize Your Greeting form.

5. Enter the required information (your name and email address, the recipient's name and email address, and an optional personal message).

6. Click the Preview Your Greeting button to preview your card.

7. Click the Send This Greeting button to send the card.

Your recipient now receives an email message from Yahoo! Greetings. This message doesn't include the card itself, but rather informs the recipient that they have a card waiting for them on the Yahoo! Greetings site. When the recipient clicks the link included in the email message, he or she is taken to the Yahoo! Greetings site, where your personalized greeting card is displayed.

THE ABSOLUTE MINIMUM

Here are the key points to remember from this chapter:

- When you want to create your own greeting cards, banners, albums, and so forth, you need home publishing software.

- Popular home publishing programs include Greeting Card Factory, Print Shop, and PrintMaster.

- You can also send greeting cards electronically, over the Internet, from a variety of greeting card Web sites—including Blue Mountain and Yahoo! Greetings.

19

LEARNING WITH EDUCATIONAL SOFTWARE

Personal computers aren't just for adults. Your PC can be a valuable learning tool for your children, especially if you get them started with the right educational software.

When you stroll the aisles of your local computer or electronics store, you'll find all manner of children's software. Not all of this software is educational; there are a lot of games (and game-like) software out there. (Don't take my word for it; turn to Chapter 20, "Playing Games," to learn more.)

Better to sit your kids down in front of your PC with a good educational program up and running. There are educational programs for all ages of kids, from preschool to high school, and beyond. Read on to learn about some of the best educational programs—including some really terrific encyclopedia software!

Finding the Best Educational Software

The following list presents some of the best educational software on the market today, organized by age group. The publishers' Web site addresses are included, so you can log onto the Internet to find out more about each program.

tip

For reviews of the very latest educational software, turn to the SuperKids Educational Software Review (www.superkids.com).

Early Learning

Early learning software is designed for your very youngest children—infant (or as soon as they can use a mouse) to preschool age. Most of this software is as fun as it is educational, with lots of brightly colored characters and fun music.

- Adventure Workshop: Preschool-1st Grade (www.broderbund.com)
- Curious George Downtown Adventure (www.vugames.com)
- Mickey Mouse Toddler/Mickey Mouse Preschool (www.disneyinteractive.com)
- Pencil Pal Preschool (www.schoolzone.com)
- Reader Rabbit (www.broderbund.com)
- Sesame Street Toddler/Sesame Street Preschool (www.encoresoftware.com)

Elementary

Educational software for elementary age children (K-6) introduces solid instructional technique, while still keeping things fun and lively.

- Adventure Workshop (www.broderbund.com)
- Discover Intensive Phonics for Yourself (www.intensivephonics.com)
- Earth's Dynamic Surface (www.tasagraphicarts.com/progeds.html)
- Flying Colors (www.magicmouse.com)
- JumpStart Series (www.vugames.com)
- Kid Performer (www.el2100.com)
- Kidspiration (www.kidspiration.com)
- Math Blaster (www.vugames.com)
- Reading Blaster (www.vugames.com)

Figure 19.1 shows one of the fun lessons in Math Blaster. Story problems were never this fun when I was a kid!

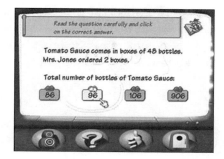

High School

Educational software for junior high and high school kids is typically heavier on the education and lighter on the fun and games. This software is particularly helpful if your child is having trouble in a particular subject; it's like having a dedicated tutor on your PC.

- Cyber Ed Chemistry (www.cybered.net)
- Inspiration (www.kidspiration.com)
- Kaplan SAT ACT PSAT Deluxe (www.kaptest.com)
- Math Advantage (www.encoresoftware.com)
- Studyworks Teaching Pro: Mathematics Complete (www.learnatglobal.com)

Continuing Education

Continuing education software is for students of all ages—equally valuable for a 40-year-old adult as for an ambitious high schooler. Particularly popular are language education programs, as well as typing tutors.

- Easy Language Deluxe (www.bmsoftware.com/easylanguageds.htm)
- LanguageNow! series—SpanishNow!, FrenchNow!, etc. (www.transparent.com)
- Learn to Speak series (www.broderbund.com)
- Mavis Beacon Teaches Typing (www.broderbund.com)

Using Encyclopedia Programs

One of the most popular types of educational software is the electronic encyclopedia. These encyclopedia programs are typically offshoots of respected print encyclopedias, supplemented with all manner of multimedia effects—including relevant audio and video clips. Some of these encyclopedia programs also link to online databases, either as part of the purchase price or for an additional subscription fee.

The Best Encyclopedia Software

The top-selling encyclopedia programs on the market today include

- Encyclopedia Britannica (www.britannica.com)
- Grolier Multimedia Encyclopedia (www.broderbund.com)
- Microsoft Encarta (encarta.msn.com)
- World Book Encyclopedia (www.worldbook.com)

Encarta is particularly popular, as it's included as part of Microsoft Works Suite—which means that if you just purchased a new PC, you probably have Encarta pre-installed.

Using Microsoft Encarta

Since Encarta is so widely available, we'll use it as an example for our tour of encyclopedia programs. To be precise, we'll look at Encarta 2004, which is included with Microsoft Works Suite 2004.

You can launch Encarta from either the Windows Start menu or the Works Task Launcher. When you launch Encarta, you'll probably be asked to insert the Encarta Encyclopedia disc. This is because Encarta is so large, so comprehensive, it can only be stored on CD-ROM. So insert the CD and get started!

When Encarta launches, it displays the Encarta Home screen, shown in Figure 19.2. To navigate within Encarta, you use the buttons on the Encarta toolbar, located at the top of the screen. This toolbar is similar to Internet Explorer's toolbar, with navigation buttons to take you back and forward through individual pages. You can also use the pull-down menus to access specific features and tools—and return to Encarta Home at any time by clicking the Home button.

FIGURE 19.2

Encarta's home page—you can find virtually anything from here!

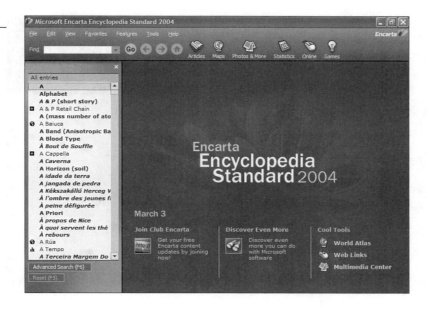

The Home screen is your gateway to all the content within the Encarta encyclopedia. From this screen you can

- Use the Find box to search for specific information.
- Choose from a master list of articles in the left-hand pane.
- Click the Articles button to view both Encarta articles and a list of countries described in the encyclopedia.
- Click the Maps button to view historical maps and Encarta's World Atlas.
- Click the Photos & More button to view lists of audio, video, and interactive content.
- Click the Statistics button to view interesting charts, tables, facts, and statistics.
- Click the Online button to get more information on the Web.
- Click the Games button to play a variety of interactive educational games.

Encarta includes traditional text-based articles (like the one shown in Figure 19.3), as well as animations, sounds, images, videos, maps, and various interactive activities. Some Encarta entries are linked to the Encarta Web site, so you can go online to get additional or updated information. All in all, using Encarta is a rich and rewarding experience—and a fun way to find all sorts of information.

FIGURE 19.3

A typical
Encarta article—
all about
molecules.

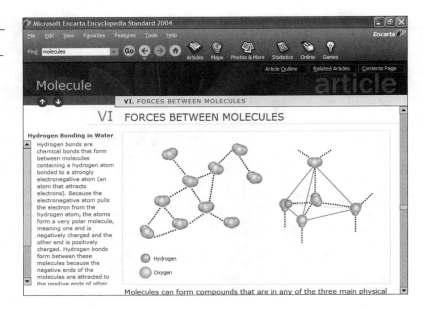

THE ABSOLUTE MINIMUM

Here are the key points to remember from this chapter:

■ There are all sorts of educational programs available for your children—
including software targeted at specific skills and age groups.

■ One of the most popular educational programs is the Microsoft Encarta encyclopedia, which is included as part of Microsoft Works Suite.

■ Encarta includes traditional text-based articles, multimedia-enhanced articles, and links to additional information on the Web.

20

PLAYING GAMES

One of the most popular uses of a personal computer has nothing to do with work—and everything to do with play. That's right, most people use their PCs, even just a little, for playing games.

There are all sorts of games you can play on your new PC. You can play traditional PC games that you buy at your local computer store and install on your PC's hard disk. You can play simple games over the Internet, where you pit your skills against a competing computer. And you can also use the Internet to link to other gamers and play sophisticated multi-player online games, which can be a real trip.

Read on to learn how to get your computer system in tip-top shape for all this game playing—and then discover the best places to play these exciting games.

Building a State-of-the-Art Gaming System

Believe it or not, it takes more computing horsepower to play games than it does to crunch numbers or surf the Web. With all those fancy graphics, gee-whiz sound effects, and high-speed action, computer games definitely put your computer system through its paces.

In fact, if you just purchased a low-end computer, you might find that it doesn't play the latest games quite as fast or as smoothly as you might have expected. (It might not even play some games at all!) To be able to play the most demanding new games, you need a truly state-of-the-art computer system—which might mean updating selected components in your current system.

What can you do to beef up your system for better game play? Here are some things to keep in mind:

- If you're using an older PC, you might think about buying a new system with a fairly powerful processor. Think Pentium 4 or AMD Athlon, running at 2.4GHz or more.

- Whether you have a newer or an older PC, you'll want to increase its memory to at least 512MB.

- You'll also need a lot of hard disk storage because the newer games take up a lot of disk space. Go for at least an 80GB hard disk—bigger if you can afford it.

- The capability to handle rapidly moving graphics is essential. Today's hottest games require a 256MB video card with 3D graphics accelerator and DirectX 9 compatibility.

- You should also consider upgrading to a DVD drive, because many new games come on single DVDs rather than multiple CDs.

- You'll probably need to upgrade your sound card, too. Consider going with a high-quality 3D sound card, and be sure you have a quality multi-speaker system, complete with subwoofer.

- Big games look better on a big screen, so think about a 19" CRT or 17" LCD monitor.

- Finally, you need something other than your mouse to control your games. You'll want to invest in a good-quality joystick or similar game controller.

Learn more about installing new hardware in Chapter 7, "Adding New Hardware and Devices to Your System."

Installing and Playing PC Games

Before you play a new PC game, you'll have to install the game software according to instructions. You might also, in some instances, need to keep the game CD in your PC's CD-ROM drive. (This is because many games access the CD to load images and sounds during the course of the game.)

You'll also need to have your game controller installed and connected, and then you're ready to play. You launch the new game from the Windows Start menu.

Every game operates a little bit differently. You typically are presented with some type of opening screen, sometimes in the form of an animated movie. Most games let you skip this animation by clicking somewhere (or anywhere) within the movie window.

After you get past the opening, you might need to configure various parameters for the game. For example, you might have to choose a user level (try starting with "beginner"), enter your player name, and so on. You should also take this opportunity to read the game's instructions, either onscreen (sometimes via the Help menu) or in an accompanying booklet.

Many games let you pause or save games in progress, so if you have to stop for the day, you can start up again tomorrow in the same spot. To save a game, follow the game's specific instructions to save your particular game file—typically by accessing some sort of "save" or "file" menu or function.

When you're ready to start playing again, all you have to do is load the previously saved game. This is typically accomplished as the game is loading, or via some type of "resume" or "file" menu. After the game is reloaded, you can resume play exactly where you stopped the day before.

caution

Don't be *too* quick about bypassing the opening animation, especially when the game is new. Sometimes information essential to the game is presented in this movie.

tip

There are several sites on the Internet that offer PC games you can download to your computer's hard disk—and a lot of them are free! Check out Free Games Net (www.free-games-net.com), GameSpot (www.gamespot.com), Gigex (www.gigex.com), and Tucows Games (games.tucows.com).

Playing Games Online

Some of the most fun PC games don't have to be installed on your hard disk. Many sites on the Web offer all sorts of games to play online—often free. Whether you're looking for a quick game of checkers or an evening-long session of Quake II, you can find dozens of sites to satisfy your craving for action and strategy.

You can play most online games by going to a gaming site and clicking the appropriate links. Everything you need to play the game is automatically loaded into your Web browser.

You'll need to read the instructions first, of course, especially if you need to find an online partner to play a particular game. Don't get too nervous about this; most sites make it extremely easy to play their most popular games.

What will you find when you log onto one of these online gaming emporiums? As you can see in Figure 20.1, most games sites include all sorts of games, including arcade games, board games, card games, casino games, puzzle games, trivia games, and word games. Most of these online games can be played free—and some sites even hand out prizes to winning players! You can log on to these sites with a minimal amount of pre-play registration and then start playing with a few clicks of your mouse.

FIGURE 20.1

Play online games at MSN Games.

If you're interested in playing some simple single-player online games, check out these Web sites:

- All Games Free (www.allgamesfree.com)
- ArcadeTown.com (www.arcadetown.com)
- Boxerjam (www.boxerjam.com)
- Games.com (play.games.com)
- Internet Chess (www.chessclub.com)
- Internet Park (www.internet-park.com)
- Lycos Gamesville (www.gamesville.lycos.com)
- MSN Games (zone.msn.com)
- Playsite (www.playsite.com)
- Pogo.com (www.pogo.com)
- Uproar (www.uproar.com)
- Yahoo! Games (games.yahoo.com)

Playing Games Against Other Players

Most PC games sold at retail today include a multiplayer option. This option lets you play the game against a human opponent. You can play another player on your local area network or find and play an opponent over the Internet.

Setting up a multiplayer game is relatively straightforward. You start by launching the game on your computer, then you connect to the Internet and log on to a specific Web site. This site can be hosted by the game manufacturer, or it can be a general gaming site that has licensing access to a particular game. In many cases, the site you need to log in to is hard-wired into the game software itself. All you have to do is pull down the menu and select the multiplayer option; then the game automatically connects itself to the proper Web site, using your normal Internet connection.

After you're logged on to the site, you access the area of the site dedicated to your particular game. You can then choose to host a game (and look for other players) or join a game already in progress. You're then connected to the other player(s), and the game begins.

tip

The faster your Internet connection, the smoother the game play you'll experience. Broadband is better than dial-up—and is required by some gaming sites.

Most sites offering multiplayer gaming operate on a subscription basis—in other words, you have to pay to play. Subscription fees vary per site but are typically assessed on an hourly, a monthly, or a yearly basis. (Fees can run as low as $20 for lifetime access or as high as $2 per hour of play.) For this fee, you get the privilege of connecting to other users, as well as using the site's services to organize and coordinate both individual match-ups and tourneys.

To find out how to play online, consult the instructions for your particular game.

Finding Videogame News and Tips Online

There are also several sites on the Web that offer videogame news and reviews, as well as tips and cheats for the latest games. These sites include

- CheatStation (www.cheatstation.com)
- Console Gameworld (www.consolegameworld.com)
- Extreme Gamers Network (www.extreme-gamers.net)
- Future Games Network (www.fgn.com)
- IGN.com (www.ign.com)
- The Magic Box (www.the-magicbox.com)
- VideoGame.net (www.videogame.net)

The Absolute Minimum

Here are the key points to remember from this chapter:

- To play games on your PC, you'll want to install a joystick or other type of game controller.
- You may also need to upgrade parts of your computer system—especially your audio and video cards—to play some of the more demanding PC games.
- There are many sites on the Internet that let you play simple single-player games, often free.
- Many computer games feature multi-player options; you can play against other players over a home network, or on the Internet.

PART V

USING THE INTERNET

21

CONNECTING TO THE INTERNET

It used to be that most people bought personal computers to do work—word processing, spreadsheets, databases, the sort of programs that still make up the core of Microsoft Works and Microsoft Office. But today, the majority of people also buy PCs to access the Internet—to send and receive email, surf the Web, and chat with other users.

Different Types of Connections

The first step in going online is establishing a connection between your computer and the Internet. To do this, you have to sign up with an Internet service provider (ISP), which, as the name implies, provides your home with a connection to the Internet.

Depending on what's available in your area, you can choose from two primary types of connections—dial-up or broadband. Dial-up is slower than broadband, but it's also lower priced. If you do a lot of Web surfing, it's probably worth a few extra dollars a month to get the faster broadband connection.

Whichever type of connection you choose, you'll connect your PC to a *modem*, which will then connect to the phone or cable line coming into your house. Most PCs have a built-in dial-up modem; if you choose broadband service, you'll get an external modem from your ISP. Read on to learn more.

Traditional Dial-Up

A dial-up connection provides Internet service over normal phone lines. The fastest dial-up connections transmit data at 56.6Kbps (kilobits per second). Most ISPs charge $20–$30 per month for normal dial-up service.

Broadband DSL

DSL is a phone line-based technology that operates at broadband speeds. DSL service piggybacks onto your existing phone line, turning it into a high-speed digital connection. Not only is DSL faster than dial-up (384Kbps to 1.5Kbps, depending on your ISP), you also don't have to surrender your normal phone line when you want to surf; DSL connections are "always on." Most providers offer DSL service for $30–$50 per month.

Broadband Cable

The most popular type of broadband connection today is available from your local cable company. Broadband cable Internet piggybacks on your normal cable television line, providing speeds in the 500Kbps to 3Mbps range, depending on the provider. Most cable companies offer broadband cable Internet for $30–$50 per month.

Broadband Satellite

If you can't get DSL or cable Internet in your area, you have another option—connecting to the Internet via satellite. Any household or business with a clear line of sight to the southern sky can receive digital data signals from a geosynchronous satellite at between 128Kbps and 400Kbps.

The largest provider of satellite Internet access is Hughes Network Systems. (Hughes also developed and markets the popular DIRECTV digital satellite system.) Hughes' DIRECWAY system (www.direcway.com) enables you to receive Internet signals via an 18-inch round dish that you mount outside your house or on your roof. The installation package (including dish and modem card) will set you back around $500 (before any specials), with monthly subscription fees in the $60–$100 range, depending on which usage plan you pick.

Before You Connect

When you sign up with an ISP, both you and the ISP have to provide certain information to each other. You provide your name, address, and credit card number; your ISP provides a variety of semi-technical information, including

- Your username and password
- Your email address
- The names of the ISP's incoming and outgoing mail servers
- Your email account name and password
- The name of your ISP's Usenet news server
- The phone number to dial into (if you're using a dial-up connection)

You'll need this information when you configure Windows for your new Internet connection—which we'll discuss next.

> **tip**
>
> For most ISPs, your username, email account name, and the first half of your email address will all be the same. It's also likely that you will be assigned a single password for both your initial login and email access.

Setting Up a New Connection

Naturally, you need to configure your computer to work with your ISP. You do this with Windows XP's New Connection Wizard. All you have to do is connect your PC's modem to your telephone line (or your computer to the broadband modem) and follow these steps:

1. Click the Start button to display the Start menu.
2. Select Connect to, Show All Connections; this displays the Network Connections window.
3. Select Create a New Connection (from the Network Tasks panel) to launch the New Connection Wizard.
4. Follow the onscreen instructions to create the appropriate type of connection.

note

If the Show All Connections option doesn't appear on your Start menu, open My Computer, select Network Places, and then select View Network Connections.

Connecting via a Commercial Online Service

A typical dial-up or broadband ISP does nothing but connect you to the Internet and provide you with an email address and inbox—and, in some cases, storage space for your own personal Web page. You can probably find a few local ISPs operating in your city or town, or you can turn to one of a handful of national ISPs. These national ISPs offer dial-up numbers all across the United States (great for when you're traveling).

If all this sounds a little confusing to you, you might want to opt for a service that provides a little more hand-holding, such as that offered by America Online (AOL) or MSN. These commercial online services function like ISPs but also provide their own unique content and interfaces. If you sign up for AOL, for example, you use AOL's software to connect to the Internet and can also access AOL-specific content and services not available anywhere else.

tip

The two largest national ISPs are AT&T Worldnet (www.att.net) and EarthLink (www.earthlink.net). You can find a list of more than 10,000 national and local ISPs at The List (thelist.internet.com).

Many new computer users prefer to connect to AOL because it's so easy to use, as you can see in Figure 21.1. On the other hand, many experienced computer users don't like being forced to use AOL's software and prefer to go with a normal ISP.

If you decide to go with a commercial online service, you'll pay between $20–$30 per month for dial-up service, higher for broadband.

FIGURE 21.1

Connecting to the Internet via America Online.

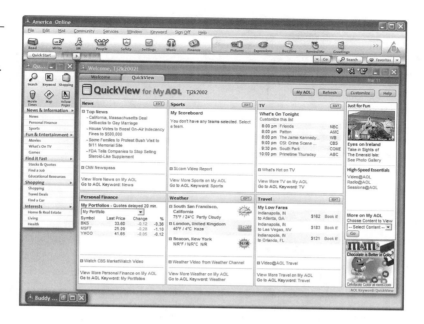

Sharing an Internet Connection

If you have more than one PC in your home, you can connect them to share a single Internet connection. This is particularly useful if you have a high-speed broadband connection.

There are several ways to share a broadband connection, and they all involve setting up some sort of home network. Which configuration you choose is dependant on how much work you want to take on, what kind of connections you want for each PC, and the type of service offered by your broadband ISP.

note

Learn more about networks in Chapter 8, "Setting Up a Home Network."

The Bridge Configuration

The most common type of network configuration for sharing an Internet connection is called a *bridge*. In this configuration, the broadband connection is routed first to the broadband modem, and then to your network hub or router. Each PC on your network is also connected to the hub, as shown in Figure 21.2.

FIGURE 21.2

A bridge config-
uration for shar-
ing an Internet
connection.

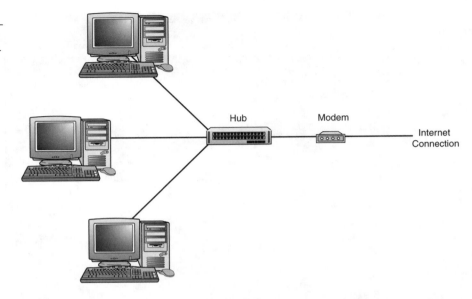

The chief advantage of the bridge configuration is that it's easy to set up and configure. It's also a popular configuration for users with wireless networks. (Most wireless
based stations also function as network hubs or routers.)

The Combination Modem/Hub Bridge Configuration

If you have a DSL connection, some DSL modems also function as network hubs. To
use a DSL modem/hub to connect multiple PCs, you create a modified bridge configuration. The broadband connection is routed directly to the modem/hub, and then
each PC is connected to the modem/hub. This type of configuration is illustrated in
Figure 21.3.

Using a modem/hub is a nice option if offered by your DSL supplier. It's probably the
easiest configuration possible, and it eliminates the need to purchase and install a
separate network hub.

FIGURE 21.3

A bridge config-
uration using a
combination
modem/hub.

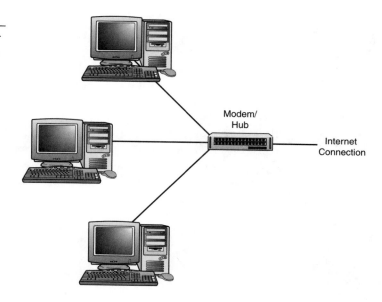

Modem/
Hub

Internet
Connection

The Gateway Configuration

This configuration uses a lead computer as a "gateway" to the Internet. This gateway computer is the only computer on your network that is visible to the Internet,
and it manages the connections for all the other PCs.

As you can see in Figure 21.4, you set up a gateway configuration
by routing the broadband connection first to your broadband
modem, and then to the gateway PC. The gateway PC then
connects to your network hub; all your other PCs
are also connected to the hub.

When you set up a home network with the
Windows XP Network Setup Wizard (as discussed
in Chapter 8), this is the type of network that you
create. It's a very secure configuration; the gateway computer can serve as a type of firewall for
the other PCs on your network. (It's also the only
configuration you can use if you're sharing a
dial-up connection; your dial-up modem has to
be attached to a computer—*not* to a hub or
router.)

caution

For a gateway configura-
tion to work, the gate-
way computer has to
have *two* network cards
installed—one connected
to the modem, and one connected
to the network hub.

FIGURE 21.4

In the gateway configuration, a lead computer serves as a gateway to the Internet for all your other PCs.

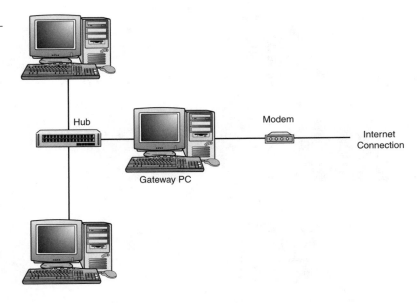

Hub

Modem

Internet Connection

Gateway PC

THE ABSOLUTE MINIMUM

When you're configuring your new PC system to connect to the Internet, remember these important points:

- You connect to the Internet through an Internet service provider; you need to set up an account with an ISP before you can connect.

- You can sign up for either dial-up (slower and less expensive) or broadband (faster and more expensive) service.

- There are three different types of broadband service—DSL, cable, and satellite.

- After you have an account with an ISP, you need to run the New Connection Wizard to configure Windows for your new account.

- If you have more than one computer at home, you can connect them in a network and share a single Internet connection.

22

SURFING THE WEB

After you're signed up with an ISP and connected to the Internet, it's time to get surfing. The World Wide Web is a particular part of the Internet with all sorts of cool content and useful services, and you surf the Web with a piece of software called a *Web browser*.

The most popular Web browser today is Microsoft's Internet Explorer, and you probably have a copy of it already installed on your new PC. This chapter shows you how to use Internet Explorer and then takes you on a quick trip around the Web—just enough to get your online feet wet!

Understanding the Web

Before you can surf the Web, you need to understand a little bit about how it works.

Information on the World Wide Web is presented in *pages*. A Web page is similar to a page in a book, made up of text and graphics. A Web page differs from a book page, however, in that it can include other elements, such as audio and video, and links to other Web pages.

It's this linking to other Web pages that makes the Web such a dynamic way to present information. A *link* on a Web page can point to another Web page on the same site or to another site. Most links are included as part of a Web page's text and are called *hypertext links*. (If a link is part of a graphic, it's called a *graphic link*.) Links are usually in a different color from the rest of the text and often are underlined; when you click a link, you're taken directly to the linked page.

Web pages reside at a Web *site*. A Web site is nothing more than a collection of Web pages (each in its own individual computer file) residing on a host computer. The host computer is connected full-time to the Internet so that you can access the site—and its Web pages—anytime you access the Internet. The main page at a Web site usually is called a *home page*, and it often serves as an opening screen that provides a brief overview and menu of everything you can find at that site. The address of a Web page is called a *URL*, which stands for uniform resource locator. Most URLs start with http://, add a www., continue with the name of the site, and end with a .com.

tip

You can normally leave off the http:// when you enter an address into your Web browser.

Using Internet Explorer

Internet Explorer (IE) is a very easy program to use. To launch IE, follow these steps:

1. Click the Start button to display the Start menu.

2. Select Internet (at the very upper-left part of the menu).

Figure 22.1 shows the various parts of the IE program, and Table 22.1 tells you what each of the buttons on the toolbar does.

note

You can use any Web browser to surf the Web—the instructions here work equally as well with Netscape or MSN Explorer, or the browser built into America Online.

Toolbar-Click these buttons to perform common functions

Address Box-Enter Web address here

FIGURE 22.1

Microsoft's
Internet Explorer
Web browser.

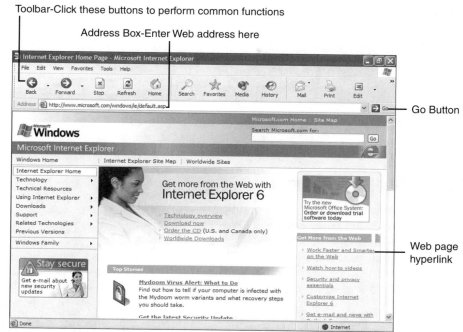

Go Button

Web page
hyperlink

Table 22.1 Internet Explorer Toolbar Buttons

	Button	Operation
Back	Back	Return to the previously viewed page
Forward	Forward	View the next page
Stop	Stop	Stop loading the current page
Refresh	Refresh	Reload the current page
Home	Home	Return to your designated start page
Search	Search	Display the Search pane and initiate a Web search
Favorites	Favorites	Display the Favorites pane
Media	Media	Display the Media pane—for listening to Internet audio and watching online videos

Table 22.1 (continued)

	Button	Operation
⊘ History	History	Display the History pane to see a list of recently viewed pages
✉ Mail	Mail	Launch your email program
🖶 Print	Print	Print the current page

Basic Web Surfing

Internet Explorer enables you to quickly and easily browse the World Wide Web—just by clicking your mouse. Here's a step-by-step tour of IE's basic functions:

tip

To change Internet Explorer's home page, drag a page's icon from Internet Explorer's Address box onto the Home button on the toolbar.

1. When you first launch Internet Explorer, it loads your predefined home page.

2. Enter a new Web address in the Address box, and press Enter (or click the Go button). Internet Explorer loads the new page.

3. Click any link on the current Web page. Internet Explorer loads the new page.

4. To return to the previous page, click the Back button (or press the Backspace key on your keyboard). If you've backed up several pages and want to return to the page you were on last, click the Forward button.

5. To return to your start page, click the Home button.

Advanced Operations

Before we take our first cruise on the Web, let's examine a few advanced operations in Internet Explorer that can make your online life a lot easier.

Saving Your Favorite Pages

When you find a Web page you like, you can add it to a list of Favorites within Internet Explorer. This way you can easily access any of your favorite sites just by selecting them from the list.

To add a page to your Favorites list

1. Go to the Web page you want to add to your Favorites list.

2. Pull down the Favorites menu, and select Add to Favorites.

3. When the Add Favorite dialog box appears, confirm the page's Name and then click the Create In button to extend the dialog box.

4. Select the folder where you want to place this link, and then click OK.

To view a page in your Favorites list

1. Click the Favorites button. The browser window will automatically split into two panes, with your favorites displayed in the left pane (see Figure 22.2).

FIGURE 22.2

Click the Favorites button to display the Favorites pane.

2. Click any folder in the Favorites pane to display the contents of that folder.

3. Click a favorite page, and that page is displayed in the right pane.

4. Click the Favorites button again to hide the Favorites pane.

Revisiting History

Internet Explorer has two ways of keeping track of Web pages you've visited, so you can easily revisit them without having to re-enter the Web page address.

To revisit one of the last half-dozen or so pages viewed in your current session, click the down-arrow on the Back button. This drops down a menu containing the last nine pages you've visited. Highlight any page on this menu to jump directly to that page.

To revisit pages you've viewed in the past several days, you use IE's History pane. Just follow these steps:

1. Click the History button. The browser window automatically splits into two panes, with your history for the past several days displayed in the left pane.

2. Your history is organized into folders for each of the past several days. Click any folder in the History pane to display the sites you visited that day.

3. Each site you visited on a particular day has its own subfolder. Click a subfolder to display the pages you visited within that particular site.

4. Click a specific page to display that page in the right pane.

5. Click the History button again to hide the History pane.

tip

To sort the sites in the History pane by site, by most visited, or by most visited today, pull down the View menu within the pane and make a new selection.

Printing

Printing a Web page is easy—just click the Print button. If you want to see a preview of the page before it prints, pull down the File menu and select Print Preview.

Let's Go Surfin'!

Okay, now you're ready to launch Internet Explorer and head out to the World Wide Web. Follow these step-by-step instructions for a quick cruise around the Web—just to see what's out there:

1. Connect to your ISP, and then launch Internet Explorer. IE appears on your desk top and displays its default home page. (Typically, this is some page on Microsoft's Web site.)

2. Let's find out what's happening out in the real world by heading over to one of the most popular news sites. Enter www.cnn.com into the Address box, and then click the Go button. This takes you to the CNN.com site, shown in Figure 22.3. Click any headline to read the complete story.

3. Now, let's do a little searching at Yahoo!, one of the Web's premier search sites. (You can learn more about searching in Chapter 23, "Finding Stuff Online.") Enter www.yahoo.com in the Address box, and then click the Go button. Ready to search? Enter que publishing in the Search the Web box at the top of the page (shown in Figure 22.4), and then click the Yahoo! Search button.

FIGURE 22.3

Get informed at CNN.com.

FIGURE 22.4

Search for other Web sites at Yahoo!

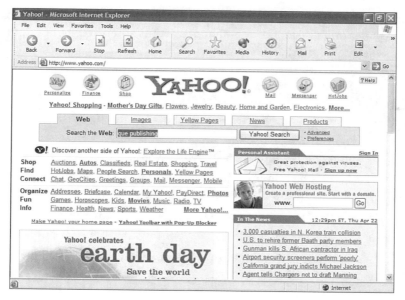

4. When the search results page appears, find the listing for Que Publishing (should be near the top) and click the link. You now should be taken to the Web site for the publisher of this book (shown in Figure 22.5). Click any link to learn more about Que and the other books they publish.

FIGURE 22.5

Learn more about this book's publisher at the Que Publishing Web site.

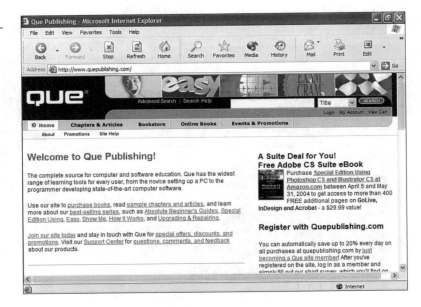

That's your quick surfing tour. You can keep surfing from here, or close Internet Explorer and disconnect from the Internet. As you can see, surfing the Web is as easy as clicking your mouse!

THE ABSOLUTE MINIMUM

Here are the key things to remember about surfing the Web:

- You surf the Web with a program called a Web browser; Internet Explorer is probably the browser installed on your new PC.
- You can go to a particular Web page by entering the page's address in the Address box and then clicking the Go button.
- Click a hyperlink on a Web page to jump to the linked page.
- Use IE's Favorites list to store your favorite Web pages for easy retrieval.
- Use the Back button or the History pane to revisit recently viewed Web pages.

23

FINDING STUFF ONLINE

Now that you know how to surf the Web, how do you find the precise information you're looking for? Fortunately, there are numerous sites that help you search the Web for the specific information you want. Not surprisingly, these are among the most popular sites on the Internet.

This chapter is all about searching the Web. You'll learn the best places to search, and the best ways to search. I'll even help you cheat a little by listing some of the most popular sites for different types of information.

So pull up a chair, launch your Web browser, and loosen up those fingers—it's time to start searching!

How to Search the Web

Most Internet search sites are actually *search engines*. They employ special software programs (called *spiders* or *crawlers*) to roam the Web automatically, feeding what they find back to a massive bank of computers. These computers then build giant *indexes* of the Web, hundreds of millions of pages strong.

When you perform a search at a search engine site, your query is sent to the search engine's index. (You never actually search the Web itself, you only search the index that was created by the spiders crawling the Web.) The search engine then creates a list of pages in its index that match, to one degree or another, the query you entered.

Constructing a Query

Almost every search site on the Web contains two basic components—a *search box* and a *search button*. You enter your query—one or more *keywords* that describe what you're looking for—into the search box, and then click the Search button (or press the Enter key) to start the search. The search site then returns a list of Web pages that match your query; click any link to go directly to the page in question.

How you construct your query determines how relevant the results will be that you receive. It's important to focus on the keywords you use, because the search sites look for these words when they process your query. Your keywords are compared to the Web pages the search site knows about; the more keywords found on a Web page, the better the match.

You should choose keywords that best describe the information you're looking for—using as many keywords as you need. Don't be afraid of using too many keywords; in fact, using too *few* keywords is a common fault of many novice searchers. The more words you use, the better idea the search engine has of what you're looking for.

Using Wildcards

But what if you're not quite sure which word to use? For example, would the best results come from looking for *auto*, *automobile*, or *automotive*? Many search sites let you use *wildcards* to "stand in" for parts of a word that you're not quite sure about.

In most instances, the asterisk character (*) is used as a wildcard to match any character or group of characters, from its particular position in the word to the end of that word. So, in the previous example, entering `auto*` would return all three words—auto, automobile, *and* automotive (as well as automatic, autocratic, and any other word that starts with "auto").

Searching for an Exact Phrase

Normally, a multiple-word query searches for Web pages that include all the words in the query, in any order. There is a way, however, to search for an exact phrase. All you have to do is enclose the phrase in quotation marks.

For example, to search for Monty Python, *don't* enter `Monty Python`. Instead, enter `"Monty Python"`—surrounded by quotation marks. Putting the phrase between quotation marks returns results about the comedy troupe, while entering the words individually returns pages about snakes and guys named Monty.

Where to Search

Now that you know how to search, *where* should you search? There's one obvious choice, and a lot of alternatives.

Google—the Most Popular Search Site on the Web

The best (and most popular) search engine today is Google (`www.google.com`). Google is easy to use and extremely fast, and returns highly relevant results. That's because it indexes more pages than any other site—more than 6 billion pages, at last count.

Most users search Google several times a week, if not several times a day. The Google home page, shown in Figure 23.1, is a marvel of simplicity and elegant Web page design. All you have to do to start a search is to enter one or more keywords into the search box, then click the Google Search button. This returns a list of results ranked in order of relevance, like the one shown in Figure 23.2. Click a results link to view that page.

FIGURE 23.1
Searching the
Web at Google.

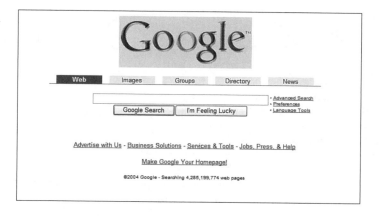

Google also offers a variety of advanced search options to help you fine-tune your
search. These options are found on the Advanced Search page, shown in Figure 23.3;
you access this page by clicking the Advanced Search link on Google's home page.
To narrow your search results, all you have to do is make the appropriate selections
from the options present.

FIGURE 23.3

Google's
Advanced
Search options.

Another neat thing about Google is all the specialty searches it offers. Table 23.1
details some of these "hidden" search features:

Table 23.1   Google Search Options

Search	URL	Description
Froogle	froogle.google.com	Comparison shopping
Google Answers	answers.google.com	Ask questions of experts (for a fee)
Google Apple Macintosh Search	www.google.com/mac/	Searches for technical information on Apple's Web site
Google Catalogs	catalogs.google.com	Display print catalogs from major catalog retailers
Google Directory	directory.google.com	Editor-selected search results
Google Groups	groups.google.com	Searches Usenet newsgroups
Google Image Search	images.google.com	Search for pictures
Google Microsoft Search	www.google.com/Microsoft.html	Searches for technical information on Microsoft's Web site
Google News	news.google.com	Searches the latest news headlines
Google U.S. Government Search	www.google.com/unclesam/	Searches U.S. government sites
Google University Search	www.google.com/options/universities.html	Searches college and university Web sites

Other Search Engines

While Google is far and away the most popular search engine, there are lots of other search engines that provide excellent (and sometimes different) results. These search engines include

- AllTheWeb (www.alltheweb.com)
- AltaVista (www.altavista.com)
- AOL Search (search.aol.com)
- Ask Jeeves! (www.askjeeves.com)
- HotBot (www.hotbot.com)

tip

You can also use Google to display maps (search for the street address), stock quotes (enter the stock ticker), answers to mathematical calculations (enter the equation), and measurement conversions (enter what you want to convert).

- Lycos (www.lycos.com)
- MSN Search (search.msn.com)
- Teoma (www.teoma.com)
- Yahoo! (www.yahoo.com)

Directories

Not all search sites use search engine technology. Some sites use human editors to evaluate and organize Web pages into a *directory*. Directories typically offer fewer but higher-quality results than pure search engines.

Among the most popular Web directories are

- About.com (www.about.com)
- LookSmart (www.looksmart.com)
- Open Directory (www.dmoz.org)
- Yahoo! (www.yahoo.com)

That's right—Yahoo! offers both search engine and directory results. (As, for that matter, does Google; the Google Directory uses listings provided by the Open Directory.) You access the Yahoo! directory by browsing through the category listings on the Yahoo! home page; you access the Yahoo! search index by entering a query into the search box at the top of the home page.

Metasearch Engines

There are also a number of search engines that let you search multiple search engines and directories from a single page—which is called a *metasearch*. The top metasearchers include

- Dogpile (www.dogpile.com)
- Excite (www.excite.com)
- GoGettem (www.gogettem.com)
- Mamma (www.mamma.com)
- MetaCrawler (www.metacrawler.com)
- Search.com (www.search.com)

Searching for People

As good as Google and other search sites are for finding specific Web pages, they're not that great for finding people. When there's a person (or an address or a phone number) you want to find, you need to use a site that specializes in people searches.

People listings on the Web go by the common name of *white pages directories*, the same as traditional white pages phone books. These directories typically enable you to enter all or part of a person's name and then search for his address and phone number. Many of these sites also let you search for personal email addresses and business addresses and phone numbers.

The best of these directories include

- AnyWho (www.anywho.com)
- InfoSpace (www.infospace.com)
- Switchboard (www.switchboard.com)
- WhitePages.com (www.whitepages.com)
- WhoWhere (www.whowhere.lycos.com)

Searching for News, Sports, and Weather

The Internet is a great place to find both news headlines and in-depth analysis. Most news-related Web sites are updated in real-time, so you're always getting the latest news—on your computer screen, when you want it.

Searching for the Latest News

Some of the biggest, most popular news sites on the Web are run by the major broadcast and cable news networks, or by the major national newspapers. You can turn to these sites to get the latest headlines, and—in many cases—live audio and video feeds.

The major news sites on the Web include

- ABC News (www.abcnews.com)
- BBC News (news.bbc.co.uk)
- CBS News (www.cbsnews.com)
- CNN (www.cnn.com)
- Fox News (www.foxnews.com)
- MSNBC (www.msnbc.com)
- *New York Times* (www.nytimes.com)

■ Reuters News Online (www.reuters.com)

■ *USA Today* (www.usatoday.com)

Searching for Sports Headlines and Scores

The Web is a great resource for sports fans of all shapes and sizes. Whether you're a fan or a participant, there's at least one site somewhere on the Web that focuses on your particular sport.

The best sports sites on the Web resemble the best news sites—they're actually portals to all sorts of content and services, including up-to-the-minute scores, post-game recaps, in-depth reporting, and much more. If you're looking for sports information online, one of these portals is the place to start:

■ CBS SportsLine (www.sportsline.com)

■ ESPN.com (msn.espn.go.com)

■ FOXSports (www.foxsports.com)

■ NBC Sports (www.nbcsports.com)

■ SI.com—Sports Illustrated (sportsillustrated.cnn.com)

■ SportingNews.com (www.sportingnews.com)

> **tip**
>
> If you follow a particular sports team, check out that team's local newspaper on the Web. Chances are you'll find a lot of in-depth coverage there that you won't find at these other sites.

Searching for Weather Reports

Weather reports and forecasts are readily available on the Web; most of the major news portals and local Web sites offer some variety of weather-related services. There are also a number of dedicated weather sites on the Web, all of which offer local and national forecasts, weather radar, satellite maps, and more.

Here are the most popular weather sites on the Web:

■ AccuWeather.com (www.accuweather.com)

■ Intellicast.com (www.intellicast.com)

■ My-Cast (www.my-cast.com)

■ NOAA (www.noaa.gov)

■ Weather Underground (www.wunderground.com)

■ Weather.com (www.weather.com)

Figure 23.4 shows the Weather.com site, from the folks at the Weather Channel.

FIGURE 23.4

Getting the latest weather reports at Weather.com.

Searching for Financial Information

The Internet is a great place to find up-to-the-minute information about stocks and other securities. Several sites and services specialize in providing real-time (or slightly delayed) stock quotes—free!

Here's a short list of the best financial sites on the Web—both free and for-a-fee:

- CBS Marketwatch (cbs.marketwatch.com)
- CNN/Money (money.cnn.com)
- Hoovers Online (www.hoovers.com)
- Motley Fool (www.fool.com)
- MSN MoneyCentral (moneycentral.msn.com)
- Yahoo! Finance (finance.yahoo.com)

Searching for Medical Information

The Internet is a fount of information of all different types. It's a particularly good research tool for health-related information.

A number of Web sites offer detailed information about illnesses, diseases, and medicines. Many of these sites focus on preventive medicine and wellness, and almost all help you match symptoms with likely illnesses and treatments. Indeed, some

caution

As useful as these health sites are, they should not and cannot serve as substitutes for a trained medical opinion.

of these sites provide access to the same medical databases used by most physicians—without waiting for an appointment!

The top medical sites on the Web include

- healthAtoZ.com (www.healthatoz.com)
- kidsDoctor (www.kidsdoctor.com)
- MedicineNet (www.medicinenet.com)
- National Library of Medicine (www.nlm.nih.gov)
- Planet Wellness (www.planetwellness.com)
- WebMD Health (my.webmd.com)

tip

You can also use the Web to search for a new or specialist physician in your area. Some of the best physician search sites include AMA Physician Select (www.ama-assn.org/aps/), Best Doctors (www.bestdoctors.com), DoctorDirectory.com (www.doctordirectory.com), and mydoctor.com (www.mydoctor.com).

THE ABSOLUTE MINIMUM

Here are the key points to remember from this chapter:

- When you need to search for specific information on the Internet, you can use one of the Web's many search engines and directories.
- The most popular Internet search engine is Google, which indexes more than 6 billion individual Web pages.
- Other popular search engines and directories include Yahoo!, AltaVista, and Ask Jeeves!
- It's better to search for people (and their phone numbers and addresses) at specific people-search sites, such as InfoSpace and Switchboard.
- The most popular news sites on the Web are those run by traditional news organizations, such as CNN and Fox News.

24

BUYING AND SELLING ONLINE

Many users have discovered that the Internet is a great place to buy things—and to sell them! All manner of online merchants make it easy to buy books, CDs, and other merchandise with the click of a mouse. And online auction sites—led by the extremely successful eBay—serve as online marketplaces for users wanting to buy and sell all manner of merchandise.

In spite of the popularity of online retailing, many users are still a little hesitant to do their shopping online. Although there certainly is some amount of online credit card theft, in general the Internet is a fairly safe place to shop—if you follow the rules, and take a few simple precautions.

Read on, then, to find out the best places to shop online—and how to shop safely.

Shopping Online

For many users, shopping online is easier than shopping at traditional "bricks-and-mortar" retailers. You can sit down in front of your computer screen at any time of the day or night, and use your PC to search the Web for just the right item you want to buy—you don't have to get dressed, start your car, or bother with boisterous crowds.

How to Shop—Safely

To purchase an item online, all you have to do is enter your name, address, and credit card number, and the online merchant will arrange to have the item delivered directly to your house within a matter of days. It's that easy!

The big online retailers are just as reputable as traditional retailers, offering safe payment, fast shipping, and responsive service. Just to be safe, look for the following features before you shop at a given site:

- Payment by major credit card. (Not being able to accept credit cards is the sign of either a very small or fly-by-night merchant.)

- A *secure server* that encrypts your credit card information—and keeps online thieves from stealing your credit card numbers. (You'll know that you're using a secure site when the little lock icon appears in the lower right corner of your Web browser.)

- Good contact information—email address, street address, phone number, fax number, and so on. (You want to be able to physically contact the retailer if something goes wrong.)

- A stated returns policy and satisfaction guarantee. (You want to be assured that you'll be taken care of if you don't like whatever you ordered.)

- A stated privacy policy that protects your personal information. (You don't want the online retailer sharing your email address and purchasing information with other merchants—and potential spammers.)

- Information *before you finalize your order* that tells you whether the item is in stock and how long it will take to ship. (More feedback is better.)

> **tip**
>
> Credit card purchases are protected by the Fair Credit Billing Act, which gives you the right to dispute certain charges and limits your liability for unauthorized transactions to $50. In addition, some card issuers offer a supplemental guarantee that says you're not responsible for *any* unauthorized charges made online. (Make sure that you read your card's statement of terms to determine the company's exact liability policy.)

Making an Online Purchase

If you've never shopped online before, you're probably wondering just what to expect. Shopping over the Web is actually quite easy; all you need is your computer and a credit card—and a fast connection to the Internet!

It really doesn't matter which retailer you shop at; the process of online shopping is pretty much the same all over. You proceed through a multiple-step process that goes like this:

1. Find a product either by browsing or searching through the site.
2. Examine the product by viewing the photos and information on a product listing page, similar to the one shown in Figure 24.1.
3. Order the product, by clicking a Buy It Now button on the product listing page, which puts the item in your online "shopping cart."
4. Check out by entering your payment and shipping information.
5. Confirm your order and wait for the merchant to ship your merchandise.

FIGURE 24.1

Examining the merchandise at Amazon.com.

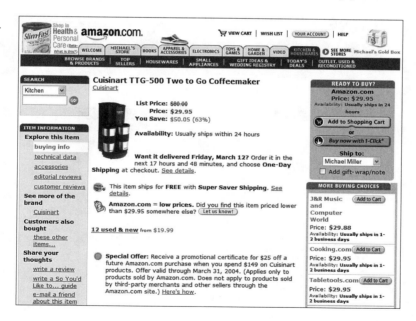

That's it! You should receive your order in a few days.

Finding the Best Prices Online

Now that you know *how* to shop, *where* should you spend your money online? Just a few short years ago, if you wanted to find the best bargains on the Web, you had to manually visit the sites of dozens of different online retailers—a very time-consuming process. Not so today, as there are numerous sites that exist to automatically do this price comparison for you. Go to a price comparison site, find the product you want, and have the site return a list of merchants offering that product, along with current prices. Choose the merchant that offers what you want, and you're ready to buy!

The best of these price comparison sites offer more than just pricing information. These full-service sites let you sort and filter their search results in a number of different ways, and often include customer reviews of both the products and the available merchants. Some even let you perform side-by-side comparisons of multiple products, which is great if you haven't yet made up your mind as to what you want to buy. (Figure 24.2 shows one such product comparison at Shopping.com.)

FIGURE 24.2

Comparing products and prices at Shopping.com.

The most popular (and useful) of these price comparison sites include

- BizRate (www.bizrate.com)
- Froogle (froogle.google.com)
- mySimon (www.mysimon.com)

- NexTag (www.nextag.com)
- PriceGrabber.com (www.pricegrabber.com)
- Shopping.com (www.shopping.com)
- Yahoo! Shopping (shopping.yahoo.com)

Buying—and Selling—at eBay Auctions

Some of the best bargains on the Web come from other consumers, just like you, selling items via *online auction*. An online auction is, quite simply, a Web-based version of a traditional auction. You find an item you'd like to own and then place a bid on the item. Other users also place bids, and at the end of the auction—typically a seven-day period—the highest bidder wins.

note

Want to find the best bargains online? Then check out my companion book, *Bargain Hunter's Secrets to Online Shopping* (Que, 2004), available in bookstores everywhere.

Far and away the largest online auction site is eBay (www.ebay.com), shown in Figure 24.3. On any given day, there are more than 24 million items listed for auction on eBay; do a search from eBay's main page, and you can find everything from rare collectibles and vintage sports memorabilia to the latest electronics equipment.

FIGURE 24.3

The world's largest online marketplace—eBay!

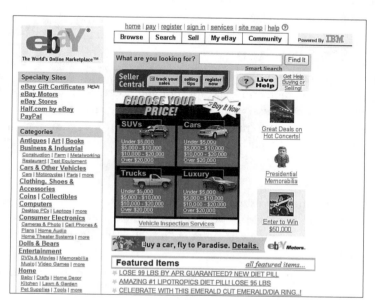

How Online Auctions Work

If you've never used eBay before, you might be a little anxious about what might be involved. Never fear; participating in an online auction is a piece of cake, something that 95 million other users have done before you. This means that you don't have to reinvent any wheels; the procedures you have to follow are well established and well documented.

eBay's online auction process is actually quite simple. It starts when a seller places a listing for a particular item and launches the auction (which typically runs for seven days). A potential buyer sees the item listing and makes a bid. Other bidders make their bids, and when the auction is over, the highest bidder wins. The seller then contacts the winning bidder with the total amount due (the final bid price plus shipping and handling). The winning bidder sends payment to the seller, and then the seller ships the item to the winning bidder.

That's it. If everything works right, it's a pretty painless process—made easy by eBay.

tip

An online auction is a great place to find things you just can't find anyplace else—especially rare collectables. It's also a great place to get rid of things that you don't want anymore; there's a good chance that somebody, somewhere, will want to buy what you want to sell.

eBay Bidding, Step-by-Step

Bidding in an online auction is kind of like shopping at an online merchant—except that you don't flat-out make a purchase. Instead, you make a bid—and you only get to purchase the item at the end of the auction if your bid was the highest bid made.

note

Learn even more about eBay auctions in my companion book, *Absolute Beginner's Guide to eBay, 2nd Edition* (Que, 2004), available where you purchased this title.

Here's how it works:

1. You begin by registering with eBay. Registration is free, and as a buyer all you have to provide is your name, address, and email. You can register directly from eBay's home page; just click the Register link at the top of the page.

2. You look for items using eBay's search function or by browsing through the product categories.

3. When you find an item you're interested in, take a moment to examine all the details. A typical item listing (like the one shown in Figure 24.4) includes a photo of the item, a brief product description, shipping and payment information, and instructions on how to place a bid.

FIGURE 24.4

An eBay item listing—ready to bid?

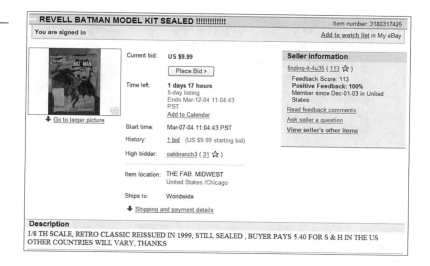

4. Now it's time to place your bid, which you do from the Ready to Bid? section near the bottom of the page. Remember, you're not buying the item at this point; you're just telling eBay how much you're willing to pay. Your bid must be at or above the current bid amount. My recommendation is to determine the maximum amount you'd be willing to pay for that item, and bid that amount—regardless of what the current bid level is.

5. eBay uses automatic proxy bidding software to automatically handle the bidding process from here. You bid the maximum amount you're willing to pay, and eBay's proxy software enters the minimum bid necessary—without revealing your maximum bid amount. Your bid will be automatically raised (to no more than your maximum amount) when other users bid.

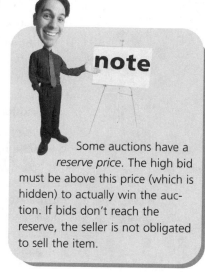

Some auctions have a *reserve price*. The high bid must be above this price (which is hidden) to actually win the auction. If bids don't reach the reserve, the seller is not obligated to sell the item.

6. The auction proceeds. Most auctions run for 7 days, although sellers have the option of running 1-, 3-, 5-, 7-, and 10-day auctions.

7. If you're the high bidder at the end of the auction, eBay informs you (via email) that you're the winner. At this point, the seller should also contact you regarding payment.

8. You pay the seller, typically by check, money order, cashier's check, or credit card. (Most eBay sellers accept credit cards via the PayPal service.) Your payment includes both the cost of the item (the winning bid amount) and a reasonable shipping/handling charge, as determined by the seller.

9. The seller ships the item.

It's important to note that even though you've been using the services of the eBay site, the ultimate transaction is between you and the individual seller. You don't pay eBay; eBay is just the middleman.

tip

To increase your chances of winning an auction, use a technique called *sniping*. When you snipe, you hold your bid until the very last seconds of the auction. If you bid high enough and late enough, other bidders won't have time to respond to your bid—and your high bid will win!

eBay Selling, Step-by-Step

Selling on eBay is a little more involved than bidding—but can generate big bucks if you do it right. Here's how it works:

1. If you haven't registered with eBay yet, do so now. You'll also need to provide eBay with a credit card number so that you can be charged the appropriate fees for your item listing.

2. Click the Sell button on eBay's home page to create the item listing for your auction. eBay displays a series of forms for you to complete; the information you enter into these forms is used to create your item listing. You'll need to select a category for your item; enter a title and description; determine how long you want your auction to run and

note

eBay makes its money by charging sellers two types of fees. (Buyers don't pay any fees to eBay.) *Insertion fees* are based on the minimum bid or reserve price of the item listed. *Final value fees* are charged when you sell an item, based on the item's final selling price. Fees are typically charged directly to the seller's credit card account.

what kind of payments you'll accept; insert a photo of the item, if you have one; and enter the amount of the desired minimum (starting) bid.

3. After you enter all the information, eBay creates and displays a preliminary version of your auction listing. If you like what you see, click OK to start the auction.

4. When the auction ends, eBay notifies you (via email) of the high bid and provides the email address of the winning bidder.

5. Email the winning bidder with an invoice containing the final bid price and the shipping/handling charges.

6. After you've been paid, pack the item and ship it out.

That's it—you've just completed a successful eBay auction!

Buying a Car Online

Shopping online isn't limited to items that can be shipped in a box or envelope. It's actually possible to buy something as large as an automobile over the Internet.

Of course, buying a new car online isn't quite the same as buying a shirt or a DVD player online. For one thing, don't expect to open your mailbox and find a car inside. No, when you use a Web site to shop for a new car, you actually end up purchasing the vehicle from a local auto dealer. The online sites simply facilitate your purchase by letting you request price quotes from local dealers; these quotes, which incorporate volume discounts arranged by the online auto site, typically are much lower than what you can negotiate on your own.

You start the process by visiting one of the many automotive portal sites, like Cars.com (shown in Figure 24.5). Once you decide on a specific model, you request price quotes. The portal sends your request to participating dealers in your area, who then contact you separately. If you like the price a dealer offers, you make the purchase.

Here are the best of these automotive portals:

- autobytel.com (www.autobytel.com)
- AutoNation.com (www.autonation.com)
- AutoSite (www.autosite.com)
- Autoweb (www.autoweb.com)
- Cars.com (www.cars.com)
- Edmunds.com (www.edmunds.com)
- Kelley Blue Book (www.kbb.com)
- MSN Autos (autos.msn.com)

tip

These automotive portals also make it easy to buy (and to sell) used cars. Browse the listings to see what's available in your area.

FIGURE 24.5

Shopping for new and used cars at Cars.com.

House Hunting Online

The biggest single purchase most people make in their entire lives is their home. Numerous home-buying resources are available on the Internet, offering everything from real estate listings to mortgage information. You can use these sites to research what kind of home you want (and can afford), and then search for a new or resale home in a particular region and price range.

Some of the more popular home-buying sites include

- eRealty.com (www.erealty.com)
- FSBO.com (www.fsbo.com)
- Homes.com (www.homes.com)
- HomeScape.com (www.homescape.com)
- iHomeowner.com (www.ihomeowner.com)
- NewHomeNetwork.com (www.newhomenetwork.com)
- Realtor.com (www.realtor.com)

Booking Travel Reservations Online

Savvy travelers use the Internet to book all their travel reservations—plane tickets, hotel rooms, rental cars, and more. To book reservations, all you need to know is where you're going and when—and all the numbers from your favorite charge card.

The Web's general travel sites all offer similar content and services, including the ability to book airline tickets, hotel rooms, and rental cars all in one place. Most of these sites (such as Expedia, shown in Figure 24.6) let you search for the lowest rates or for flights and lodging that match your specific requirements.

Here are the best of these "online travel agents":

- Expedia (www.expedia.com)
- Hotwire (www.hotwire.com)
- Orbitz (www.orbitz.com)
- Priceline (www.priceline.com)
- TravelNow.com (www.travelnow.com)
- Travelocity (www.travelocity.com)

tip

When you make reservations online, look for a site that employs real people behind-the-scenes—and offers a 24/7 800 number to contact those people if something goes wrong. Talking to a real person over the phone can be a lifeline if you're stranded somewhere without a reservation.

FIGURE 24.6

Shopping for airline and hotel reservations at Expedia.

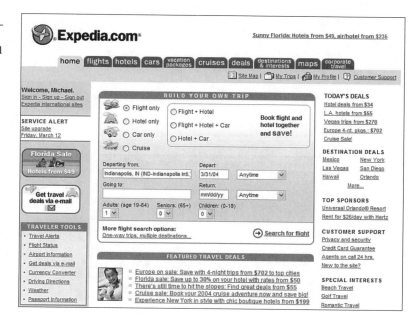

The Absolute Minimum

Here are the key points to remember from this chapter:

- You can find just about any type of item you want to buy for sale somewhere on the Internet.

- Internet shopping is very safe, especially if you buy from a major merchant that offers a secure server and a good returns policy.

- To find the best prices online, use a price comparison site such as Shopping.com or Froogle.

- If you have an item you want to sell, use an online auction site, such as eBay. (eBay is also a great place to buy merchandise—especially rare collectables!)

- Online shopping isn't limited to small items; you can also purchase airline tickets, new cars, and houses over the Web.

25

SENDİNG AND RECEİVİNG EMAİL

Email is the modern way to communicate with friends, family, and colleagues. An email message is like a regular letter, except that it's composed electronically and delivered almost immediately via the Internet.

There are several programs you can use to send and receive email messages. If you're in a corporate environment, or running Microsoft Office, you can use Microsoft Outlook for your email. (Outlook is also a scheduler and personal information manager.) If you're connecting from home, the simpler Outlook Express is probably a better choice; it's easier to learn and use than its bigger brother, Outlook. Plus, Outlook Express is pre-installed on all Windows PCs free.

Using Outlook Express to send and receive email is a snap. Once you get it configured for your particular Internet service provider and email account, checking your messages is as easy as clicking a button.

Setting Up Your Email Account

Back in Chapter 21, "Connecting to the Internet," you learned how to configure your computer for your particular Internet service provider. When you did your main configuration, you should have entered information about your email account.

If you later change email providers, or add a new email account, you'll have to access your email settings separately. To configure Outlook Express for a new email account, you'll need to know the following information:

- The email address assigned by your ISP, in the format *name@domain.com*.
- The type of email server you'll be using; it's probably a POP3 server. (It could also be an HTTP, IMAP, or SMTP server, but POP3 is more common.)
- The address of the incoming email server and the outgoing mail server.
- The account name and password you use to connect to the email servers.

Once you have this information (which should be supplied by your ISP), you can enter it manually into Outlook Express by following these steps:

1. From within Outlook Express, select Tools, Accounts to display the Internet Accounts dialog box.
2. Select the Mail tab.
3. To change the settings for an existing account, select the account and click Properties.
4. To enter a new account, click the Add button and select Mail.
5. When the Properties dialog box appears, select the General tab, then enter a name for this account, your name (first and last), and the email address assigned by your ISP.
6. Select the Servers tab and enter the following information: type of server, incoming email server address, outgoing email server address, your assigned account name, and your password.
7. Click OK.

You're now ready to send and receive email.

tip

To avoid entering your password every time you check your email, select the Remember Password option in the Properties dialog box.

Understanding the Outlook Express Window

Before we start working with email, let's take a look at the Outlook Express window. As you can see in Figure 25.1, the basic Outlook Express window is divided into three panes. The pane on the left is called the Folder list, and it's where you access your Inbox and other message folders. The top pane on the right is the Message pane, and it lists all the messages stored in the selected folder. Below that is the Preview pane, and it displays the contents of the selected message.

FIGURE 25.1

Use Outlook Express to send and receive email.

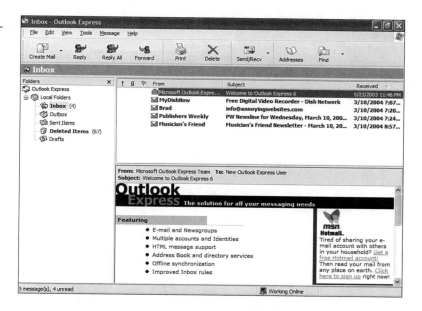

The way it all works is that you select a location in the Folder List (typically your inbox), select a message header in the Message pane, and view the contents of that message in the Preview pane.

Managing Your Email

Using Outlook Express is easy—and composing a new email message isn't much different from writing a memo in Microsoft Word. You just have to know which buttons to push!

Composing a Message

It's easy to create a new email message. Just follow these steps:

1. Click the Create Mail button on the Outlook Express toolbar; this launches a New Message window, similar to the one shown in Figure 25.2.

FIGURE 25.2

Use the New Message window to compose a new email message.

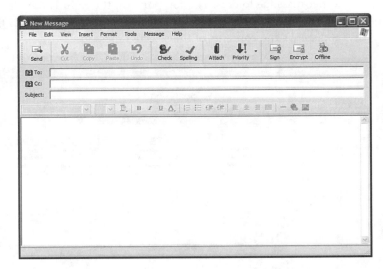

2. Enter the email address of the recipient(s) in the To field, then enter the address of anyone you want to receive a carbon copy in the Cc box. You can enter multiple addresses, as long as you separate multiple addresses with a semicolon (;), like this: `mmiller@molehillgroup.com; gjetson@sprockets.com`.

3. Move your cursor to the main message area and type your message.

4. When your message is complete, send it to the Outbox by clicking the Send button.

tip

You can test your email account by sending a message to yourself; just enter your own email address in the To field.

Now you need to send the message from your Outbox over the Internet to the intended recipient (you!). You do this by clicking the Send/Recv button on the Outlook Express toolbar. Assuming your computer is connected to the Internet, your message will now be sent.

Reading New Messages

When you receive new email messages, they're stored in the Outlook Express Inbox. To display all new messages, select the Inbox icon from the Folders list. All waiting messages now appear in the Message pane.

To read a specific message, select its header in the Message pane. The contents of that message are displayed in the Preview pane.

tip

You also can double-click a message header to display the message in a separate window.

Replying to a Message

To reply to an email message, follow these steps:

1. Select the message header in the Message pane.
2. Click the Reply button on the Outlook Express toolbar; this opens a Re: window, which is just like a New Message window except with the text from the original message "quoted" in the text area and the email address of the recipient (the person who sent the original message) pre-entered in the To field.
3. Enter your reply text in the message window.
4. Click the Send button to send your reply back to the original sender.

Sending Files via Email

The easiest way to share a file with another user is via email, as an *attachment*.

Attaching a File to an Email Message

To send a file via email, you attach that file to a standard email message. When the message is sent, the file travels along with it; when the message is received, the file is right there, waiting to be opened.

To attach a file to an outgoing email message, follow these steps:

1. Start with a new message and then click the Attach button in the message's toolbar; this displays the Insert Attachment dialog box.
2. Click the Browse button to locate and select the file you want to send.
3. Click Attach.

The attached file is now listed in a new Attach: field below the Subject: field in the message window. When you click the Send button, the email message and its attached file are sent together to your Outbox.

Opening an Email Attachment

When you receive a message that contains a file attachment, you'll see a paper clip icon in the message header and a paper clip button in the preview pane header. You can choose to view (open) the attached file or save it to your hard disk.

To view or open an attachment, click the paper clip button in the Preview pane header, and then click the attachment's filename. This opens the attachment in its associated application. (If you're asked whether you want to save or view the attachment, select view.)

To save an attachment to your hard disk, click the paper clip button in the preview pane header, and then select Save Attachments. When the Save Attachments dialog box appears, select a location for the file and click the Save button.

Protecting Against Email Viruses

Computer viruses are files that can attack your system and damage your programs and documents. Most viruses are spread when someone sends you an email message with an unexpected file attachment—and then you open the file. It's just too easy to receive an email message with a file attached, click the file to open it, and then launch the virus file. Boom! Your computer is infected.

Viruses can be found in many types of files. The most common file types for viruses are .EXE, .VBS, .PIF, and .COM. Viruses can also be embedded in Word (.DOC) or Excel (.XLS) files. You *can't* catch a virus from a picture file, so viewing a .JPG, .GIF, .TIF, and .BMP file is completely safe.

The best way to avoid catching a virus via email is to *not open any files attached to incoming email messages.* Period.

> **note**
>
> Learn more about computer viruses in Chapter 30, "Protecting Your PC from Viruses, Spam, and Other Nuisances."

That includes messages where you know the sender, because some viruses are capable of taking over an email program and "spoofing" other users' addresses. An email message might look like it's coming from a friend, but it's really coming from another machine and includes a virus. (Pretty tricky, eh?)

By default, Outlook Express is configured to automatically reject files that might contain viruses. You can verify this setting (or turn it off, if you want to receive a file), by opening the Options dialog box, selecting the Security tab, and checking both options in the Virus Protection section.

Using Address Book to Manage Your Contacts

Windows includes a contact manager application, called the *Address Book*, that you can use to store information about your friends, family, and business associates. You can then import this contact information into Outlook Express (to send email), Microsoft Works Calendar (to remind you of birthdays), and Microsoft Word (to personalize letters and address envelopes and labels).

To add a new contact to your Address Book, click the New button on the Address Book toolbar, then select New Contact. Enter all the information you know (you don't have to fill in *all* the blanks), then click OK.

You can also add contacts from any email messages you receive. Just right-click the sender's name in the email message and select Add Sender to Address Book. This creates a new contact for that person; you can then go to the Address Book and add more detailed information later—as described next.

To send email to one of your contacts, all you have to do is click the To button in your new Outlook Express message. This displays the Select Recipients dialog box, shown in Figure 25.3. Select the contact(s) you want, then click either the To, Cc, or Bcc buttons. Click OK when you're done adding names.

caution

Remember, you activate a virus only when you open a file attached to an email message. You can't activate the virus just by viewing the message itself.

note

Address Book is included with both Outlook Express and Microsoft Works Suite.

note

A Cc (carbon copy) message is one that is sent to someone other than the main recipient. A Bcc (blind carbon copy) is just like a Cc, except the Bcc recipient is hidden from the other recipients.

FIGURE 25.3

Sending email
to contacts in
your Address
Book.

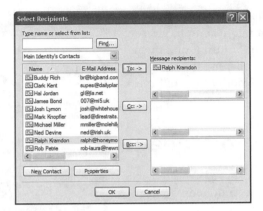

THE ABSOLUTE MINIMUM

Here are the key points to remember from this chapter:

- Email is a fast and easy way to send electronic letters over the Internet.

- You can send and receive email messages using the Outlook Express program, pre-installed on most new PCs.

- Sending a new message is as easy as clicking the Create Mail button; reading a message is as easy as selecting it in the Message pane (and viewing it in the Preview pane).

- Don't open any unexpected files attached to incoming email messages—they might contain computer viruses!

- You can store frequently used email addresses in the Address Book utility.

26

USING INSTANT MESSAGING AND CHAT

People like to talk—even when they're online.

There are two primary means of "talking" to other users via the Internet, both of which let you carry on text-based conversations in real time. When you want to hold a private one-on-one talk, you use an application called *instant messaging*. When you want to talk publicly, with a large group of people, you use *Internet chat*.

Instant messaging is the ideal medium for very short, very immediate messages. Online chat is better for longer discussions, and for group discussions. (And neither one is great for longer, more formal communications; email is best for those sort of messages.)

If you want to compare each method of online communication with their offline equivalents, think of email as the online version of written letters, online chat as the online version of phone conferences, and instant messaging as the online version of paging. Read on to learn more about both instant messaging and chat—and then get ready to start talking!

Sending and Receiving Instant Messages

Instant messaging lets you communicate one on one, in real-time, with your friends, family, and colleagues. It's faster than email and less chaotic than chat rooms (discussed later in this chapter). It's just you and another user—and your instant messaging software.

There are several big players in the instant messaging market today, including

- AOL Instant Messenger (www.aim.com)
- ICQ (web.icq.com)
- Windows Messenger *also known as* MSN Messenger (messenger.msn.com)
- Yahoo! Messenger (messenger.yahoo.com)

Unfortunately, many of these products don't work well (or at all) with each other; if you're using Windows Messenger, for example, you won't be able to communicate with someone running AOL Instant Messenger. That means you'll be messaging with other users of the same program you're using.

Depending on your computer configuration, you probably have either MSN Messenger or Windows Messenger installed on your new PC. (MSN Messenger is a version of Windows Messenger for users of the MSN online service.) We'll use Windows Messenger for our examples in this chapter, although all instant messaging programs work pretty much the same way.

> **caution**
>
> Instant messaging only works if both parties are online at the same time; you can't send an instant message to someone who isn't available.

Getting Connected

You launch Windows Messenger from the Windows Start menu. The first time you use the program, you need to sign up for Microsoft's .NET Messenger service. The sign-up is free and lets you choose your own unique sign-in name that other users will know you by. Click the Click Here to Sign In link to register; then follow the onscreen instructions.

Adding New Contacts

To send an instant message to another user, that person has to be on your Messenger contact list.

To add a contact to your list, follow these steps:

1. From within Messenger, click the Add a Contact link to launch the Add a Contact Wizard.

2. To add a contact manually, select By Email Address or Sign-In Name and click Next; when the next page appears, enter the user's email address, then click Next. If the user you specified has a Microsoft Passport, that contact will be added to your contact list; if not, you'll be notified.

3. To search for a contact, select the Search for a Contact option and click Next; when the next page appears, enter his or her first name, last name, and country, then select to search from either the Hotmail Member Directory or the address book on your hard disk, and click Next. Any users matching your search will now be listed; select the name you want to add and click Next to add them to your contact list.

After you add contacts to your list, they appear in the main Messenger window, as shown in Figure 26.1. Contacts who are currently online are listed in the Online section; those who aren't are listed as Not Online. To remove a contact from your list, right-click the name and then select Delete Contact.

FIGURE 26.1
Choose a contact to send an instant message to.

Sending a Message

To send an instant message to another user, follow these steps:

1. Double-click a name in your contact list to open the Conversation window, shown in Figure 26.2.

FIGURE 26.2

Send and receive instant messages via the Conversation window.

2. Enter your message in the lower part of the window.

3. Click the Send button (or press Enter).

Your message now appears in the top part of the window, as will your contact's reply. Continue talking like this, one message after another. Your entire conversation is displayed in the top part of the window, and you can scroll up to reread earlier messages.

Receiving a Message

When someone else sends you an instant message, Windows lets out a little bleeping sound and then displays an alert in the lower-right corner of your screen. To open and reply to the message, click the alert. (Naturally, you have to be connected to the Internet to receive these messages.)

If you happen to miss the alert, Windows displays a flashing message button in the taskbar. You can click this button to read your message.

Chatting with Friends Online

An online chat is different from an instant message. Whereas instant messaging describes a one-to-one conversation between two users, online chat involves real-time discussions between large groups of users. These chats take place in public *chat rooms* (sometimes called *chat channels*).

You can find chat rooms at any number of Web sites, accessible via Internet Explorer or any other Web browser.

Chatting at Yahoo!

One of the most popular chat sites is Yahoo! Chat, which is part of the giant Yahoo! portal. You access Yahoo! Chat by clicking the Chat link on the Yahoo! home page or by going directly to chat.yahoo.com.

The main Yahoo! Chat page is your home page for all of Yahoo!'s chat activities. From here you can access featured chat rooms and chat events or click the Complete Room List link for a list of all available Yahoo! Chat rooms.

tip

The first time you visit Yahoo! Chat, you'll be prompted for your Yahoo! ID and password; if you don't yet have a Yahoo! ID, take this opportunity to register. (It's free.)

After you select a chat room, Yahoo! loads special chat software into your Web browser. This is done automatically, and takes just a few minutes.

When you enter a chat room, you see the screen shown in Figure 26.3. All messages are displayed in the Chat pane; everyone chatting in the room is listed in the Chatters pane.

FIGURE 26.3

A typical Yahoo! chat room— enter a message in the Send box, and then chat away!

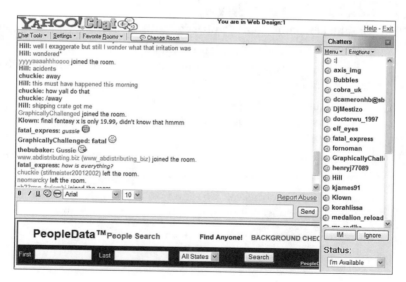

You enter your messages in the Send box and then click the Send button or press Enter to send the message to the room. After you send a message, it appears in the Chat pane, listed in-line with all the other messages.

Everybody else in your chat room is listed in the Chatters list. In addition, you can display a list of all the participants in every Yahoo! Chat room by clicking the Who's Chatting button in the Tools section.

If you want to change chat rooms, click the Change Room button in the Tools section. When you click this button, Yahoo! displays the chat room list; click a room name to change to that room.

Other Chat Sites

If you're serious about online chat, you might want to check out some of the other major chat communities on the Web. These sites include

- Excite Super Chat (chat.excite.com)
- Internet TeleCafe (www.telecafe.com)
- MSN Chat (chat.msn.com)
- Talk City (www.talkcity.com)

If you're a subscriber to America Online, you can also access AOL's proprietary chat rooms. These are some of the busiest chat rooms on the Internet, and they're reserved exclusively for AOL members.

THE ABSOLUTE MINIMUM

Here are the key points to remember from this chapter:

- Where email is great for longer, more formal messages, instant messaging is better for short one-on-one conversations—and Internet chat is good for more public discussions.
- There are many different incompatible instant messaging networks, including AOL Instant Messenger, ICQ, MSN/Windows Messenger, and Yahoo! Messenger.
- To message another user, you both must be online at the same time, using the same instant messaging software.
- Internet chat rooms can be found on many different Web sites, such as Yahoo! Chat—as well as part of the America Online service.

27

USING NEWSGROUPS, MESSAGE BOARDS, AND BLOGS

The Internet is a great way for people with special interests to gather and exchange ideas. Whether you're into model trains, European soccer, or soap operas, you can find a legion of similar fans online.

There are three primary types of *online communities*: newsgroups, message boards, and blogs. The best way to think of these communities is that they're like old-fashioned bulletin boards. A user begins by posting a message regarding a specific topic. Other members of the community respond to that message and post replies. Before long you have a intricate *thread* of messages, all branching out from that initial posting.

So go online and learn how to interact with others who share your specific interests. Chances are, there's an online community waiting just for you—and it's no further away than your computer keyboard.

Reading and Posting to Usenet Newsgroups

Usenet is a subset of the overall Internet, and its host to more than 30,000 topic-specific *newsgroups*. A newsgroup is kind of like an online bulletin board where users post messages (called *articles*) about a variety of topics; other users read and respond to these articles. The result is a kind of ongoing, freeform discussion, in which hundreds of users can participate.

You use a *newsreader* program to access Usenet newsgroups. Outlook Express, the email program we discussed back in Chapter 25, "Sending and Receiving Email," doubles as a newsreader.

Reading Newsgroup Articles

If you're using Outlook Express, you access Usenet newsgroups by clicking the icon in the folder list for your particular news server. Now click the Newsgroups button on the Outlook Express toolbar; this opens the Newsgroups dialog box, which lists all available newsgroups.

When you find a newsgroup you want to read, select it and click the Go To button. All the articles from that newsgroup will now appear in Outlook Express's Message pane, as shown in Figure 27.1. Click a message header to read the contents of that article in the Preview pane.

By the way, a newsgroup name looks a little like a Web site address, with single words or phrases separated by periods. Newsgroup names are more logical, however, in that each break in the name signifies a different subset of the major topic. For example, the `rec.arts.cinema` group tells you that the newsgroup is in the *recreational* section of Usenet and that it discusses the *art* of the *cinema*.

tip

When you're communicating in one of these online forums, you need to follow proper *netiquette*. This includes not writing in ALL CAPITAL LETTERS; not posting off-topic messages; not *cross-posting* the message in multiple forums; not advertising or spamming; and, above all else, using common courtesy.

note

Outlook Express should have been set up for your newsgroup server when you first configured your computer for your specific Internet service provider.

FIGURE 27.1
Reading articles
in a Usenet
newsgroup.

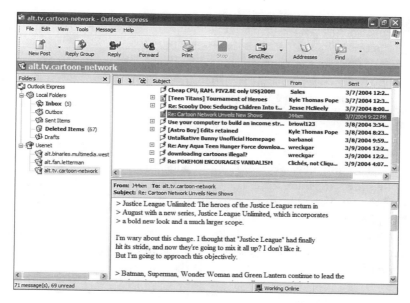

Creating and Posting Newsgroup Articles

To reply to a newsgroup article, select the message in the Message pane and then click the Reply button. To create a new article, click the New Post button. Enter your message in the New Message window, and then click the Send button to post the message to the current newsgroup.

tip

If you're interested in viewing older Usenet articles, you can search the newsgroup archives housed at the Google Groups Web site (groups.google.com).

Participating in Web-Based Message Boards

Web-based message boards are similar to Usenet newsgroups in that they let you post and read messages related to a specific topic. They differ from newsgroups in that they're not part of an Internet-wide network; message boards are tied to specific Web sites.

There are thousands of Web sites that offer topic-specific message boards. Most message boards work in a similar fashion, so we'll look at the largest message host—Yahoo! Message Boards—to learn how message boards work.

Using Yahoo! Message Boards

To access Yahoo! Message Boards, click the Message Boards link on the Yahoo! home page, or go directly to `messages.yahoo.com`. When the Yahoo! Message Boards page appears, you can choose to browse for boards by category, or search for a specific board.

After you've selected a specific message board, you'll see the message board's main page, like the one shown in Figure 27.2. The theme of the board (in the form of a "starter" message) is sometimes displayed at the top of the page; all the message threads are listed (by topic) below the Topic heading. Click a topic to read the first message in a thread.

FIGURE 27.2

Reading the messages at Yahoo! Message Boards.

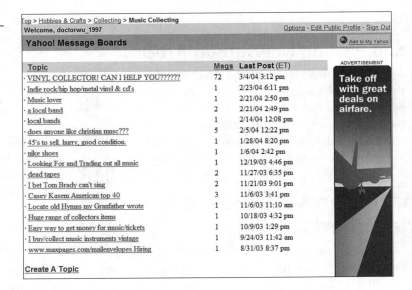

Top > Hobbies & Crafts > Collecting > **Music Collecting**
Welcome, doctorwu_1997   Options - Edit Public Profile - Sign Out

Yahoo! Message Boards   Add to My Yahoo

Topic	Msgs	Last Post (ET)
· VINYL COLLECTOR! CAN I HELP YOU??????	72	3/4/04 3:12 pm
· Indie rock/hip hop/metal vinyl & cd's	1	2/23/04 6:11 pm
· Music lover	1	2/21/04 2:50 pm
· a local band	2	2/21/04 2:49 pm
· local bands	1	2/14/04 12:08 pm
· does anyone like christian musc???	5	2/5/04 12:22 pm
· 45's to sell. hurry, good condition.	1	1/28/04 8:20 pm
· nike shoes	1	1/6/04 2:42 pm
· Looking For and Trading out all music	1	12/19/03 4:46 pm
· dead tapes	2	11/27/03 6:35 pm
· I bet Tom Brady can't sing	2	11/21/03 9:01 pm
· Casey Kasem American top 40	3	11/6/03 3:41 pm
· Locate old Hymns my Granfather wrote	1	11/6/03 11:10 am
· Huge range of collectors items	1	10/18/03 4:32 pm
· Easy way to get money for music/tickets	1	10/9/03 1:29 pm
· I buy/collect music instruments vintage	1	9/24/03 11:42 am
· www.maxpages.com/mailenvelopes Hiring	1	8/31/03 8:37 pm

Create A Topic

ADVERTISEMENT

Take off with great deals on airfare.

Each message in the thread appears in its own page. Click the Next link to read the next message in the thread; click the Previous link to back up and read the previous message. To reply publicly to a message, click the Reply link; to send a private email to the author of the message, click the author's name.

To post a new message in a new thread, click the Create a Topic link on the main message board page. When the next page appears, enter a subject for your message in the Type Message Subject box, and then enter the text of your message in the Type Message box. When you're ready to send your message, click the Post Message button; remember, any message you post will be visible to anyone visiting this message board!

Where to Find Message Boards

There are several different portals, like Yahoo! Message Boards, that offer a collection of message boards. The most popular of these are Excite Message Boards (boards.excite.com) and ezboard (www.ezboard.com).

You can also find message boards on many topic-specific Web sites. For example, Ancestry.com (www.ancestry.com), a big genealogy site, offers genealogy-focused message boards; the ABC News site (abcnews.go.com) offers messages boards to discuss news stories and current events.

Similar to message boards are *group communities*. These sites typically offer message boards as part of a larger set of community functions, such as chat, instant messaging, photo albums, file hosting, and the like. The two most popular group communities are MSN Groups (groups.msn.com) and Yahoo! Groups (groups.yahoo.com).

Joining the Blog Community

The newest type of Web community is called a *Weblog*, or just *blog* for short. Blogs are personal Web sites, like the one in Figure 27.3, that are updated frequently with commentary, links to other sites, and anything else the author might be interested in. Many blogs also let visitors post their comments, resulting in a community that is very similar to that of a message board.

There are literally tens of thousands of blogs on the Web, covering just about any topic you can think of. To find a particular blog, check out the following blog directories:

- Blog Search Engine (www.blogsearchengine.com)
- Blogger (www.blogger.com)
- BlogHop (www.bloghop.com)
- Daypop (www.daypop.com)
- Feedster (www.feedster.com)

tip

If you want to create your own blog, many Web site hosting communities offer blogging features. Learn more in Chapter 29, "Creating Your Own Web Page."

- Globe of Blogs (www.globeofblogs.com)
- Weblogs.com (www.weblogs.com)

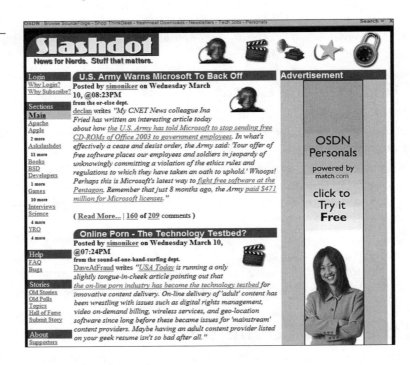

THE ABSOLUTE MINIMUM

Here are the key points to remember from this chapter:

- Usenet is a collection of more than 30,000 topic-specific newsgroups that you access with a newsreader program, such as Outlook Express.

- Web-based message boards are similar to physical bulletin boards, in that they enable users to exchange messages about a common topic.

- Community groups such as MSN Groups and Yahoo! Groups offer message boards in conjunction with other features, such as chat, photo albums, and file hosting.

- Blogs are Web sites updated constantly with personal commentary and links to other sites.

28

DOWNLOADING FILES

The Internet is a huge repository for computer files of all shapes and sizes, from utilities that help you better manage your disk drive to full-featured email and newsgroup programs. There are hundreds of thousands of these programs available *somewhere* on the Internet; if you can find them, you can download them to your computer.

Many of the programs you find online are available free; these programs are called *freeware*. Other programs can be downloaded for no charge, but they require you to pay a token amount to receive full functionality or documentation; these programs are called *shareware*. (Both types of programs are in contrast to the software you buy in boxes at your local computer retailer, which is *commercial software*.)

Finding Files Online

Before you can use any of the programs available online, you first have to find them and then download them from their current locations to your PC. There are some variations to the procedure, but overall, it's pretty straightforward. In a nutshell, all you have to do is the following:

1. Create a special download folder on your computer's hard drive—typically in the My Documents folder

2. Find and download the file you want.

3. If the file was compressed (with a ZIP extension), decompress the file using Windows XP Extraction Wizard, as discussed in Chapter 6, "Working with Files and Folders."

4. If the file you downloaded was a software program, you'll need to install the software. Installation instructions are usually included somewhere on the download information page or in a readme file included with the file download. In most cases, installation involves running a file named setup.exe or install.exe; after the setup program launches, follow the onscreen instructions to complete the installation.

5. Delete the compressed file you originally downloaded.

caution

If you download files from less-recognized Web sites, you might be at risk of downloading a file infected with a computer virus. To learn more about viruses, see Chapter 30, "Protecting Your PC from Viruses, Spam, and Other Nuisances."

Downloading from a File Archive

Where do you find all these wonderful files to download? The best places to look are Web sites dedicated to file downloading. These sites are called *file archives*, and they typically store a huge variety of freeware and shareware programs and utilities.

Downloading a file from any of these archives is typically easy. Once you locate the file you want, you're prompted to click a specific link to begin the download. Some sites will begin the download automatically; other sites will prompt Windows to display a dialog box asking if you want to save or open the file (you want to save it), and where you want to save it. Follow the onscreen instructions to begin the download.

When you're looking for files to download, here are some of the best download repositories on the Internet:

- Download.com (download.cnet.com)
- IT Pro Downloads (www.itprodownloads.com)
- Jumbo (www.jumbo.com)
- Tucows (www.tucows.com)

Figure 28.1 shows the main page at Tucows, one of the most popular of these download sites. Just look at all the different types of software you can download!

There are several good reasons to download from one of these well-established sites. First, they all have really big collections; the more files available, the more likely it is you'll find what you're looking for. Second, they all make the download process relatively easy. And third, they all check their files for viruses before offering them to the public. In other words, these sites make downloading safe and easy.

Downloading Files from Any Web Page

You don't necessarily have to go to a software archive to find files to download. You can actually download files you find on any Web page—especially graphics files. That's because if you see a pretty picture on a page, that picture is actually a graphics file; any background on a Web page is also a file. And any graphics file on a Web page can be downloaded to your PC.

To download a graphics file from a Web page, all you have to do is right-click the picture and select Save Picture As from the pop-up menu. When prompted, select a location for the file, then click Save. The graphics file will now be downloaded to the location you specified.

If a Web page contains a link to a file (of any type), you can download that file directly from the link—without actually jumping to the file. Just right-click the link to the file and select Save Target As from the pop-up menu. When prompted, select a location for the file, and then click Save to start the download.

THE ABSOLUTE MINIMUM

Here are the key points to remember from this chapter:

- The Internet is a great place to find computer software and utilities of all different types—many of which are available free.

- The best places to find files to download are the major software download archives, such as Tucows and Download.com.

- You can download any graphic you find on any Web page, by right-clicking the picture and selecting Save Picture As from the pop-up menu.

29

CREATING YOUR OWN WEB PAGE

It seems like everybody and their brother has their own personal Web pages these days. If you want to keep up with the Joneses (and the Smiths and the Berkowitzes), you need to create a personal Web page of your own.

All Web pages are based on a special programming code, called Hypertext Markup Language (HTML). Fortunately, you don't need to learn HTML to create a simple Web page. That's because there are a number of software programs and Web sites that make it easy to generate good-looking pages without you having to learn any fancy programming.

Building a Web Page at a Home Page Community

If you want a one-stop solution to creating and hosting your own Web pages, turn to one of the major *home page communities* on the Web. These sites not only help you create your own Web pages, they even host your pages on the Web. And, in many cases, this basic hosting service is free!

Visiting the Communities

The most popular of these home page communities include

- Angelfire (angelfire.lycos.com)
- Tripod (www.tripod.lycos.com)
- Yahoo! GeoCities (geocities.yahoo.com)

Many Internet service providers also offer free personal home pages to their subscribers; check with your ISP to see what services are available. In addition, if you're an America Online member, you can avail yourself of the AOL Hometown home page community. (AOL Hometown is accessible from within the AOL service, or on the Web at hometown.aol.com.)

tip

Both Angelfire and Tripod offer tools for building and hosting your own personal weblog, or blog. Learn more about blogs in Chapter 27, "Using Newsgroups, Message Boards, and Blogs."

Creating a Home Page at Yahoo! GeoCities

The oldest—and the largest—home page community is Yahoo! GeoCities, shown in Figure 29.1. The site offers several different ways to build a page:

- **Yahoo! PageWizards.** The easiest way to build a simple Web page; just answer a few questions and the form-based engine will generate your page automatically.

- **Yahoo! PageBuilder.** PageBuilder is a Java-based application that runs on your desktop while you're online, and provides a step-by-step page-building environment. You pick a category and a template for your page, and then modify the template for your own personal needs.

- **HTML Editor.** If you want to create more sophisticated Web pages, you have to get down and dirty with the underlying HTML code. Yahoo! GeoCities provides the Advanced Editor, just for this purpose. You can enter HTML code directly into the Advanced Editor window; GeoCities converts that code into a finished Web page.

FIGURE 29.1

Yahoo! GeoCities: The largest home page community on the Internet.

The easiest way to create a simple Web page is to use the PageWizard feature. Just follow these steps:

1. Click the Yahoo! PageWizards link on the Yahoo! GeoCities home page.

2. When the Yahoo! PageWizards page appears, as shown in Figure 29.2, click the page design you want to use.

FIGURE 29.2

As simple as filling in a form: Yahoo! PageWizards.

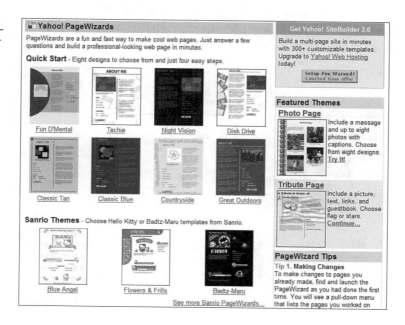

3. A new Quick Start Web Page Wizard window will now appear on your desktop. Press the Begin button to proceed.

4. When the Choose a Look for Your Page page appears, select a style for your page. (The style you originally selected should be checked; you can continue with this style, or change to another style.) Click the Next button to proceed.

5. When the Enter Your Page Title and Text page appears, enter a title to appear at the top of your page, and then enter the text to appear in the body of your page. Click the Next button to proceed.

6. When the Pick Your Picture page appears, click the Browse button to select a picture file from your hard disk, then enter a caption for the picture. (If you want to use the stock picture for this page style, skip this step without selecting a picture.) Click the Next button to proceed.

7. When the Enter Your Favorite Links page appears, enter up to four other Web sites (both the name and the address). Click the Next button to proceed.

8. When the Enter Your Information page appears, enter your name and email address. If you use Yahoo! Instant Messenger and want your Web page to display a graphic when you're online, click the Put This On My Page option. Click the Next button to proceed.

9. When the Name Your Page page appears, enter a name for your page. (This will appear as part of the page's URL.) Click the Next button to complete the process.

The wizard now displays a Congratulations page. The URL for your new page will be displayed here; write it down for future reference, or click the link to view your page. Figure 29.3 shows the kind of page you can create with the PageWizard.

FIGURE 29.3
A personal Web page created with the Yahoo! PageWizard.

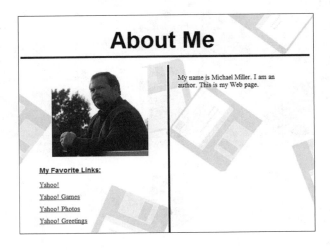

Using Page-Building Software

The Web page you create at Yahoo! GeoCities is a relatively simple one. If you want to create more sophisticated pages—or multiple pages, in a complete Web site—you need a more powerful tool. Fortunately, there are numerous software programs available you can use to build really fancy Web pages.

Here's a short list of some of the most popular page-building software available today:

- Adobe GoLive (www.adobe.com)
- Dreamweaver (www.macromedia.com)
- Microsoft FrontPage (www.microsoft.com/frontpage/)

Figure 29.4 shows Microsoft FrontPage, one of the most popular page builder programs. FrontPage lets you build everything from simple personal pages to sophisticated e-commerce Web sites—and it's easy to use, thanks to its Office-like interface.

tip

You can edit any pages you created with PageWizard with Yahoo! PageBuilder. Just relaunch PageBuilder, click the Open button, and select the page you want to edit.

FIGURE 29.4

Build sophisticated Web pages and sites with Microsoft FrontPage.

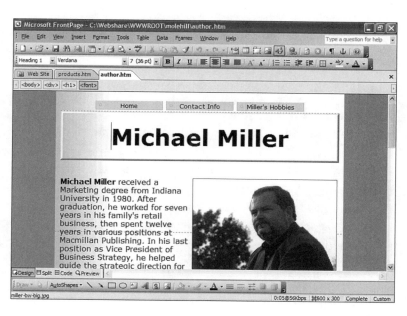

Uploading Your Pages

Web pages with one of these software programs, you still have to find a site on the Web to host your pages. Yahoo! GeoCities and the other home page communities offer separate page hosting services (usually for a fee), geared towards personal Web pages. If you need a host for a complete Web site (or for small business purposes), you should probably examine a service that specializes in more sophisticated Web site hosting.

A Web site hosting service will manage all aspects of your Web site. For a monthly fee, you'll receive a fixed amount of space on their servers, your own Web site address (and your own personal domain, if you want to pay for it), and a variety of site management tools. Pricing for these services typically start at $10 or so a month, and goes up from there.

The best way to look for a Web site host is to access a directory of hosting services. Most of these directories let you search for hosts by various parameters, including monthly cost, disk space provided, programming and platforms supported, and extra features offered. Among the best of these host search sites are the following:

- HostIndex.com (www.hostindex.com)
- HostSearch (www.hostsearch.com)
- TopHosts.com (www.tophosts.com)
- Web Hosters (www.webhosters.com)

THE ABSOLUTE MINIMUM

Here are the key points to remember from this chapter:

- Web pages are built using the HTML programming language—although you don't have to know how to program to create a simple Web page.
- To create a personal Web page, check out one of the large page building communities, such as Yahoo! GeoCities.
- To create a more sophisticated Web page or Web site, use a dedicated page building program, such as Microsoft FrontPage.

30

PROTECTING YOUR PC FROM VIRUSES, SPAM, AND OTHER NUISANCES

When you connect your PC to the Internet, you open up a whole new world of adventure and information for you and your family. Unfortunately, you also open up a new world of potential dangers— viruses, spam, computer attacks, and more.

Fortunately, it's easy to protect your computer and your family from these dangers. All you need are a few software utilities—and a lot of common sense!

Safeguarding Your System from Computer Viruses

A *computer virus* is a malicious software program designed to do damage to your computer system by deleting files or even taking over your PC to launch attacks on other systems. A virus attacks your computer when you launch an infected software program, launching a "payload" that oftentimes is catastrophic.

Signs of Infection

How do you know whether your computer system has been infected with a virus?

In general, whenever your computer starts acting different from normal, it's possible that you have a virus. You might see strange messages or graphics displayed on your computer screen or find that normally well-behaved programs are acting erratically. You might discover that certain files have gone missing from your hard disk or that your system is acting sluggish—or failing to start at all. You might even find that your friends are receiving emails from you (that you never sent) that have suspicious files attached.

If your computer exhibits one or more of these symptoms—especially if you've just downloaded a file from the Internet or received a suspicious email message—the prognosis is not good. Your computer is probably infected.

How to Catch a Virus

Whenever you share data with another computer or computer user, you risk exposing your computer to potential viruses. There are many ways you can share data and many ways a virus can be transmitted:

- Opening an infected file attached to an email message
- Launching an infected program file downloaded from the Internet
- Sharing a floppy disk that contains an infected file
- Sharing a computer file over a network that contains an infected file

Of all these methods, the most common means of virus infection is via email. Whenever you open a file attached to an email message, you stand a good chance of infecting your computer system with a virus—even if the file was sent by someone you know and trust. That's because many viruses "spoof" the sender's name, thus making you think the file is from a friend or colleague. The bottom line is that no email attachment is safe unless you were expressly expecting it.

Practicing Safe Computing

Because you're not going to completely quit doing any of these activities, you'll never be 100% safe from the threat of computer viruses. There are, however, some steps you can take to reduce your risk:

- Don't open email attachments from people you don't know—or even from people you *do* know, if you aren't expecting them.
- Share disks and files only with users you know and trust.
- Download files only from reliable Web sites.
- Don't execute programs you find in Usenet newsgroups.
- Don't click links sent to you from strangers via instant messaging or in a chat room.
- Use antivirus software.

These precautions—especially the first one about not opening email attachments—should provide good insurance against the threat of computer viruses.

caution

If you remember nothing else from this chapter, remember this: *Never open an unexpected file attachment.* Period!

Disinfecting Your System with Antivirus Software

Antivirus software programs are capable of detecting known viruses and protecting your system against new, unknown viruses. These programs check your system for viruses each time your system is booted and can be configured to check any programs you download from the Internet. They're also used to disinfect your system if it becomes infected with a virus.

The most popular antivirus programs include

- Kaspersky Anti-Virus Personal (www.kaspersky.com)
- McAfee VirusScan (www.mcafee.com)
- Norton AntiVirus (www.symantec.com)
- PC-cillin (www.trendmicro.com)

Whichever antivirus program you choose (Norton AntiVirus is shown in Figure 30.1), you'll need to go online periodically to update the virus definition database the program uses to look for known virus files. As new viruses are created every week, this file of known viruses must be updated accordingly.

caution

Your antivirus software is next to useless if you don't update it at least weekly. An outdated antivirus program won't be capable of recognizing—and protecting against—the very latest computer viruses.

FIGURE 30.1

Use Norton
AntiVirus to
protect against
computer
viruses.

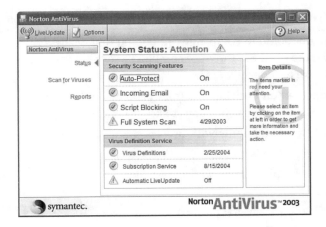

Fighting Email Spam

Viruses aren't the only annoying things delivered via email. If you're like most users, well over half the messages delivered to your email inbox are unsolicited, unauthorized, and unwanted—in other words, *spam*. These spam messages are the online equivalent of the junk mail you receive in your postal mailbox, and it's a huge problem.

Although it's probably impossible to do away with 100% of the spam you receive (you can't completely stop junk mail, either), there are steps you can take to reduce the amount of spam you have to deal with. The heavier your spam load, the more steps you can take.

Protecting Your Email Address

Spammers accumulate email addresses via a variety of methods. Some use high-tech methods to harvest email addresses listed on public Web pages and message board postings. Others use the tried-and-true approach of buying names from list brokers. Still others automatically generate addresses using a "dictionary" of common names and email domains.

One way to reduce the amount of spam you receive is to limit the public use of your email address. It's a simple fact: The more you expose your email address, the more likely it is that a spammer will find it—and use it.

To this end, you should avoid putting your email address on your Web page, or your company's Web page. You should also avoid including your email address in any postings you make to Web-based message boards or Usenet newsgroups. In addition, you should most definitely not include your email address in any of the conversations you have in chat rooms or via instant messaging.

Another strategy is to actually use *two* email addresses. Take your main email address (the one you get from your ISP) and hand it out only to a close circle of friends and family; do *not* use this address to post any public messages or to register at any Web sites. Then obtain a second email address (you can get a free one at www.hotmail.com or mail.yahoo.com) and use that one for all your public activity. When you post on a message board or newsgroup, use the second address. When you order something from an online merchant, use the second address. When you register for Web site access, use the second address. Over time, the second address will attract the spam; your first email address will remain private and relatively spam-free.

Blocking Spammers in Outlook Express

If you use Outlook Express, you can manually block messages from known spammers by using the Blocked Senders List feature. When you receive a spam message in your inbox, just tell Outlook Express to ignore all future messages from this spammer.

All you have to do is select the message from the sender you want to block, and then select Message, Block Sender. In the future, all messages from this sender will automatically deleted.

Fighting Spam with Microsoft Outlook

An even better spam fighter is built into Microsoft Outlook 2003, the email program that comes with Microsoft Office 2003. Outlook's spam-blocking feature alone might be worth upgrading from Outlook Express to Outlook 2003.

You access Outlook's anti-spam tools by selecting Actions, Junk E-Mail, Junk E-Mail Options. This opens the Junk E-Mail Options dialog box, shown

tip

If you do have to leave your email address in a public forum, you can insert a *spamblock* into your address—an unexpected word or phrase that, although easily removed, will confuse the software spammers use to harvest addresses. For example, if your email address is johnjones@myisp.com, you might change the address to read johnSPAMBLOCKjones@myisp.com. Other users will know to remove the SPAMBLOCK from the address before emailing you, but the spam harvesting software will be foiled.

note

Outlook Express doesn't actually block any email messages; the messages are still received by your computer, but sent immediately to the Delete folder—where they can still be viewed until you delete the contents of the folder.

in Figure 30.2. Select the Options tab to view the level of spam protection available. You can choose from the following options:

FIGURE 30.2

Activating
Microsoft
Outlook's
spam-blocking
features.

- **No Automatic Filtering.** Turns off Outlook's spam filter.
- **Low.** Blocks the most obvious spam messages.
- **High.** Blocks the majority of spam messages—but might also block some non-spam email.
- **Safe Lists Only**. Blocks all email except messages from people on your Safe Senders List.

You can also have Outlook block messages from specific senders. Just select a message from a sender you want to block, and then select Actions, Junk E-Mail, Add Sender to Blocked Senders List.

> **tip**
>
> For most users, I recommend the High option; it will catch a high percentage of spam with minimal blocking of regular messages. You can minimize the downside by telling Outlook not to block messages from people in your Contacts list. Just select the Safe Senders tab in the Junk E-Mail Options dialog box and click the Also Trust E-Mail From My Contacts option.

Using Anti-Spam Software

If the amount of spam in your inbox becomes particularly onerous, you might want to consider using an anti-spam software program. Most anti-spam software uses some combination of spam blocking or content filtering to keep spam messages from ever reaching your inbox; their effectiveness varies, but they will decrease the amount of spam you receive to some degree.

The most popular anti-spam software includes

- ANT 4 MailChecking (www.ant4.com)
- MailWasher (www.mailwasher.net)
- Norton AntiSpam (www.symantec.com)
- RoadBlock (www.roadblock.net)
- SpamKiller (www.mcafee.com)

Hunting Down Spyware

Another growing nuisance is the proliferation of *spyware* programs. These are programs that install themselves on your computer and then surreptitiously send information about the way you use your PC to some interested third party. Spyware typically gets installed in the background when you're installing another program. One of the biggest sources of spyware are KaZaA and other peer-to-peer music-trading networks; when you install the file-trading software, the spyware is also installed.

note

Learn more about music-trading networks in Chapter 33, "Downloading and Playing Digital Music."

Having spyware on your system is nasty, almost as bad as being infected with a computer virus. Some spyware programs will even hijack your computer and launch pop-up windows and advertisements when you visit certain Web pages. If there's spyware on your computer, you definitely want to get rid of it.

Unfortunately, most antivirus programs won't catch spyware because spyware isn't a virus. To track down and uninstall these programs, then, you need to run an anti-spyware utility, such as Spybot Search & Destroy (shown in Figure 30.3).

Here are some of the best of these spyware fighters:

- Ad-Aware (www.lavasoftusa.com)
- McAfee AntiSpyware (www.mcafee.com)
- Spy Sweeper (www.webroot.com)
- Spybot Search & Destroy (www.safer-networking.org)

FIGURE 30.3

Finding hidden spyware programs with Spybot Search & Destroy.

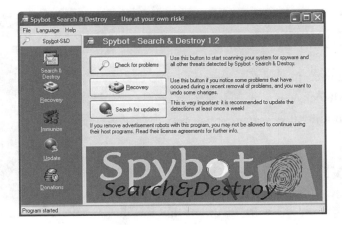

Defending Against Computer Attacks

Connecting to the Internet is a two-way street—not only can your PC access other computers online, but other computers can also access *your* PC. Which means that, unless you take proper precautions, malicious hackers can read your private data, damage your system hardware and software, and even use your system (via remote control) to cause damage to other computers.

You protect your system against outside attack by blocking the path of attack with a *firewall*. A firewall is a software program that forms a virtual barrier between your computer and the Internet. The firewall selectively filters the data that is passed between both ends of the connection and protects your system against outside attack.

caution

The risk of outside attack is even more pronounced if you have an always-on connection, such as that offered with DSL and cable modems.

Using the Windows XP Internet Connection Firewall

If you're running Windows XP, you already have a firewall program installed on your system. You can make sure that Windows' Internet Connection Firewall is activated by following these steps:

1. Click the Windows Start button to display the Start menu.

2. Select Connect To, Show All Connections to open the Network Connections folder.

3. Right-click the connection you use for your ISP and select Properties from the pop-up menu; this displays the Properties dialog box.

4. Select the Advanced tab.

5. Make sure that the Internet Connection Firewall option is checked.

Using Third-Party Firewall Software

A number of third-party firewall programs are also available—most of which are more robust and offer more protection than Windows XP's built-in firewall. The best of these programs include

- ■ BlackICE (blackice.iss.net)
- ■ Kerio Personal Firewall (www.kerio.com)
- ■ McAfee Personal Firewall (www.mcafee.com)
- ■ Norton Personal Firewall (www.symantec.com)
- ■ Sygate Personal Firewall (www.sygate.com)
- ■ ZoneAlarm (www.zonelabs.com)

Shielding Your Children from Inappropriate Content

The Internet contains an almost limitless supply of information on its tens of billions of Web pages. Although most of these pages contain useful information, it's a sad fact that the content of some pages can be quite offensive to some people—and that there are some Internet users who prey on unsuspecting youths.

As a responsible parent, you want to protect your children from any of the bad stuff (and bad people) online, while still allowing access to all the good stuff. How do you do this?

Using Content Filtering Software

If you can't trust your children to always click away from inappropriate Web content, you can choose to install software on your computer that performs filtering functions for all your online sessions. These safe-surfing programs guard against either a preselected list of inappropriate sites or a preselected list of topics—and then block access to sites that meet the selected criteria. Once you have the software installed, your kids won't be able to access the really bad sites on the Web.

The most popular filtering programs include

- Cybersitter (www.cybersitter.com)
- Net Nanny (www.netnanny.com)
- Norton Internet Security (www.symantec.com)
- SurfControl (www.surfcontrol.com)

Kids-Safe Searching

If you don't want to go to all the trouble of using content filtering software, you can at least steer your children to some of the safer sites on the Web. The best of these sites offer kid-safe searching so that all inappropriate sites are filtered out of the search results.

The best of these kids-safe search and directory sites include

- AltaVista—AV Family Filter (www.altavista.com; go to the Settings page and click the Family Filter link)
- Ask Jeeves for Kids (www.ajkids.com)
- Fact Monster (www.factmonster.com)
- Google SafeSearch (www.google.com; go to the Preferences page then choose a SafeSearch Filtering option)
- Yahooligans! (www.yahooligans.com)

> **tip**
>
> If you're an America Online subscriber, check out AOL's built-in (and very effective) Parental Controls feature. You can select different filtering options for different AOL screen names and choose from four age-rated categories—Kids Only (12 and under), Young Teen (13-15), Mature Teen (16-17), and General Access (18+).

> **tip**
>
> Kids-safe search sites are often good to use as the start page for your children's browser because they are launching pads to guaranteed safe content.

Encouraging Safe Computing

Although you using content-filtering software and kids-safe Web sites are good steps, the most important thing you can do, as a parent, is to create an environment that encourages appropriate use of the Internet. Nothing replaces traditional parental supervision, and at the end of the day, you have to take responsibility for your children's online activities. Provide the guidance they need to make the Internet a fun and educational place to visit—and your entire family will be better for it.

Here are some guidelines you can follow to ensure a safer surfing experience for your family:

- Make sure that your children know never to give out any identifying information (home address, school name, telephone number, and so on) or to send their photos to other users online.

- Provide each of your children with an online pseudonym so they don't have to use their real names online.

- Don't let your children arrange face-to-face meetings with other computer users without parental permission and supervision. If a meeting is arranged, make the first one in a public place and be sure to accompany your child.

- Teach your children that people online might not always be who they seem; just because someone says that she's a 10-year-old girl doesn't necessarily mean that she really is 10 years old, or a girl.

- Consider making Internet surfing an activity you do together with your younger children—or turn it into a family activity by putting your kids' PC in a public room (such as a living room or den) rather than in a private bedroom.

- Set reasonable rules and guidelines for your kids' computer use. Consider limiting the number of minutes/hours they can spend online each day.

- Monitor your children's Internet activities. Ask them to keep a log of all Web sites they visit; oversee any chat sessions they participate in; check out any files they download; even consider sharing an email account (especially with younger children) so that you can oversee their messages.

- Don't let your children respond to messages that are suggestive, obscene, belligerent, or threatening—or that make them feel uncomfortable in any way. Encourage your children to tell you if they receive any such messages, and then report the senders to your ISP.

- Install content-filtering software on your PC, and set up one of the kid-safe search sites (discussed earlier in this section) as your browser's start page.

- Subscribe to America Online. AOL offers great filtering options for younger users; you can set up your kids' email accounts so that they can't receive files or pictures in their messages. AOL's filtering options can also be configured to keep younger users away from chat rooms and other inappropriate content both on AOL and the Web.

Teach your children that Internet access is not a right; it should be a privilege earned by your children and kept only when their use of it matches your expectations.

The Absolute Minimum

Here are the key points to remember from this chapter:

- Avoid computer viruses by not opening unsolicited email attachments and by using an anti-spam software program.

- Fight email spam by keeping your email address as private as possible, upgrading to Microsoft Outlook 2003, and using anti-spam software.

- Use anti-spyware tools to track down and remove spyware programs from your computer.

- Protect your computer from Internet-based attack by using a firewall program.

- To protect against inappropriate content on the Internet, install content filtering software—and make sure that your children use kids-safe Web sites.

PART VI

WORKING WITH MUSIC, MOVIES, AND PHOTOS

31

PLAYING CDS AND DVDS

Your personal computer can do more than just compute. It can also serve as a fully functional audio/video playback center.

That's right, you can use your PC to listen to your favorite audio CDs, and to watch the latest movies on DVD. Of course, the playback quality is limited by your PC's (small) speakers and (also small) screen, but it's a pretty convenient way to entertain yourself when you're working at the old keyboard.

Understanding CD/DVD Playback

In most cases, playing a CD or DVD is as simple as inserting a disc into your computer's CD or DVD drive. This should automatically launch a media player program, which should start playing your music or movie.

Which media player program you use depends on what's installed on your PC. Chances are your PC actually has multiple players installed, since most are available free. Some of the most popular media player programs include:

- Musicmatch Jukebox (www.musicmatch.com)
- RealPlayer (www.real.com)
- Sonique Media Player (sonique.lycos.com)
- UltraPlayer (www.ultraplayer.com)
- WinAmp (www.winamp.com)

Using Windows Media Player

For most users, however, the media player of choice is the one that comes free with Microsoft Windows. *Windows Media Player* (WMP) is a great little program you can use for many purposes—playing CDs and DVDS, ripping and burning CDs, listening to Internet radio broadcasts, and watching video Webcasts. It works similarly to most other media players, so if you know how to use WMP, you should be able to figure out any other media player program.

Whether you're playing a CD, DVD, or digital audio file, you use the controls located at the bottom of the WMP window, shown in Figure 31.1. These are the normal transport buttons you find on a cassette deck or VCR, including Play/Pause, Stop, Rewind, and Fast Forward. WMP also includes Next and Previous track buttons, along with a volume control and Mute button.

tip

By default, WMP is launched in its Full mode. If you'd rather display the player without all the extraneous controls, you can switch to the more compact Skin mode by clicking the Switch to Skin Mode button—or by pulling down the View menu and selecting Skin Mode. When you're in Skin mode, a small anchor window appears at the bottom left of your desktop; double-click this window to return to Full mode.

FIGURE 31.1
Playing CDs
and other audio
files with the
Windows Media
Player.

Taskbar   Video/Visualization Window

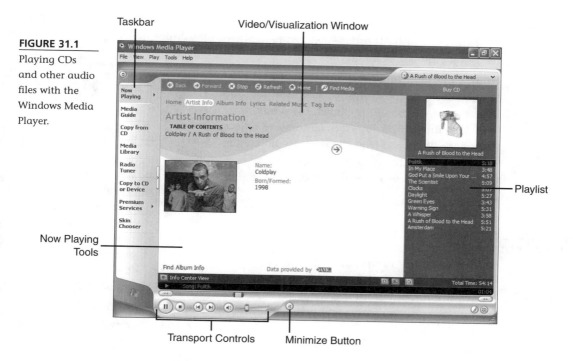

Now Playing
Tools

Transport Controls   Minimize Button

Playlist

The biggest part of the WMP window is the video/visualization window. When you're watching a DVD, this is where the movie appears. When you're listening to CDs or digital music, you can choose to have this area display information about the current album or artist (the info center view) or what Microsoft calls "visualizations." (Think of a visualization as a kind of "live" wallpaper that moves along with your music.) You can choose which visualizations are displayed by pulling down the View menu, selecting Visualizations, and then making a choice. If you'd rather see the album and artist info, select View, Info Center View, Always Show.

To the right of the video/visualization window is the Playlist area. Individual tracks of the CD or DVD are listed here. This area also displays the songs in any playlists that you create from the digital music files stored on your hard drive. (You'll learn more about playlists and digital music files in Chapter 33, "Downloading and Playing Digital Music.")

note

To display info center information, your computer must be connected to the Internet. WMP automatically goes out to the Internet to retrieve information about any commercial CD or DVD you're playing.

Between the playback controls and the video/visualization window is an area called the Now Playing Tools area. This area typically displays information about the currently playing CD or audio file.

Finally, the eight buttons along the left of the window (contained in what is called the Taskbar) link to key features of the player. Click a button and the entire player interface changes to reflect the selected feature—Now Playing, Media Guide, Copy from CD, Media Library, Radio Tuner, Copy to CD or Device, Premium Services, or Skin Chooser.

Playing a CD

If WMP doesn't start automatically when you load a CD into your PC's CD-ROM drive, you can launch it manually from the Windows Start menu. You can then start playback by clicking WMP's Play button.

To pause playback, click the Pause button (same as the Play button); click Play again to resume playback. To skip to the next track, click the Next button. To replay the last track, click the Previous button. You stop playback completely by clicking the Stop button.

Playing a DVD

If you have a DVD drive in your computer, it's a snap to use WMP to play DVD movies on your computer monitor.

Using Windows Media Player to Play DVDs

When you insert a DVD in your DVD drive, playback should start automatically. Your system should sense the presence of the DVD, launch Windows Media Player, and start playing the movie. (You can also initiate playback from within WMP by pulling down the Play menu and selecting DVD.)

As you can see in Figure 31.2, the picture from the DVD displays in WMP's video window. The individual tracks on the DVD are displayed in the Playlist area to the

> **tip**
>
> If the sound is too loud (or not loud enough), you can change the volume by dragging the Volume slider—to the right of the transport controls—to the right (louder) or left (softer). If you need to mute the sound quickly, click the Mute button to the left of the Volume slider. Click the Mute button again to unmute the sound.

> **tip**
>
> To play the songs on a CD in a random order, select Play, Shuffle—or click the Turn Shuffle On button. WMP will now shuffle randomly through the tracks on the CD.

right of the screen, and information about the DVD (including the DVD cover) is displayed beneath the video window.

FIGURE 31.2

FIGURE 31.2

Watching a
DVD movie with
Windows Media
Player.

Changing Display Size

You can watch your movie in WMP's video window,
or you can view the DVD using your entire computer screen. Just click the Full Screen button (at the
lower-right corner of the video window)—or select
View, Full Screen—and the movie will enlarge to fill
your entire screen. Press Esc to return to normal
viewing mode.

Navigating DVD Menus

Almost all DVDs come with their own built-in
menus. These menus typically lead you to special
features on the disc and allow you to select various
playback options and jump to specific scenes.

note

You have to be connected to the Internet for
WMP to find and display this DVD
information and cover art.

To display the DVD's main menu, select View, DVD Features, Title Menu. To display
the DVD's special features menu, pull down the View menu and select DVD Features,
Top Menu. When the special features menu is displayed, you can click any of the
options onscreen to jump to a particular feature.

Changing Audio Options

Many DVDs come with an English-language soundtrack, as well as soundtracks in other languages. Some DVDs come with different types of audio—mono, Dolby Pro Logic surround, Dolby Digital 5.1 surround, and so on. Other DVDs come with commentary from the film's director or stars on a separate audio track.

You can select which audio track you listen to by selecting View, DVD Features, Audio and Language Tracks. This displays a list of available audio options. Select the track you want to listen to, and then settle back to enjoy the movie.

Playing in Slow Motion—or Fast Motion

WMP provides a variety of special playback features. You can pause a still frame, advance frame-by-frame, or play the movie in slow or fast motion. To access these special playback features, select View, Now Playing Tools, DVD Controls. This displays a set of special controls in the Now Playing Tools area of the WMP window. Use these tools to vary the playback speed or pause the movie on a still frame.

Displaying Subtitles and Closed Captions

Many DVDs include subtitles in other languages. To turn on subtitles, select View, DVD Features, Subtitles and Captions, and then select which subtitles you want to view.

Other DVDs include closed captioning for the hearing impaired. You can view closed captions by selecting View, DVD Features, Subtitles and Captions, Closed Captions.

The Absolute Minimum

Here are the key points to remember from this chapter:

- To play CDs and DVDS on your PC, you use a media player program—such as Windows Media Player (WMP).
- WMP's transport controls (pause, fast forward, and so on) are just like those on a CD or DVD player.
- When WMP is connected to the Internet, it will automatically download information about the currently playing CD or DVD.
- When you're playing an audio CD, you can minimize WMP by switching to Skin mode; when you're playing a DVD you can maximize the movie by switching to full-screen mode.

IN THIS CHAPTER

- Understanding Digital Audio Formats
- Get the Right Software
- Ripping Songs from CD to Your PC
- Burning Your Own CDs

32

RIPPING AND BURNING CDS

Your computer's hard disk stores all sorts of information. Many users use their hard disks to store digital copies of their favorite songs. You can then play your digital music on your PC, using a music player program like Windows Media Player or Musicmatch Jukebox.

In addition, if you have a recordable CD drive (called a *CD burner*) in your computer system, you can make your own audio mix CDs. You can take any combination of songs on your hard disk and "burn" them onto a blank CD—and then play that CD in your home, car, or portable CD player. You can also use your PC to make copies of any CD you own.

And the good thing is, all of this is extremely easy to do. You don't have to be a geek to create your own computerized music library!

Understanding Digital Audio Formats

Anyone with a personal computer—and the right software—can make digital copies of music from CDs, and then store these copies on their computer's hard disk. These digital audio files can also be traded with other users, over the Internet.

We'll learn more about playing digital music in Chapter 33, "Downloading and Playing Digital Music." But before we get into the mechanics of creating your own digital music library, you need to understand the various audio file formats available for your use.

You see, there are many different ways to make a digital recording. Each format has its plusses and minuses, as described in Table 32.1.

Table 32.1   Digital Audio File Formats

Format	Pros	Cons
AAC	Compresses songs into small files	Not CD quality
	Used by Apple's iPod portable music player and iTunes software	Not compatible with many music player programs and portable music players
AIFF	CD quality	Large file size
		Not compatible with many music player programs and portable music players
MP3	Compresses songs into small files	Not CD quality
	The most universal of all audio file formats; compatible with virtually all music player programs and portable music players	
WAV	CD quality	Large file size
WMA	Compresses songs into small files	Not CD quality
	Used by most online music stores	Not compatible with Apple's iPod
	Compatible with most music player programs and portable music players	

Here's the lowdown. The AIFF and WAV formats are used to create commercial CDs, and therefore have the best sound quality. These formats result in extremely large files, however, which makes them inappropriate for downloading and use with portable music players.

The other three formats create much smaller files, at the expense of sound quality. These formats compress the sound to some degree, which is noticeable to some audiophiles—although you probably can't tell when listening via headphones or PC speakers.

Of these three formats, the MP3 format is the oldest and most universal; almost every music player program and portable music player is MP3-compatible. The WMA format was developed by Microsoft, and is used by most commercial online music stores; it's compatible with all music player programs except Apple's iTunes, and with all portable music players except Apple's iPod. The AAC format is Apple's proprietary format, and is used by both iTunes and iPod; it's not compatible with many other music player programs and portable music players.

If you're downloading music, you probably don't have a choice of formats; you have to take the music in the format that it's in. When you're copying files from your CD to your PC, however, you have your choice of format.

Get the Right Software

Before you start copying digital music files to and from CDs, you need to have the proper software installed on your PC. Fortunately, most of these programs are free downloads—and the ones that aren't don't cost that much.

Here are some of the most popular programs you can use for both burning and ripping digital audio files to and from CD:

- Magix MP3 Maker (www.magix.net)
- Musicmatch Jukebox (www.musicmatch.com)
- RealPlayer (www.real.com)
- RioPort Audio Manager (www.rioport.com)

Ripping Songs from CD to Your PC

If you have a decent compact disc collection and a CD-ROM drive in your computer system, you can make your own digital music files from the songs on your CDs. You can then listen to these files on your computer, transfer the files to a portable music player for listening on the go, share them with other users via the Internet, or use these files to burn your own custom mix CDs.

The process of copying files from a CD to your hard disk is called *ripping*. You use an enhanced digital music player program, such as Musicmatch Jukebox, to rip your files.

How Ripping Works

The ripping process is fairly simple. You start by inserting the CD you want to copy from into your PC's CD-ROM drive. Then you launch the ripper program and select which songs on your CD you want to rip. You'll also need to select the format for the final file (MP3, WAV, or WMA) and the *bit rate* you want to use for encoding; the higher the bit rate, the better the sound quality. (And the larger the file size!) After you've set up everything, click the appropriate button to start the encoding process.

caution

After you've started the ripping process, do *not* use your computer to do anything else while encoding; doing so runs the risk of adding "skips" to your digital music files.

Ripping a CD with Musicmatch Jukebox

The most popular ripping program today is Musicmatch Jukebox. That's because it's so easy to use—practically the entire process is automated.

Musicmatch Jukebox rips in MP3, WAV, and WMA formats. To rip a CD, follow these steps:

1. Connect to the Internet, then launch the Musicmatch software, shown in Figure 32.1.

2. Click the Rip from CD button; this opens the Recorder window, shown in Figure 32.2.

3. Insert the CD you want to copy from into your PC's CD-ROM drive. Musicmatch will now synch up (over the Internet) with CDDB, an online database, to obtain track information.

FIGURE 32.1

Use Musicmatch
Jukebox to con-
vert a CD to dig-
ital audio files.

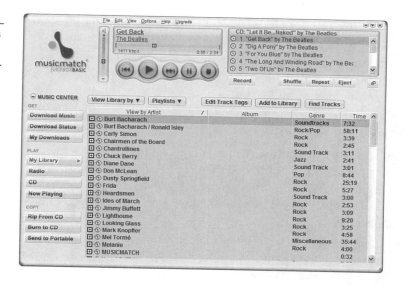

FIGURE 32.2

Getting ready to
rip a CD with
Musicmatch
Jukebox's
Recorder.

4. To set the bit rate and format for recording, click the Options button to display the Settings dialog box. Select the Recorder tab, pull down the Recording
   Format list, and select a file format; you can then select the desired quality
   level, below this list. Click OK when ready to proceed.

5. Back in the main window, check the boxes next to the tracks you want to
   copy.

6. When you've selected which tracks to rip, click the Record button.

Musicmatch now copies the selected files from your CD to the My Music folder on
your hard disk. That's it—you're ready to listen to digital music!

Burning Your Own CDs

Unlike ripping songs from a CD, burning digital music to CD doesn't require you to
set a lot of format options. That's because whatever format the original file is in,
when it gets copied to CD it gets encoded into the CD Audio (CDA) format. All music

CDs use the CDA format, so whether you're burning an MP3 or WMA file, your CD burner software translates it to CDA before the copy is made.

There are no quality levels to set, either. All CDA-format files are encoded at the same bit rate. So you really don't have any configuration to do—other than deciding which songs you want to copy.

How CD Burning Works

The easiest way to burn a CD full of songs is to assemble a playlist beforehand (in your CD burner program), and then copy that entire playlist. You can record up to 74 minutes (650MB) worth of music on a standard CD-R disc, or 80 minutes (700MB) on an enhanced disc.

After you've decided which songs to copy, load a blank CD-R disc into your computer's CD-R/RW drive, launch your CD burner software, and then follow the program's instructions to start translating and copying the song files. After the ripping begins, the digital music files on your hard drive are converted and copied onto a blank CD-R in standard CD Audio format.

tip

To play your new CD in a regular (non-PC) CD player, record in the CD-R format and use a blank CD-R disc specifically labeled for audio use. (CD-RW discs will not play in most home CD players.)

Burning CDs with Musicmatch Jukebox

Most CD burner software works in much the same fashion. Since you've just learned how to use Musicmatch Jukebox to rip CDs, you might as well use it to burn your CDs, too. Follow these steps:

tip

Windows Media Player can also be used to burn CDs.

1. From the main Musicmatch window, select those songs you want to copy to CD. (Hold down the Ctrl key to select multiple files.)

2. Click the Burn to CD button; this opens the Burner Plus window.

3. In the Burner Plus window, click the Click Here to Add Files Currently Selected in Your Library button. (Alternately, you can drag files from the main Musicmatch Jukebox window onto the Burner Plus window.) The songs you selected are now displayed in the Burner Plus window, as shown in Figure 32.3

FIGURE 32.3

Getting ready to burn a new CD.

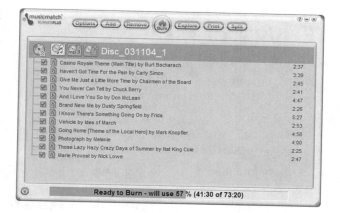

4. To add additional songs to the burn list, click the Add button and select songs from the Open Music dialog box.

5. To change the order of songs on the burn list, select a song and drag it to a new position.

6. If you've added more songs than you have room for, select some songs to delete and click the Remove button.

7. When you've added all the songs you want to burn, click the Burn button.

The songs are now burned to your blank CD. When the burning process is completed, the CD is ejected.

tip

To create labels for your custom CDs, use a label maker program like cdrLabel (www.ziplabel.com) or the Neato CD Labeler Kit (www.neato.com).

Copying CDs

Making a copy of a CD is pretty much a combination of ripping and burning. That is, you rip the files from your original CD to your hard disk, then burn those files to a new CD. Just make sure you rip the files to WAV format, to retain the original audio fidelity.

An even easier solution is to use a program specifically designed for CD copying, such as Easy CD & DVD Creator (www.roxio.com). This program makes copying an audio CD pretty much a one-button operation; just click the Disc Copier button and follow the onscreen instructions.

note

Some new PCs come with a limited version of this program, called Easy CD Creator, preinstalled. This version is perfect for copying CDs—it just doesn't have the added DVD copying capability.

THE ABSOLUTE MINIMUM

Here are the key points to remember from this chapter:

- The process of copying songs from a CD to your hard disk is called *ripping*; the process of copying digital audio files from your hard disk to a blank CD is called *burning*.

- For best audio quality, rip files using the WAV format; for best compatibility with music player programs and portable music players, use the MP3 format.

- You can use the Musicmatch Jukebox program to both rip digital music files and burn audio CDs.

- To make an exact copy of an audio CD, use the Easy CD & DVD Creator Program.

33

DOWNLOADING AND PLAYING DIGITAL MUSIC

Downloading music from the Web is a big deal. Originally popularized by college students (with fast university Internet connections), users of all ages are now using the Internet for at least part of their music listening.

A wealth of music is available online that you can download and then play back on your PC, from a variety of sources—online music stores, file trading networks, Internet radio stations, and the like. It's like having the world's biggest jukebox available to you, over the Internet.

Downloading from Online Music Stores

One of the great things about digital music is that you can listen to just the songs you want. You're not forced to listen to an entire album; you can download that one song you really like and ignore the rest. Even better, you can take songs you like from different artists and create your own playlists; it's like being your own DJ or record producer!

Where do you go to download your favorite songs? You have a lot of choices, but the easiest is to shop at an online music store. These are Web sites that offer hundreds of thousands of songs from your favorite artists, all completely legal. You pay about a buck a song and download the music files directly to your computer's hard disk.

caution

When you're downloading music, it's best to have a high-speed broadband Internet connection. Although nothing's stopping you from downloading via a dial-up connection, the process can get a tad tedious. These are big files to download!

iTunes Music Store

The most popular online music store today is Apple's iTunes Music Store. The iTunes Music Store (`www.apple.com/itunes/store/`) offers more than 400,000 songs for just 99 cents each. All songs are in Apple's proprietary AAC file format, which means that they won't play in most third-party music player programs, or on most non-Apple portable music players. But you can use Apple's iTunes software to play the files, and (of course) play all downloaded songs on your Apple iPod.

To use the iTunes Music Store, you first have to download the iTunes software. We'll examine this software in more detail in Chapter 34, "Using Your PC with a Portable Music Player," but don't worry—it's a fairly easy program to use. To download the software, all you have to do is click the Download Now button on the iTunes Music Store home page, and then follow the onscreen instructions.

note

Learn more about AAC, MP3, WMA, and other audio file formats in Chapter 32, "Ripping and Burning CDs."

Once the iTunes software is up and running on your computer, you access the iTunes Music Store by clicking the Music Store icon in the Source pane. As you can see in Figure 33.1, there are several different ways to find music in the iTunes Music Store. You can browse by genre, view new releases, or use the search box (in the top right corner) to search for specific songs or artists.

The results of your search are now listed, as shown in
Figure 33.2. To purchase and download a song, click
the Buy Song button. After you confirm your purchase, the song will be downloaded automatically
to your PC and added to your iTunes Library. You
can listen to your downloaded music in the iTunes
music player, using the transport controls at the top
of the window.

Napster 2.0

If you don't have an Apple iPod, you'll want to
check out some of the non-Apple online music
stores that offer songs in Microsoft's WMA file format. WMA files can be played in most music
player programs (including Windows Media Player)
and portable music players—Apple's iPod being the notable exception.

note

The first time you
make a purchase from the
iTunes Music Store, you'll be
prompted to create a new
account and enter your credit
card information.

One of the best online music stores today is Napster 2.0 (www.napster.com). This is a
completely new digital music service named after the pioneering (and long defunct)
Napster online music site. The new Napster offers more than a half-million songs for
downloading at 99 cents apiece; entire albums can be downloaded for $9.95.

FIGURE 33.2

Downloading
songs from the
iTunes Music
Store.

Napster is similar to the iTunes Music Store in that before you can use the site, you have to download the Napster software. When you launch the Napster software, it takes you to the main Napster site and displays the Home page, as shown in Figure 33.3. You'll need to sign up for Napster membership before you can download any music; basic membership is free.

You can browse the Napster site for the music you want or search for specific songs or artists. Buying a track is as simple as clicking the Buy Track or Buy Only button next to a song listing. After you make your purchase, the song is automatically downloaded to your PC.

One unique aspect to Napster is the fact that it's more than just an online music store—it's also a subscription music service. For $9.95 per month, Napster Premium provides streaming audio, access to a number of Internet radio stations, and the ability to download an unlimited number of songs for playback on your PC. When you subscribe to Napster Premium, you can listen to almost any song available on the Napster service without purchasing it separately. (You still have to purchase tracks individually if you want to burn them to CD or transfer to a portable music player, however.)

note

Learn more about streaming audio and Internet radio in the "Listening to Internet Radio" section, later in this chapter.

I like to connect to Napster and pick a Napster Radio stream to listen to while I'm working on my computer; it's great music, no downloading necessary!

FIGURE 33.3

More music to download from Napster 2.0.

Other Online Music Stores

iTunes Music Store and Napster are just two of many new online music stores. All offer similar pricing, although the selection tends to differ from site to site. When you're shopping for songs to download, here are some of the other big online music stores to check out:

- BuyMusic.com (www.buymusic.com)
- eMusic (www.emusic.com)
- Musicmatch Downloads (www.musicmatch.com)
- RealPlayer Store (www.real.com)
- Rhapsody (www.listen.com)
- Wal-Mart Music Downloads (musicdownloads.walmart.com)

Downloading from Free Music Sites

You don't have to pay to download music. A lot of sites offer free music downloads— no purchase or subscription necessary.

Of course, a free music download site isn't going to have the selection of a paid site. Most of these free sites lack music by major artists and labels, instead focusing on songs by new or independent artists. Still, free is free—and it's a great way to check out some new music!

Most of these free music sites offer songs for downloading in the industry-standard MP3 format. You can play MP3 files on virtually every music player program and portable audio player.

Here are some of the most popular free music download sites:

tip

When you're searching for a particular song or artist anywhere on the Internet, check out an MP3 search engine site, such as Lycos Music (`music.lycos.com`), MP3 Search (`mp3search.astraweb.com`), or Musicseek (`www.musicseek.net`).

- Ampcast (`www.ampcast.com`)
- ARTISTdirect (`www.artistdirect.com`)
- BeSonic (`www.besonic.com`)
- Peoplesound (`www.peoplesound.com`)

Downloading from File-Trading Networks

Some of the best music on the Internet doesn't come from any Web site—it comes from other users. Over the past few years, the Web has seen a profusion of file-trading networks, where you can swap music files with your fellow computer users. You connect your computer (via the Internet) to the network, which already has thousands of other users connected; when you find a song you want, you transfer it directly from the other computer to yours.

Of course, file trading works in both directions. When you register with one of these services, other users can download digital audio files from *your* computer, as long as you're connected to the Internet.

tip

One bonus to accessing a file-sharing network is that you can often find more than just music files. It's common to find movie files, software applications, and even dirty pictures on a file-trading network. You just never know what's available online.

Where to Trade Files Online

Most file-trading networks require you to download a copy of their software and then run that software whenever you want to download. You use their software to search for the songs you want; the software then generates a list of users who have that file stored on their computers. You select which computer you want to connect to, and then the software automatically downloads the file from that computer to yours.

The most popular of these file-sharing services include

- Gnutella (www.gnutelliums.com)
- Grokster (www.grokster.com)
- iMesh (www.imesh.com)
- LimeWire (www.limewire.com)
- KaZaA Media Desktop (www.kazaa.com)
- Morpheus (www.morpheus.com)

Downsides to File Trading

There are a few downsides to swapping music over a file-trading network—and they're serious enough to keep many users away.

First, if you're trading copyrighted songs (which you probably are), it's illegal. The Recording Industry Association of America keeps itself quite busy filing lawsuits against file swappers—regular users, like you and me. This is serious stuff; if you don't want to risk getting sued, you shouldn't use a file-trading network.

Second, when you install some file-trading programs, you also install spyware. As you learned in Chapter 30, "Protecting Your PC from Viruses, Spam, and Other Nuisances," spyware can track everything you do on your computer and feed that information back to some marketing service. KaZaA is particularly notable for its intrusive spyware, which apparently pays for its otherwise free service. If you don't like spyware inhabiting your PC, stay away.

Third, many file-trading networks are rife with computer viruses. You might think that you're downloading an audio file, but instead find yourself loading the latest computer virus onto your hard disk. These file-trading networks don't have any oversight (unlike paid sites), so you never know what you're actually downloading. Unless you're extremely diligent about using antivirus software and checking every file you access, download at your own risk.

These risks, however, are unique to file-trading networks. If you download from a reputable online music store, or even one of the free music download sites, you don't face any of these issues. Files downloaded from Napster 2.0 and the iTunes Music Store are legal and free from spyware and viruses. If you want a guaranteed safe downloading experience, stick with one of the commercial sites—and stay clear of the file-trading networks.

Playing Digital Music with Windows Media Player

After you've downloaded a fair number of digital audio files, it's time to start listening to them—which you do with a music player program. As you learned in Chapter 31, "Playing CDs and DVDs," the most popular music player program is Windows Media Player (WMP), which is provided free with Microsoft Windows, and is probably already installed on your PC.

Playing Digital Audio Files

To play a digital audio file with Windows Media Player, you follow these steps:

1. Select the Now Playing tab.
2. Select File, Open.
3. When the Open dialog box appears, select the file you want to play; the file you selected will start playing automatically.

WMP stores your favorite files in what it calls the Media Library (shown in Figure 33.4). To add a file to the Media Library, select File, Add to Media Library; then select either Add Currently Playing Track (to add the song you're listening to) or Add File or Playlist (to add another file stored on your hard disk).

FIGURE 33.4

Store your favorite MP3 files in WMP's Media Library.

Creating a Playlist of Your Favorite Songs

Files in your WMP Media Library can be combined into *playlists*. You can create playlists from the files you have stored on your hard disk, in any order you want—just like listening to a radio station's playlist.

To create a new playlist, follow these steps:

1. Select the Media Library tab.
2. Click the Playlists button and select New Playlist.
3. When the New Playlist dialog box appears, shown in Figure 33.5, enter a name for the playlist.
4. The left side of the New Playlist dialog box displays all the songs in your Media Library. (Pull down the View Media Library list to display songs by artist, album, genre, and so on.) Click a song to add it to your playlist.
5. Click OK when done.

Playing an entire playlist is as simple as going to the Media Library and double-clicking a playlist in the left-hand pane. WMP will start playing the first song in your playlist, and go on from there.

> **tip**
>
> To play the songs in a playlist in random order, click the Turn Shuffle On button or select Play, Shuffle.

FIGURE 33.5
Add songs to your new playlist.

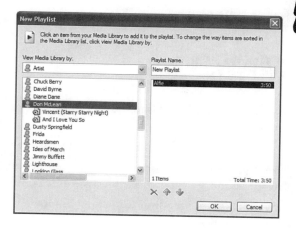

Listening to Internet Radio

Many real-world radio stations—as well as Web-only stations—broadcast over the Internet using a technology called *streaming audio*. Streaming audio is different from downloading an audio file. When you download a file, you can't start playing that file until it is completely downloaded to your PC. With streaming audio, however, playback can start before an entire file is downloaded. This also enables live broadcasts—both of traditional radio stations and made-for-the-Web stations—to be sent from the broadcast site to your PC.

Internet radio can be listened to with most music player programs. For example, Windows Media Player has a Radio Tuner tab that facilitates finding and listening to a variety of Internet radio stations. In addition, many Internet radio sites feature built-in streaming software or direct you to sites where you can download the appropriate music player software.

When you're looking for Internet radio broadcasts (of which there are thousands, daily), you need a good directory of available programming. Here's a list of sites that offer links to either traditional radio simulcasts or original Internet programming:

tip

Although you can listen to Internet radio over a traditional dial-up connection, you'll hear better quality sound over a broadband connection.

- LAUNCH (launch.yahoo.com)
- Live@ (www.live-at.com)
- Live365 (www.live365.com)
- Radio-Locator (www.radio-locator.com)
- RadioMOI (www.radiomoi.com)
- SHOUTcast (yp.shoutcast.com)
- Web-Radio (www.web-radio.com)

THE ABSOLUTE MINIMUM

Here are the key points to remember from this chapter:

- You can download songs from iTunes Music Store, Napster, and other online music stores for just 99 cents apiece.
- Some Web sites offer free MP3 files from new and independent artists.
- You can also swap music files with other users, using a file-trading network such as KaZaA—although trading copyrighted songs is both illegal and risky.
- You can use any audio player program—such as Windows Media Player—to play back digital audio files.
- If you prefer to listen to a stream of digital music, Internet radio is the way to go; hundreds of real-world and Web-only radio stations are broadcasting on the Internet.

34

USING YOUR PC WITH A PORTABLE MUSIC PLAYER

One of the hottest consumer electronics gadgets today is the portable music player, sometimes called an MP3 player. I'm not talking about the old Sony Walkman or even about portable CD players. These new players store thousands of digital audio files on micro hard drives or in flash memory, and can fit in the palm of your hand.

What's cool about these portable players is that they get their songs from your computer. The music you rip from CD or download from the Internet is transferred from your PC to the portable audio player. You can even use your PC to organize the player's songs into playlists!

Working with the Apple iPod

The most popular portable music player today is the Apple iPod. Apple sells several different versions of the iPod, including the standard-sized iPod shown in Figure 34.1 and the compact iPod Mini. And, unlike every other product that Apple sells, the iPod is the one device that works equally well with Macintosh or Windows computers.

To use the iPod with your PC, you first have to install Apple's iTunes software. iTunes is a music player program, like Windows Media Player, that is fine-tuned to work with both the iPod and with Apple's iTunes Music Store. You use iTunes to transfer music files to your iPod, as well as to purchase and download digital music from the ITunes Music Store site on the Web.

note

The iPod's chief drawback is that it only plays digital audio files in the AAC and MP3 formats. (AAC is somewhat propriety to Apple.) It does *not* play files in Microsoft's WMA format. So you won't be able to play WMA files downloaded from Napster and similar sites on your iPod device.

FIGURE 34.1

The extremely popular Apple iPod portable music player. (Photo courtesy of Apple.)

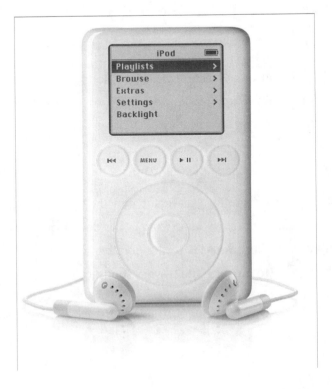

Connecting an iPod to Your PC

Connecting the iPod to your PC is as simple as connecting a cable from the iPod to a USB or FireWire port on your computer. When the iPod is connected, your PC automatically launches the iTunes software and downloads any new songs and playlists you've added since the last time you connected.

Managing Your Music with iTunes

The key to managing the music on your iPod is mastering Apple's iTunes software. As you can see in Figure 34.2, iTunes looks like most other music player programs. You have a set of transport controls (for playing music on your PC) in the upper left corner, a list of music files in the main window, and a list of playlists in the Source pane on the left. Select a source or playlist in the Source pane, and its contents are displayed in the main window

caution

The iPod is a USB 2.0 device. If your PC uses the older USB 1.0 ports, you'll need to upgrade by installing a USB 2.0 card.

FIGURE 34.2

Managing music files with the iTunes player.

Your master collection of songs is stored in the Library, which is the first source in the Source pane. When you first install the iTunes software, it imports all AAC, AIFF, MP3, and WAV format files in your My Documents folder and lists them in the Library. (iTunes isn't compatible with Microsoft's WMA format, so it just ignores those files.)

To transfer songs to your iPod, all you have to do is check them. The next time you connect your iPod, all checked songs in your Library will be downloaded.

Assembling Playlists

Most users like to assemble collections of their favorite songs, in the form of playlists. iTunes provides two different ways to create playlists for use on your iPod.

The easiest type of playlist to create is the Smart Playlist. This is a playlist that iTunes automatically assembles from information you provide. You can create Smart Playlists based on artist, album, genre, file size, beats per minute, and other attributes. All you have to do is select File, New Smart Playlist. This displays the Smart Playlist dialog box, shown in Figure 34.3; select the criteria you want, click OK, and iTunes finds all matching songs. For example, to create a playlist of all the Coldplay songs in your Library, choose Artist from the first drop-down list and enter Coldplay in the right-hand box.

FIGURE 34.3

Creating a
Smart Playlist.

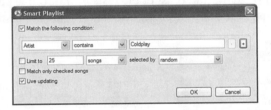

You can also create playlists manually. Just follow these steps:

1. Select File, New Playlist to add a new playlist to the Source pane.

2. Click the new playlist twice to edit the title.

3. Add songs to the new playlist by dragging songs from the Library onto the new playlist icon.

Once you've added songs to a playlist, you can view the contents of the playlist by selecting it as your source. Then you can rearrange the songs by dragging them into the order you prefer.

The next time you connect your iPod, your new playlists will be transferred to the portable device.

caution

You can't manually add songs to (or arrange songs within) a Smart Playlist.

Downloading Songs from the iTunes Music Store

Back in Chapter 33, "Downloading and Playing Digital Music," you learned how to download music from various online music sites. As discussed in that chapter, one of the most popular online music stores is Apple's iTunes Music Store. The entire iTunes Music Store is designed for users of the iPod and the iTunes software.

Connecting to the iTunes Music Store is as easy as clicking the Music Store icon in the iTunes Source pane. Once you're online, you purchase songs as described in Chapter 33; all the songs you purchased are automatically added to your iTunes Library. Then, the next time you connect your iPod, the songs are automatically transferred to your portable device.

Transferring Songs to Other Portable Music Players

If you have another brand of portable music player, you'll use other methods to transfer music from your PC to your portable device. Some portable players have their own transfer/player software, similar to iTunes. Others appear to your PC as a new disk drive and require you to copy files using My Computer.

Still other portable music players let you copy songs using Windows Media Player. It's not that hard a process, as long as you prepare a playlist to copy beforehand. Then you connect your player and follow these steps:

note

Learn about copying files with My Computer in Chapter 6, "Working with Files and Folders."

1. From within WMP, select the Copy to CD or Device screen, shown in Figure 34.4.

2. In the left pane, pull down the Items to Copy list and select the playlist you want to transfer.

3. In the right pane, pull down the Items on Device list and select your portable music player.

4. Click the Copy button in the top right corner.

That's it; the playlist you selected will now be copied to your portable device.

FIGURE 34.4

Using Windows Media Player to transfer songs.

THE ABSOLUTE MINIMUM

Here are the key points to remember from this chapter:

- Copying digital music files from your PC to a portable music player is typically as easy as connecting the player to your PC.

- You manage the files you want to copy on your PC beforehand—even creating playlists of your favorite songs.

- The most popular portable music player today is the Apple iPod, which uses the iTunes software to manage all of its song transfers.

- Other portable music players use either their own propriety transfer software or Windows Media Player to move songs from your PC to the portable device.

35

EDITING YOUR OWN HOME MOVIES

If you have a camcorder and make your own home movies, you can use your computer system to make those movies a lot more appealing. With the right hardware and software, you can turn your PC into a video editing console—and make your home movies look a *lot* more professional.

And the neat thing is, you probably don't have to buy anything extra to do your video editing. If you're using Windows XP and have one of the latest digital video recorders, all you have to do is hook up a few cables and start editing!

Configuring Your System for Video Editing

Preparing your PC for video editing is fairly simple. All you have to do is connect your camcorder or VCR to your PC system unit. How you do this depends on what type of camcorder or VCR you have.

If you have an older VHS, VHS-C, SVHS, 8mm, or Hi8 recorder, you'll need to buy and install an analog-to-digital video capture card in your PC. (You can buy one at most computer stores.) You'll plug your recorder in to the jacks in this card (typically using standard RCA connectors), and it will convert the analog signals from your recorder into the digital audio and video your computer understands.

If you have one of the latest digital video (DV) recorders in the Digital8 or MiniDV formats, you don't need a video capture card. What you do need is an IE1394 FireWire interface, which is included with many new PCs. This type of connection is fast enough to handle the huge stream of digital data pouring from your DV recorder into your PC. (Using any other type of connection, including USB 2.0, is not only slower but might result in some degree of frame loss.)

tip

For best results, you should strive for a completely digital chain. Start with digital video shot on Digital8 or MiniDV, edit the video digitally with Windows Movie Maker, and then output the completed movie to a CD or DVD in WMV format.

Choosing a Video Editing Program

PC-based video editing software performs many of the same functions as the professional editing consoles you might find at your local television station. You can use video editing software to cut entire scenes from your movie, rearrange scenes, add fancy transitions between scenes, add titles (and subtitles), and even add your own music soundtrack. The results are amazing!

The most popular Windows-compatible video editing programs include

- Adobe Premiere Pro (www.adobe.com)
- Pinnacle Studio (www.pinnaclesys.com)
- Ulead MediaStudio Pro (www.ulead.com/msp/)

In addition, Windows XP includes its own video editing software, called Windows Movie Maker (WMM). Although its not quite as sophisticated as some of the other video editing programs, WMM includes all the features you need to do basic home video editing—and it's free!

Working with Windows Movie Maker

Windows Movie Maker works by dividing your home movie into scene segments it calls *clips*. You can then rearrange and delete specific clips to edit the flow of your movie.

The basic WMM window is divided into four main parts, as shown in Figure 35.1.

tip

Make sure that you're working with the latest version of Windows Movie Maker, WMM 2. If you need to upgrade, go to Microsoft's WMM Web site (www.microsoft.com/ windowsxp/moviemaker/).

Tasks/Collections Pane   Contents Pane   Monitor

FIGURE 35.1
Editing home movies with Windows Movie Maker.

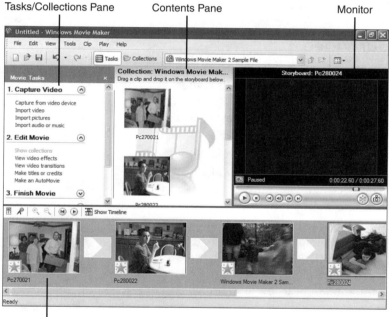

Storyboard/Timeline

Recording from a Camcorder

Each movie you create with WMM is called a *project*. For most WMM projects, your main source material will be your original videotape(s). You use Windows Movie Maker to record the tape as you play it back on your VCR or camcorder.

After you have the camcorder or VCR connected and turned on, select File, Capture Video. This launches the Video Capture Wizard. Follow the onscreen instructions to select the capture device you want to use, specify where you want the captured video (and audio) file to be saved, and choose the video setting (the level of recording quality).

After you click the Record button in the wizard, press the Play button on your camcorder or VCR. WMM now automatically records the playback from your input device. (Recording will stop when you press the Stop button, or after two hours, whichever comes first.) The new clips you create will now appear in the Collections area of the Movie Maker window.

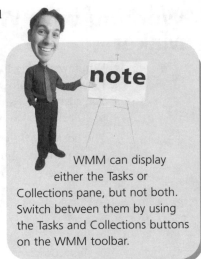

note

WMM can display either the Tasks or Collections pane, but not both. Switch between them by using the Tasks and Collections buttons on the WMM toolbar.

Editing Your Video

You create your movie in the Storyboard area at the bottom of the Movie Maker window. You create a movie by dragging clips down into the Storyboard. You can insert clips in any order, and more than once if you want to. After the clips are in the Storyboard, you can drag them around in a different order. This is how you edit the flow of your movie.

When you get the basic flow of your movie in place, you can switch from Storyboard to Timeline view, shown in Figure 35.2. You switch views by clicking the Show Timeline/Show Storyboard button just above the Storyboard/Timeline. In the Timeline view, you see the timing of each segment, and can overlay background music and narration.

tip

As you work, you can preview your project-in-process with the Movie Maker Monitor. Just select one or more clips in the Storyboard/ Timeline, and then click the Play button on the Monitor.

FIGURE 35.2

Displaying your clips in Timeline view.

Working with Movie Maker's clips is fairly intuitive. Just drag things into place and move them around as you like, and you have 90% of it mastered. The major operations are described in Table 35.1.

Table 35.1 Windows Movie Maker Clip Operations

Operation	Instructions
Add a clip	Use your mouse to drag the new clip from the Contents pane into position in the Storyboard/Timeline.
Move a clip	Grab the clip with your mouse and drag it to the new position.
Remove a clip	Select the clip and select Edit, Delete.
Trim a clip	Set the clip's start and end *trim points*; everything outside these two points will be trimmed.
Split a clip	Begin playing the clip in the monitor; when you reach the point where you want to make the split, click the Pause button, and then select Clip, Split.
Combine two or more clips	Select the clips (by holding down Ctrl while clicking each clip) and then select Clip, Combine.

Titles, Transitions, and Other Options

WMM 2 also lets you add some neat bells and whistles to your video movies. For example, you can add

- Titles and credits (select Tools, Titles and Credits)
- Transitions between clips (select Tools, Video Transitions)
- Special effects, such as blurs, fades, film-aging, sepia tones, and double-speed and half-speed effects (select Tools, Video Effects)
- Background music (insert an audio clip the same way you insert a video clip)
- Narration (select Tools, Narrate Timeline)

Saving—and Watching—Your Movie

When you're done editing, you save your project by selecting File, Save Project. This does not save a movie file, however—it only saves the component parts of your project.

When your project is absolutely, positively finished, you actually make the movie. Select File, Save Movie to launch the Save Movie Wizard. From here, you select where to save the movie file, the name for the movie file, and the quality of the saved file. When you finish the wizard, WMM creates your movie and saves it as a WMV-format file. (Be patient—creating a movie can take some time!)

Burning Your Movie to DVD

Once you've created your WMV-format movie file, you can use third-party software to burn the file to DVD so that it can be viewed by anyone with a DVD player. Learn more about DVD-burning software, such as Sonic MyDVD, in Chapter 36, "Burning and Copying DVDs."

THE ABSOLUTE MINIMUM

Here are the key points to remember from this chapter:

- For the best results, stay all-digital throughout the entire video editing process; this means recording your original movie in Digital8 or MiniDV format.

- Windows Movie Maker is a digital video editing program, included with Windows XP, that you can use to edit your home movies originally recorded on videotape.

- The bits and pieces of your project are called *clips*; you put together your movie by dragging clips into the Workspace area at the bottom of the Movie Maker window.

- Windows Movie Maker saves your movie in a WMV-format file; you can then use a DVD-burning program to copy the movie to DVD for playback.

36

BURNING AND COPYING DVDs

CD burners are standard equipment with most new PCs, but some new systems also come with DVD burners. If you have a DVD burner installed in your PC, you can use it to burn your home movies to DVD and to make copies of your personal DVDs.

Burning a DVD is a lot like burning a CD—but with movies instead of music. So read on to learn how to use your PC to burn your own DVD movies.

Choosing a DVD Creation Program

Chances are, your DVD burner came with some DVD creation software pre-installed. If so, great! If not, you probably want to check out some of the many programs you can use to burn your own DVDs. Here are some of the most popular:

- DVD X Maker (www.dvdxcopy.com)
- Easy CD & DVD Creator (www.roxio.com)
- Sonic MyDVD (www.sonic.com)
- Ulead MovieFactory (www.ulead.com)
- Ulead CD & DVD PictureShow (www.ulead.com)

Perhaps the easiest to use and most widely distributed DVD creation program is Sonic MyDVD, which is what we'll use for all the examples in this chapter.

Creating a Movie DVD Direct from Tape

When you first launch MyDVD, you're presented with three choices. If all you want to do is transfer an existing videotape to DVD, select Transfer Video Direct-to-DVD.

When you select this option, the program opens the Direct-to-DVD Wizard, shown in Figure 36.1. You now work your way through a simple process:

FIGURE 36.1
Using MyDVD to create a DVD from an existing videotape.

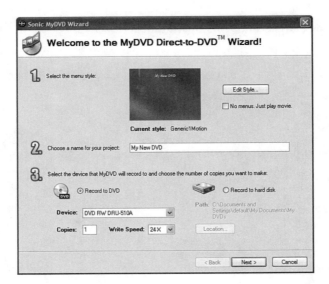

1. Click the Edit Style button to select the style of menus you want on the DVD. (You can also select the No Menus option if you want the movie to play automatically with no startup menu.) You can select different background animations, button styles, and background music for the menu screen. You can also opt for plain or animated buttons.

2. Enter a name for your project.

3. Select a location for the finished project—either your DVD recorder or a folder on your hard disk, and then click Next.

4. When the next screen appears, choose how often you want to add chapter points (to start new chapters on the disc).

5. Now make sure that your VCR or camcorder is connected to your PC; then click the Start Capturing button and initiate playback on your VCR.

6. When the playback is complete, click the Stop Capturing process.

MyDVD will now start building the new DVD. This can take some time (an hour or more), so be patient! When it's done, your new DVD will be ready to play.

Creating a Movie DVD from Video Files

If you've used Windows Movie Maker or another video editing program to create movie files on your computer's hard disk, MyDVD can combine one or more of these files into a movie DVD, complete with menus. To initiate this process, select Create or Modify a DVD Video Project on the opening screen.

This opens MyDVD's main project window, shown in Figure 36.2. To create a movie DVD, follow these steps:

1. Click the Edit Style button to select the style of menus you want on the DVD.

2. Click the menu title text to add your own title to the main menu screen.

3. Add a video file to your DVD by clicking the Get Movies button. This opens the Add Movie(s) to Menu dialog box; select the file(s) you want to add, and then click Open.

4. The movie file you selected is now added to your project, and a button is added to the main menu. Click the filename under the button to rename the button.

5. Repeat steps 3 and 4 to add other movie files to your project.

6. To create a submenu under the main menu, click the Add Submenu button. This adds an "untitled menu" button to the main menu; click this text to change the name of the button.

FIGURE 36.2
Using MyDVD to
create a movie
DVD from
movie files.

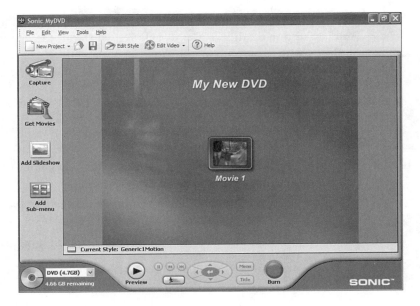

7. To add movies to the submenu, double-click the submenu button; this takes you to the submenu screen. Follow steps 3 and 4 to insert movie files. Double-click the Home button to return to the main menu.

8. When you've finished building menus and adding movie files, make sure that you've saved your project; then click the Burn button.

tip

Preview your new DVD at any time by clicking the Preview button. If you want to see animated buttons in action, click the Build Motion Menu button first.

MyDVD will now start building the new DVD. Remember, this is a long process—feel free to go out and get a pizza or something while you wait.

Creating a DVD Slideshow

One especially neat thing about these DVD creation programs is that almost all let you create animated slideshows of your digital photographs, which can play on most consumer DVD players. If you have a lot of photos in your collection, it's easy to burn them to DVD and then distribute the discs to your friends and family. It's a lot more convenient than passing around a photo print album!

With MyDVD, the process of creating a slideshow is almost identical to the process of creating a movie DVD. The only difference is that instead of adding a movie file to a menu, you add a slideshow. This lets you include multiple slideshows on a single disc.

To add a slideshow to a DVD project, follow these steps:

note

Learn more about digital photographs in Chapter 38, "Working with Digital Pictures."

1. From MyDVD's project window, click the Add Slideshow button; this opens the Create Slideshow window, shown in Figure 36.3.

2. To add pictures to the slideshow, click the Get Pictures button; when the Open dialog box appears, select the picture(s) to add, and then click the Open button.

FIGURE 36.3
Using MyDVD to create a photo slideshow.

3. The pictures you selected are now added to the slideshow filmstrip. You can rearrange the pictures by dragging any picture to a new position in the filmstrip.

4. To change the length of time each picture appears onscreen, click the Settings button to display the Slideshow Settings dialog box; select the Basic tab, and then adjust the Duration setting as desired. Click OK when done.

5. To add music to your slideshow, click the Settings button to display the Slideshow Settings dialog box; select the Basic tab, check the Audio Track option, and then click the Choose button to select a music file. Click OK when done.

6. By default, MyDVD adds a cross-fade transition between each slide. To use a different type of transition, click the Settings button to display the Slideshow Settings dialog box; select the Advanced tab, and then pull down the Transitions list and choose a new transition. Click OK when done.

7. To choose a button image for the slideshow (on the DVD menu), select a picture and click the Button Image button. This sets the selected picture as the button image.

8. When you're done adding pictures to the slideshow, click the OK button; your slideshow is now added to the current DVD menu.

Repeat this entire process to create additional slideshows on your DVD.

> **tip**
>
> To have MyDVD store copies of each picture file on the DVD (so that others can download the pictures to their own PCs), open the Slideshow Settings dialog box, select the Advanced tab, and select the Archive Original Pictures on Disc option.

Copying a DVD

Copying a DVD is somewhat more problematic than copying a CD. There are two reasons for this:

- Dual-layer commercial DVDs hold up to 9.4GB of data, where blank DVD-R discs only hold 4.7GB. This means that it's impossible to copy a movie onto a single disc; you either have to break the movie into two halves (on two separate discs) or compress the movie to fit, thus compromising quality.

- Many commercial DVDs are protected by a sophisticated encryption scheme, which prevents copying.

So if you want to copy a DVD, you're pretty much limited by the original material. If you want to copy a DVD you've created, you're okay. If you want to copy a commercial DVD movie—even if it's just a backup copy for your personal use—you're probably out of luck. (There's no harm in trying, however; not all commercial DVDs feature copy-protection encryption.)

That said, there are many programs that let you make copies of your personal DVDs. With most of these programs, the process is as simple as clicking a button or two; some programs let you compress longer DVDs to fit on a standard blank DVD or break long DVDs into two shorter ones.

Here are some of the most popular DVD copy programs:

- DVD Wizard Pro (www.dvdwizardpro.com)
- DVD X Copy (www.dvdxcopy.com)
- Easy CD & DVD Creator (www.roxio.com)
- EZ DVD Copy (www.ezdvdcopy.com)
- Pinnacle Instant CD/DVD (www.pinnaclesys.com)
- Ulead MovieFactory (www.ulead.com)

THE ABSOLUTE MINIMUM

Here are the key points to remember from this chapter:

- If you have a DVD burner in your PC system, you can create movie DVDs from your existing home movies.
- MyDVD lets you create DVDs direct from videotape or from edited movie files.
- You can also create DVDs that contain slideshows of your digital photographs.
- While it's possible to copy your personal DVDs, copying commercial movie DVDs is more problematic—because of both file size and copy-protection issues.

37

CONNECTING A DIGITAL CAMERA OR SCANNER

More and more people are trading in their old film cameras for new digital cameras—and connecting those cameras to their PCs. You can use your digital camera and PC together to transfer all the photos you take to your hard disk, and then edit your pictures to make them look even better.

There are several different ways to get your photos into your computer—you can transfer digital files directly from your camera's memory card, download pictures from your camera via a USB or FireWire connection, or even scan existing photo prints. We'll discuss them all next.

Making the Connection

Connecting a digital camera or scanner to your PC is extremely easy, especially if you have a newer model with a USB or FireWire connection. With this type of setup, Windows will recognize your camera or scanner as soon as you plug it in and install the appropriate drivers automatically.

If Windows does not recognize your camera or scanner, you can use the Scanners and Cameras utility to install the new device on your system. From the Control Panel, select Printers and Other Hardware, and then Scanners and Cameras; when the Scanners and Cameras utility appears, click Add an Imaging Device. This launches the Scanner and Camera Installation Wizard. Follow the onscreen instructions to identify the make and manufacturer of your device and complete the installation.

Transferring Pictures from a Digital Camera

The main reason you connect your digital camera to your PC is to transfer photos to your hard disk. Whether you connect via USB or FireWire, one of three things is likely to happen:

- If this launches a propriety picture management program that came with your digital camera, use this program to transfer photos from your camera to your PC's hard disk.

- If this opens Windows' Choose Pictures to Copy dialog box, click Acquire Photos; this launches the Scanner and Camera Wizard. As you can see in Figure 37.1, you're presented with thumbnails of all the photos currently stored in your camera. Select which photos you want to copy, and then click the Next button. When the Picture Name and Destination screen appears, select the destination folder and filenames for your folders, and then click Next to copy the selected pictures.

- If nothing happens, click the Start menu, select My Pictures, and then click Get Pictures From Camera or Scanner. This should open the Choose Pictures to Copy dialog box, as just described.

If none of these methods work for you, you might need to open My Computer and double-click the icon for your digital camera. When the digital camera window opens, copy the files you want to a location on your hard disk.

note

Once you've saved a digital picture file to your hard disk, you can then use picture-editing software to edit and otherwise manipulate the picture. Learn more in Chapter 38, "Working with Digital Pictures."

FIGURE 37.1

Use the Scanner and Camera Wizard to transfer pictures from your digital camera to your PC's hard disk.

Transferring Pictures from a Memory Card Reader

Copying digital pictures via USB can be a trifle slow. For many users, a faster—and easier—method is to use a memory card reader. A memory card reader is a low-cost external peripheral that connects to a USB port on your PC. You then insert the memory card from your digital camera into the memory card reader, and your PC recognizes the card as if it were another hard disk. You can then use either the Scanner and Camera Wizard or My Computer to transfer the digital photo files from the memory card to your PC's hard disk.

tip

Many color photo printers include memory card slots that let you print directly from your camera's memory card, bypassing your computer entirely.

Scanning a Picture

If your photos are of the old-fashioned print variety, you can still turn them into digital files, using a flatbed scanner. When you initiate a scan, Windows automatically launches the now-familiar Scanner and Camera Wizard. As you can see in Figure 37.2, the scanner part of this wizard lets you control how your picture is scanned. All you have to do is follow these steps:

1. Select one of the Picture Type options: Color Picture, Grayscale Picture, Black and White Picture or Text, or Custom. You can also click the Options button to change the resolution of the scan.

2. Click the Preview button. The wizard now displays a preview of what you're scanning.

FIGURE 37.2

Preview your
scan before you
accept it.

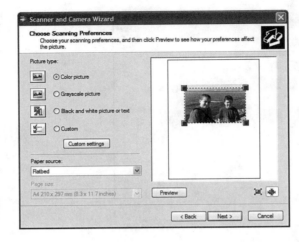

3. If you want to crop the item you're scanning, use the handles around the preview area to crop to a smaller area.

4. If you like what you see, click the Next button; then enter the name, file format, and location for this group of scans.

5. Click the Next button to complete the scan.

6. When the next screen appears, select Nothing if you're done with this scan, and then click Next.

7. Click Finish to exit the wizard.

tip

If you don't like the preview scan, reposition the item on your scanner and click the Preview button to start a new scan.

That's all there is to it. Your print photo is now scanned into a new digital file and saved on your hard disk for future use.

The Absolute Minimum

Here are the key points to remember from this chapter:

- You can connect a digital camera to your PC via USB or FireWire or use a memory card reader to transfer files from the camera's media card.

- Some cameras, when connected, launch proprietary picture transfer software; in other cases, connecting your camera will launch the Camera and Scanner Wizard, which you use to transfer picture files to your PC.

- When you scan a photo print, the Camera and Scanner Wizard lets you edit your picture before it's saved to hard disk.

38

WORKING WITH DIGITAL PICTURES

Once you've transferred a digital photo from your camera to your PC, a lot of options are available to you. A digital picture file is just like any computer file, which means that you can copy it, move it, delete it, or whatever. You can also use special picture editing software to manipulate your photos—to touch up bad spots and red eye, crop the edges, and apply all sorts of special effects.

After you've touched up all your photos, you can choose to create digital photo albums, use them in all manner of picture-related projects and documents, or print them out—either on your own four-color printer, or at a traditional photo processor. The combination of digital photography and personal computing is definitely the way to go—and it's a lot more versatile than traditional film-based photography!

Managing Your Photos

By default, Windows XP stores all your picture files in the My Pictures folder, shown in Figure 38.1. This folder includes a number of features specific to the management of picture files, found in the Picture Tasks panel. These features include

- View as a slide show
- Order prints online
- Print this picture
- Set as desktop background
- Copy to CD

FIGURE 38.1

Use the My Pictures folder to store and organize your digital pictures.

You can also change the way files are displayed in this folder. To display a thumbnail of each file, select View, Thumbnails. To view the selected file as a large image with all the other files in a scrolling list, select View, Filmstrip. To view details about each picture (its size, when it was taken, and so on), select View, Dimensions.

Choosing a Photo Editing Program

When it comes time to touch up your digital photos, you need a photo editing program. You can choose a low-priced, consumer-oriented program or a high-priced program targeted at professional photographers. For most of us, the consumer-oriented programs are more than adequate—and, in fact, you might have received one bundled with your new PC or digital camera.

If you're in the market for a low-priced photo editing program, here are the most popular programs in use today:

- Adobe Photoshop Elements (www.adobe.com)
- CorelDRAW Essentials (www.corel.com)
- Paint Shop Pro (www.jasc.com)
- Microsoft Picture It! Photo (www.microsoft.com/products/imaging/)
- Roxio PhotoSuite (www.roxio.com)

My favorite of these programs is Adobe Photoshop Elements—not to be confused with the much more expensive (and harder to use) Adobe Photoshop. The Elements program is extremely easy to use, with one-button operation for most common photo editing tasks—as you'll see next.

Editing Your Photos with Adobe Photoshop Elements

Not all the pictures you take are perfect. Sometimes the image might be a little out of focus or off center, or maybe your subject caught the glare of a flash for a "red eye" effect. The nice thing about digital pictures is that you can easily edit them to correct for these and other types of flaws.

Let's look at how you can use Adobe Photoshop Elements for these simple picture-editing tasks.

Opening a Picture for Editing

Photoshop Elements offers two ways to open a picture for editing. You select File, Open to use the standard Open dialog box, or select File, Browse to use Elements' File Browser. The File Browser is perhaps an easier approach, as you can see thumbnails of all the pictures available for editing.

When you open a specific picture, it's displayed in a window within the work area, which you can see in Figure 38.2. Along the top of the work area are the typical menus and toolbars, along with the following unique elements:

- **Options bar**—Which provides options for using a particular tool.
- **Palette well**—Which provides tabbed access to different editing palettes—you can also pull palettes out of the well to display in separate windows.
- **Toolbox**—A free-floating collection of editing tools.

tip

View the names of the Toolbox tools by hovering your cursor over each button.

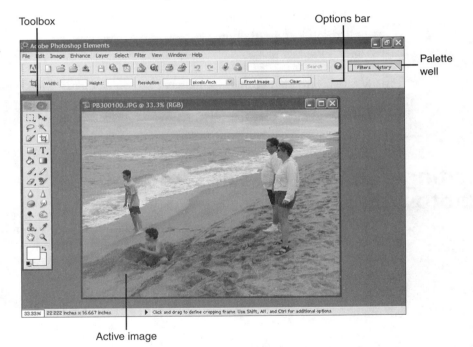

Toolbox

Options bar

Palette well

FIGURE 38.2
The Photoshop Elements work area.

Active image

Touching Up a Picture

Most basic touchup operations can be performed from Elements' Quick Fix utility. Select Enhance, Quick Fix to display the Quick Fix dialog box, shown in Figure 38.3.

Table 38.1 shows some of the things you can do with the Quick Fix utility.

FIGURE 38.3

Use the Quick
Fix tool for most
basic touchups.

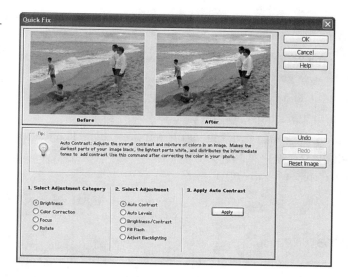

Table 38.1 Quick Fix Operations

Operation	Steps
Automatically adjusts overall contrast	Brightness, Auto Contrast, Apply
Automatically adds contrast to a flat picture	Brightness, Auto Levels, Apply
Manually adjusts brightness and contrast	Brightness, Brightness/Contrast, adjust Brightness and Contrast sliders
Lightens a dark photo	Brightness, Fill Flash, adjust Lighter and Saturation sliders
Brings out lost detail in the background	Brightness, Adjust Backlighting, adjust Darker slider
Automatically fixes color problems	Color Correction, Auto Color, Apply
Manually adjusts color and tint	Color Correction, Hue/Saturation, adjust Hue, Saturation, and Lightness sliders
Automatically sharpens a blurry photo	Focus, Auto Focus, Apply
Automatically softens the focus	Focus, Blur, Apply
Rotates a picture	Rotate, select adjustment, Apply

Removing Red Eye

If you use flash photography, sooner or later you're going to run into the problem of
red eye, which can make ordinary people look like the spawn of the devil himself.

Elements includes a special red eye removal tool, which is really easy to use. Follow these steps:

1. Select the Zoom tool from the Toolbox, and then zoom in closer by clicking on the eyes you want to fix.

2. Select the Red Eye Brush tool from the Toolbox.

3. In the Options bar, click the Default Colors button.

4. Position the cursor over one of the red eyes; then click the mouse button and drag the cursor over the eye until all the red color is removed.

5. Repeat step 4 for the other eye.

That's all there is to it—you've essentially "painted out" the red eye!

Cropping a Picture

One of the more common picture flaws comes when the subject of the picture isn't ideally positioned. You can fix this type of flaw by *cropping* the picture to eliminate unwanted areas of the image.

To crop a picture with Photoshop Elements, follow these steps:

1. Select the Crop tool from the Toolbox.

2. Position the cursor at where you want the top left corner of your image to be.

3. Click and drag your mouse down and to the right until you've selected the entire final image area.

4. Release the mouse button; the area you want to crop to is now highlighted, and the area outside this image is dimmed, as shown in Figure 38.4.

5. Double-click within the final image area to complete the crop.

Resizing a File for the Internet

If you use the entire multi-megapixel capacity of your digital camera, you'll end up creating some really digital pictures—both physically and in terms of file size. Big files are good when you want high-quality pictures for printing, but when it comes to putting a picture on a Web page or sending it via email, you need to work with something a lot smaller.

Fortunately, Elements makes it easy to resize your pictures for Internet use. Just follow these steps:

1. Select File, Save for Web to display the Save for Web dialog box, shown in Figure 38.5.

2. In the New Size section, make sure that the Constrain Proportions option is selected, and then enter either a new Width and Height for the picture or enter a Percent of the original picture. Click Apply to apply your changes.

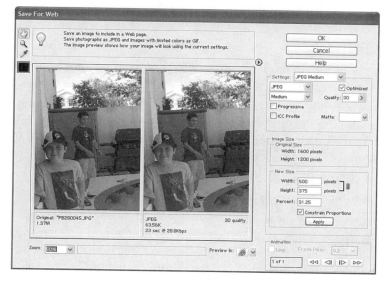

3. Pull down the Settings list and select either JPEG Low (smallest files, lowest picture quality) or JPEG Medium (slightly larger files, better picture quality).

4. Click OK, and when the Save Optimized As dialog box appears, enter a new filename.

That's it—you've created a new, smaller file, and your original picture file remains untouched.

Printing Your Photos

After you've touched up (or otherwise manipulated) your photos, it's time to print them—a task that's really easy in Windows XP.

Choosing the Right Printer—and Paper

If you have a color printer, you can make good-quality prints of your image files. Even a low-priced color inkjet can make surprisingly good prints, although the better your printer, the better the results.

Some manufacturers sell printers specifically designed for photographic prints. These printers use special photo print paper and output prints that are almost indistinguishable from those you get from a professional photo processor. If you take a lot of digital photos, one of these printers might be a good investment.

The quality of your prints is also affected by the type of paper you use. Printing on standard laser or inkjet paper is okay for making proofs, but you'll want to use a thicker, waxier paper for those prints you want to keep. Check with your printer's manufacturer to see what type of paper it recommends for the best quality photo prints.

Making the Print

Any photo editing program will let you print your pictures from within the program. You can also print directly from Windows XP via the Photo Printing Wizard.

You launch this wizard by opening the My Pictures folder, selecting a picture, and then selecting the Print Pictures option in the Picture Tasks panel. The Photo Printing Wizard then appears and walks you step-by-step through the printing process. Here are some of the options you can select:

- Which pictures to print
- Which printer to use
- Which layout to use
- How many prints to print

When you complete the wizard, the printing starts just as you specified.

Printing Photos Online

If you don't have your own photo-quality printer, you can use a professional photo-processing service to print your photos. There are a number of ways you can create prints from your digital photos:

- Copy your image files to disk and deliver the disk by hand to your local photo finisher.
- Go to the Web site of an online photo-finishing service and transfer your image files over the Internet.
- Use the Order Prints from the Internet option in Windows XP's My Pictures folder.

The first option is kind of old-fashioned and not always convenient. For many users, it's a lot less hassle to order photo prints from the comfort of their computer keyboards—however you do it.

Ordering from a Photo-Processing Site

Dozens and dozens of Web sites offer photo-processing services. They all operate in pretty much the same fashion.

After you register with the site, you upload the pictures you want printed from your hard drive to the Web site. Most sites accomplish this by giving you a few buttons to click and forms to fill out; a handful of sites let you send them your picture files as email attachments. After you upload the photos, you choose what size prints and how many copies you want, along with how fast you want them shipped. Enter your name, address, and credit card number, and your order is complete.

If you're looking for online photo services, here are some of the most popular sites to consider:

- Club Photo (www.clubphoto.com)
- FotoTime (www.fototime.com)
- Ofoto (www.ofoto.com)
- PhotoAccess (www.photoaccess.com)
- PhotoFun.com (www.photofun.com)
- PhotoWorks (www.photoworks.com)
- Shutterfly (www.shutterfly.com)
- Snapfish (www.snapfish.com)

Ordering from Within Windows XP

If you're running Windows XP, you can order prints directly from the My Pictures folder. All you have to do is select the files you want to print and then click the Order Prints from the Internet option in the Picture Tasks panel.

This launches the Internet Print Ordering Wizard. The wizard lets you pick which service you want to use, as well as what type and how many prints to make. You have to fill in all the normal shipping and payment information, of course. You'll receive your prints in a few days, just as you would if you ordered directly from that site via your Web browser.

tip

A lower-priced alternative to making a lot of photo prints is to create your own online photo album that your friends and family can view over the Internet. Check with your favorite online photo site to see what kind of online photo album options it offers.

THE ABSOLUTE MINIMUM

Here are the key points to remember from this chapter:

- By default, your digital pictures are stored in the My Pictures folder.
- You can use a photo editing program, such as Adobe Photoshop Elements, to touch up or edit your photos.
- Some of the most popular "touch ups" include removing red eye, adjusting brightness and contrast, changing color and tint, cropping the edges of the photo, and sharpening or blurring the picture.
- You can print your photos to any four-color printer or sent them (via the Internet) to an online photo processor for printing.

Index

How can we make this index more useful? Email us at indexes@quepublishing.com

How can we make this index more useful? Email us at indexes@quepublishing.com

Q-R

How can we make this index more useful? Email us at indexes@quepublishing.com

How can we make this index more useful? Email us at indexes@quepublishing.com

informIT